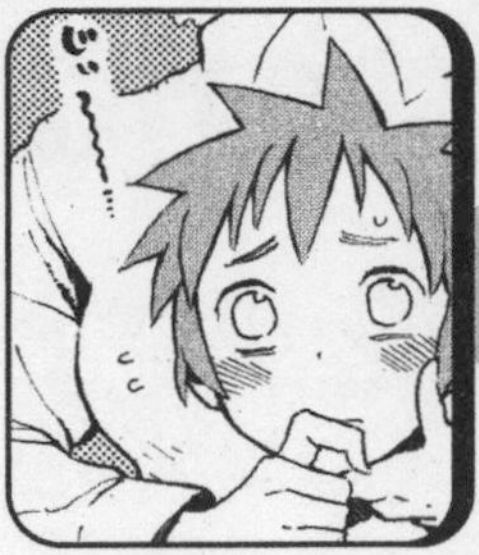

Dullahan

Kyoko Machi
Class 1-B

- A demi of Irish folklore whose head and body are separate.
- Likes her head to be held.
- In love with Takahashi-sensei.

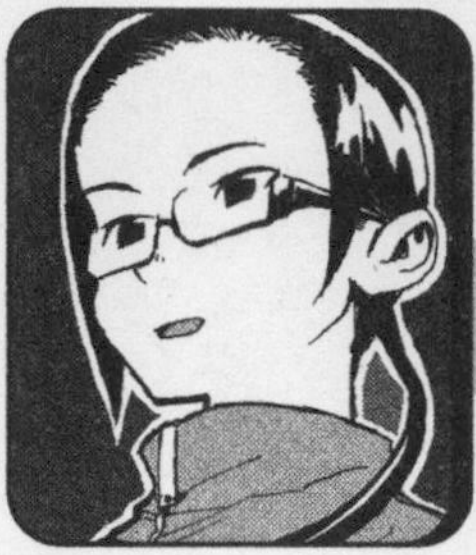

Succubus

Sakie Sato

- Math teacher.
- Lives in an isolated, dilapidated house so as not to unintentionally arouse anyone.
- Romantic history: zilch.
- Has a crush on Takahashi-sensei.

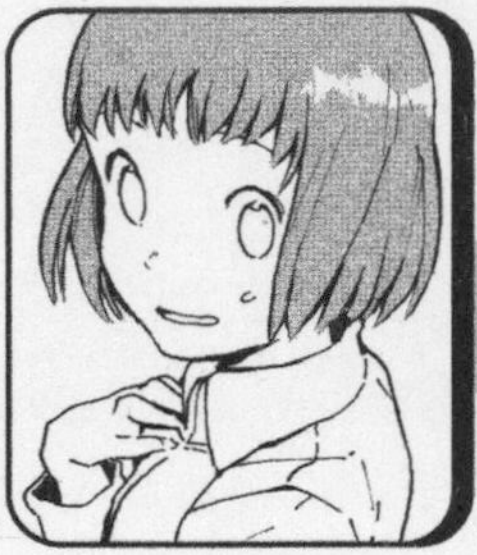

Snow Woman

Yuki Kusakabe
Class 1-A

- Exudes cold air and weeps ice under stress.
- At first, avoided contact with others due to doubts about her own nature.

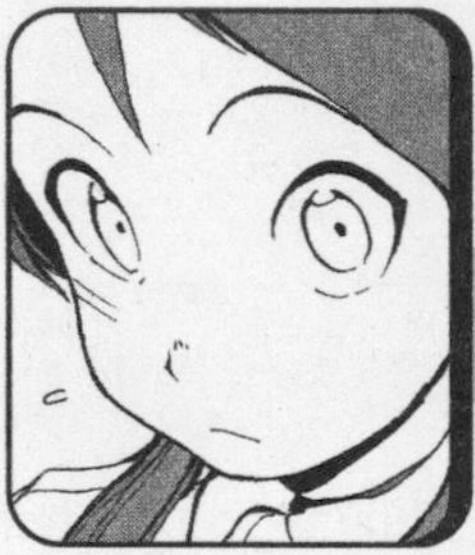

Himari Takanashi
Class 1-C

- Human
- Hikari's younger twin sister.
- Good grades, mature attitude—polar opposite of her sister.

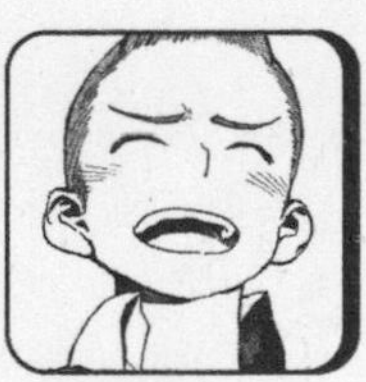

Satake
Class 1-A

- Classmate of the demis.
- Easy-going.

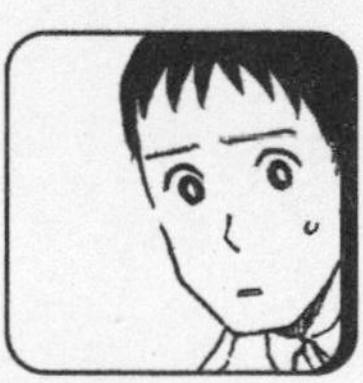

Ota
Class 1-A

- Classmate of the demis.
- Often seen with Satake.

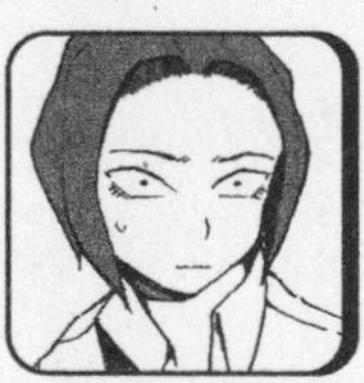

Kimura
Class 1-C

- Classmate of the demis.

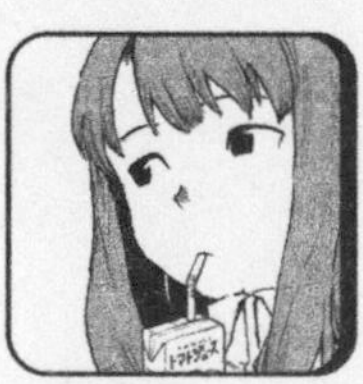

Imori
Class 1-C

- Classmate of the demis.
- Talked about Yuki behind her back with Kimura.

"Demi-humans" are just a little different from us—
these days, they go by "Demis."
Their problems are as adorable as they are.

*DEMIS: SHORT FOR "DEMI-HUMANS."

INTERVIEWS WITH MONSTER GIRLS

CONTENTS

Chapter 24: My Sister, My Mirror

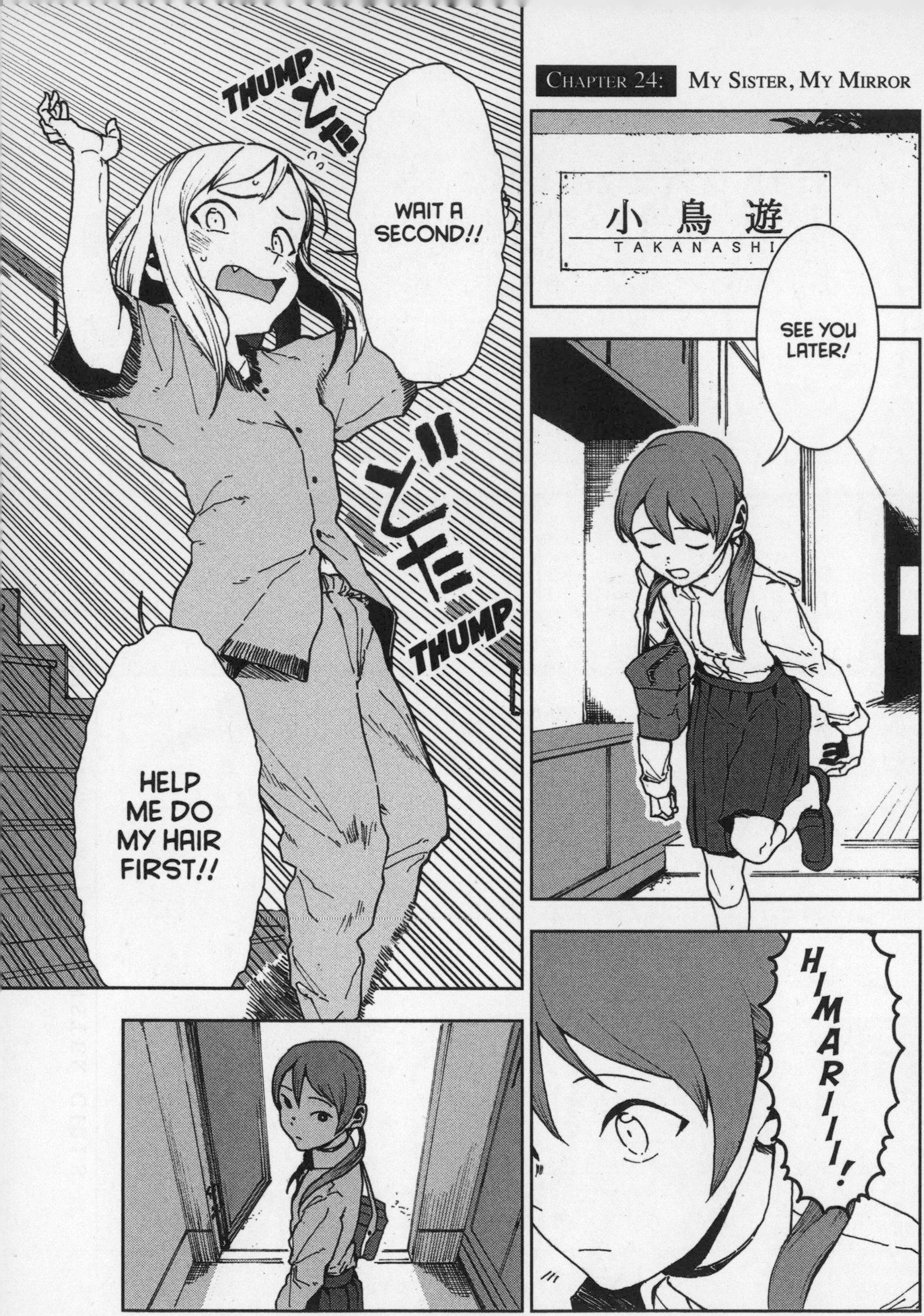

小鳥遊
TAKANASHI
SEE YOU LATER!
THUMP
WAIT A SECOND!!
THUMP
HELP ME DO MY HAIR FIRST!!
HIMARIIII!

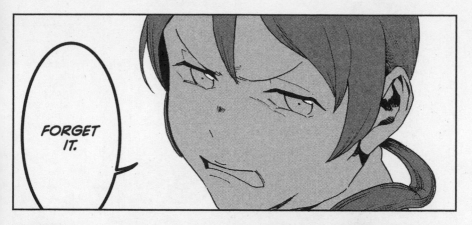

FORGET IT.
READING ROOM
AND...
...THAT'S ...
...HOW I HELPED MY SISTER BECOME A LITTLE MORE INDEPENDENT.
THAT'S SOME TOUGH LOVE, HIMARI-CHAN!
I CAN JUST PICTURE HIKARI'S FACE!
SHE'S SUCH A BUM.
SHE'S IN HIGH SCHOOL NOW! IT'S TIME TO GROW UP.

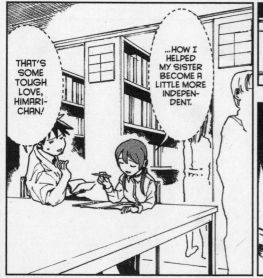

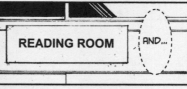

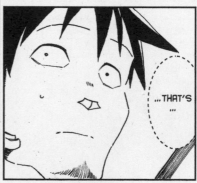

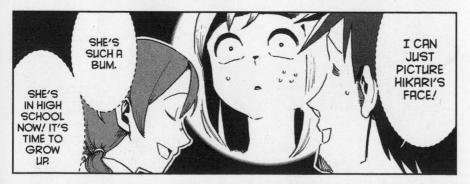

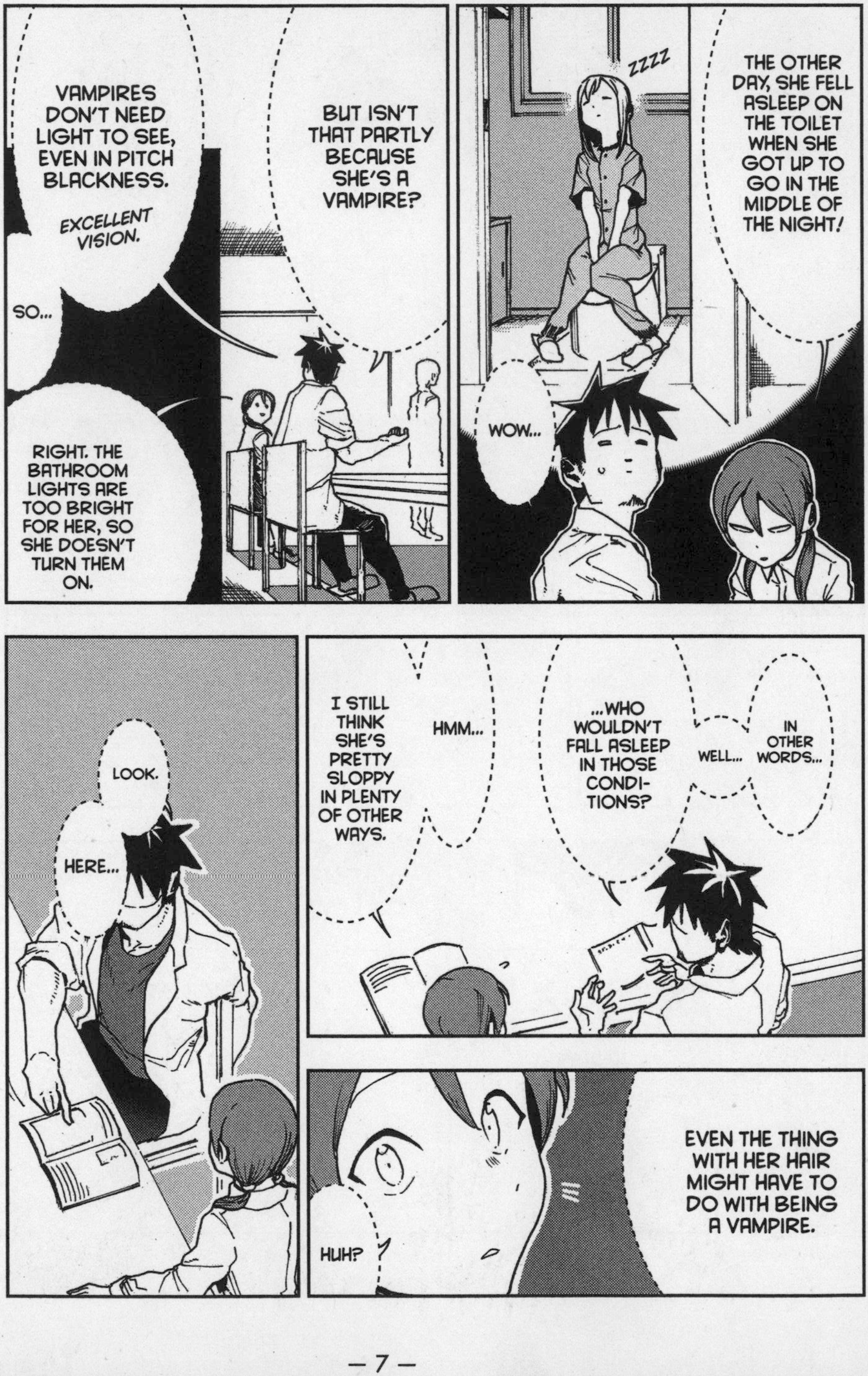
THE OTHER DAY, SHE FELL ASLEEP ON THE TOILET WHEN SHE GOT UP TO GO IN THE MIDDLE OF THE NIGHT!
ZZZZ
WOW...
BUT ISN'T THAT PARTLY BECAUSE SHE'S A VAMPIRE?
VAMPIRES DON'T NEED LIGHT TO SEE, EVEN IN PITCH BLACKNESS.
EXCELLENT VISION.
SO...
RIGHT. THE BATHROOM LIGHTS ARE TOO BRIGHT FOR HER, SO SHE DOESN'T TURN THEM ON.
IN OTHER WORDS...
WELL...
...WHO WOULDN'T FALL ASLEEP IN THOSE CONDI-TIONS?
HMM...
I STILL THINK SHE'S PRETTY SLOPPY IN PLENTY OF OTHER WAYS.
EVEN THE THING WITH HER HAIR MIGHT HAVE TO DO WITH BEING A VAMPIRE.
HUH?
LOOK.
HERE...

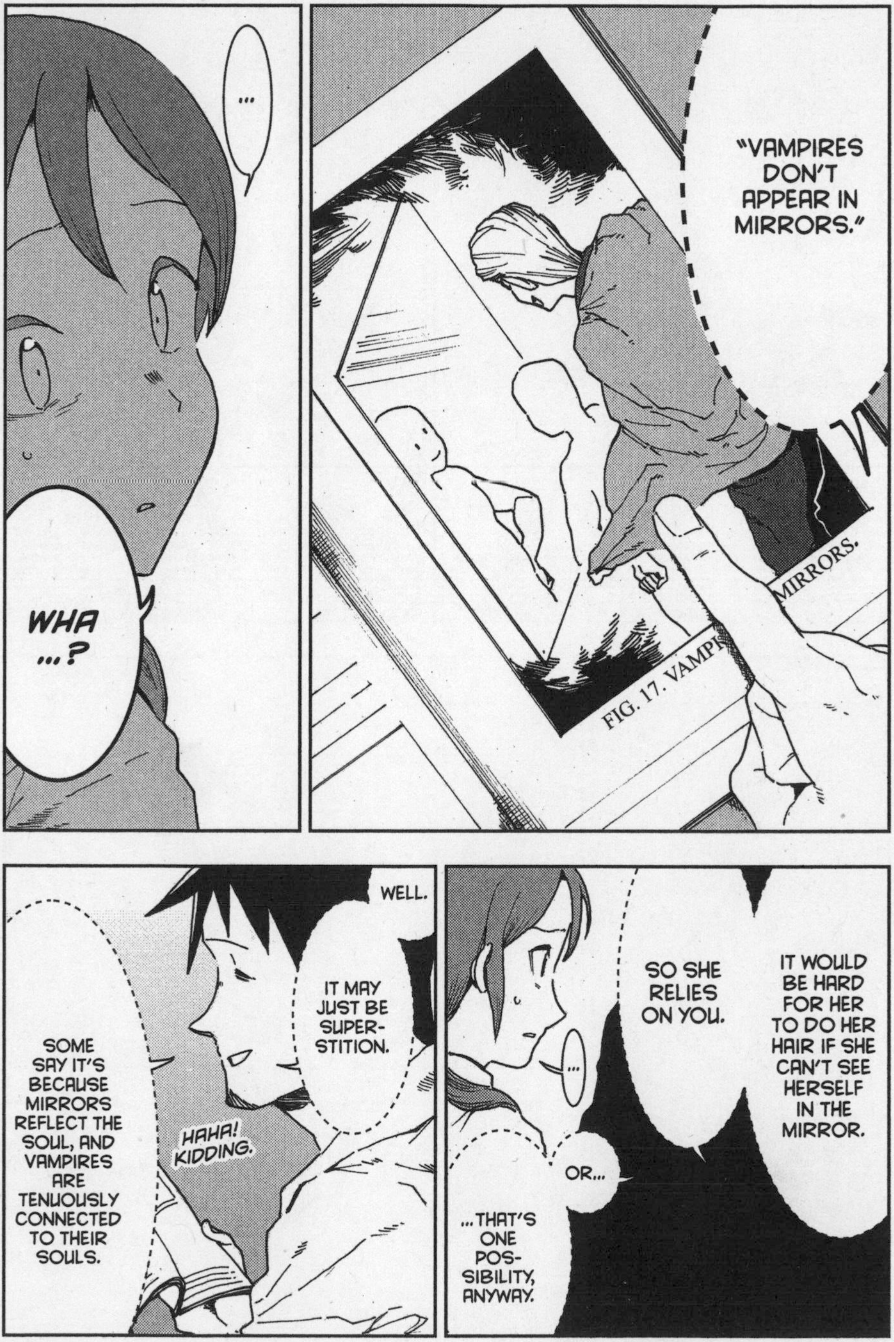
"VAMPIRES DON'T APPEAR IN MIRRORS."
FIG. 17. VAMP
MIRRORS.
...
WHA ...?
IT WOULD BE HARD FOR HER TO DO HER HAIR IF SHE CAN'T SEE HERSELF IN THE MIRROR.
SO SHE RELIES ON YOU.
...
OR...
...THAT'S ONE POS-SIBILITY, ANYWAY.
WELL.
IT MAY JUST BE SUPER-STITION.
HAHA! KIDDING.
SOME SAY IT'S BECAUSE MIRRORS REFLECT THE SOUL, AND VAMPIRES ARE TENUOUSLY CONNECTED TO THEIR SOULS.

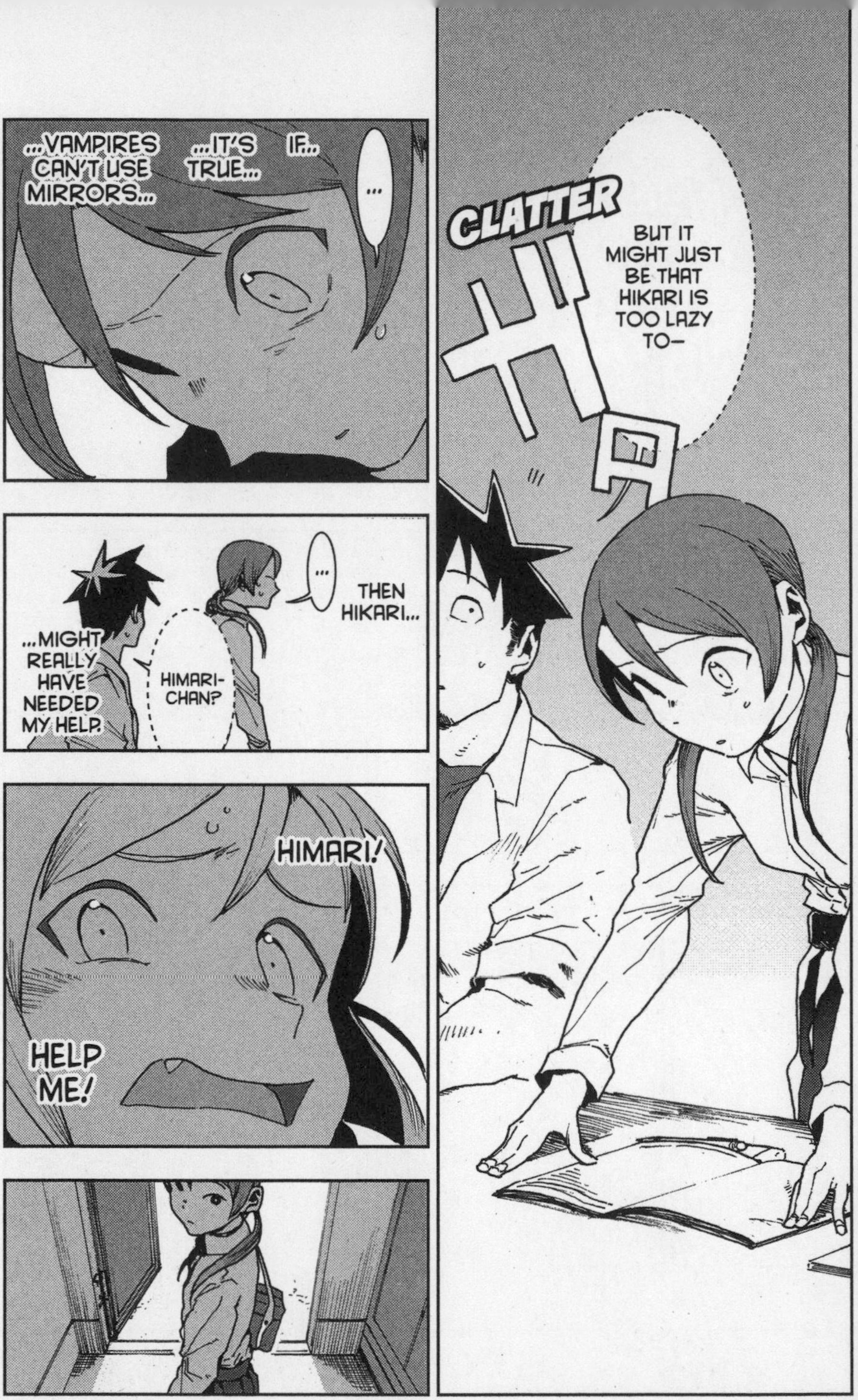
CLATTER
BUT IT MIGHT JUST BE THAT HIKARI IS TOO LAZY TO—
...
IF...
...IT'S TRUE...
...VAMPIRES CAN'T USE MIRRORS...
THEN HIKARI...
...
HIMARI-CHAN?
...MIGHT REALLY HAVE NEEDED MY HELP.
HIMARI!
HELP ME!

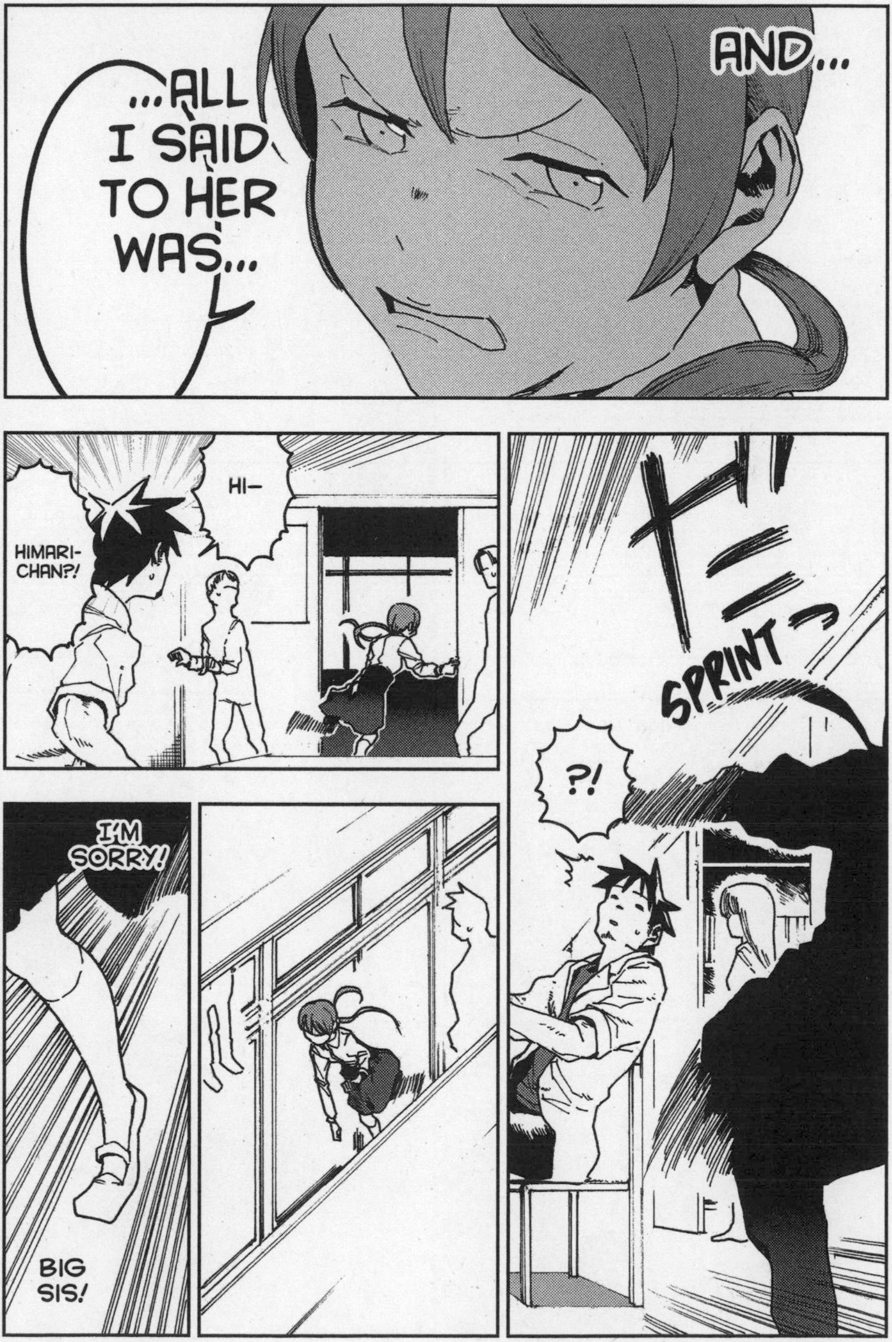
AND...
...ALL I SAID TO HER WAS...
SPRINT
?!
HI—
HIMARI-CHAN?!
I'M SORRY!
BIG SIS!

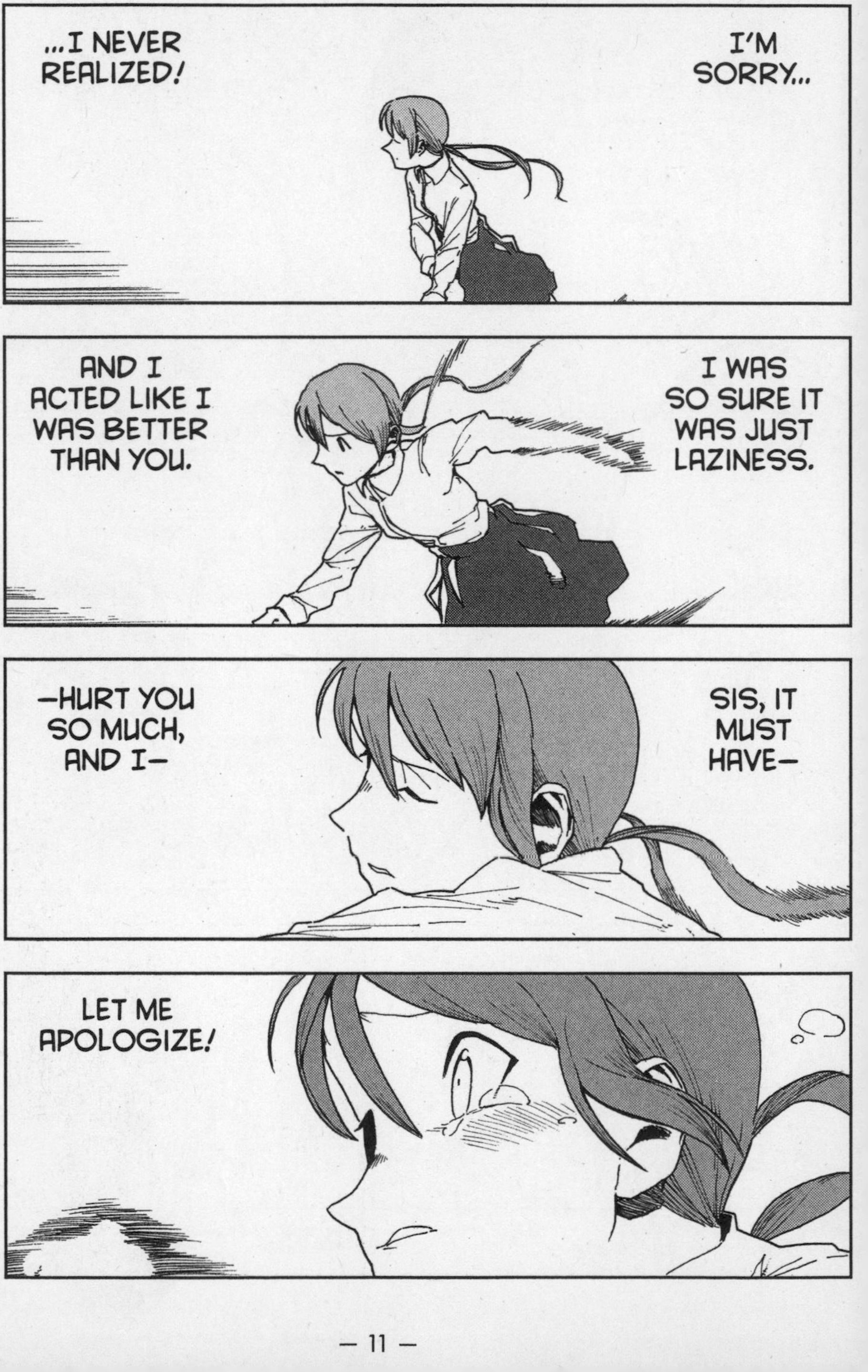
I'M SORRY...
...I NEVER REALIZED!
I WAS SO SURE IT WAS JUST LAZINESS.
AND I ACTED LIKE I WAS BETTER THAN YOU.
SIS, IT MUST HAVE—
—HURT YOU SO MUCH, AND I—
LET ME APOLOGIZE!

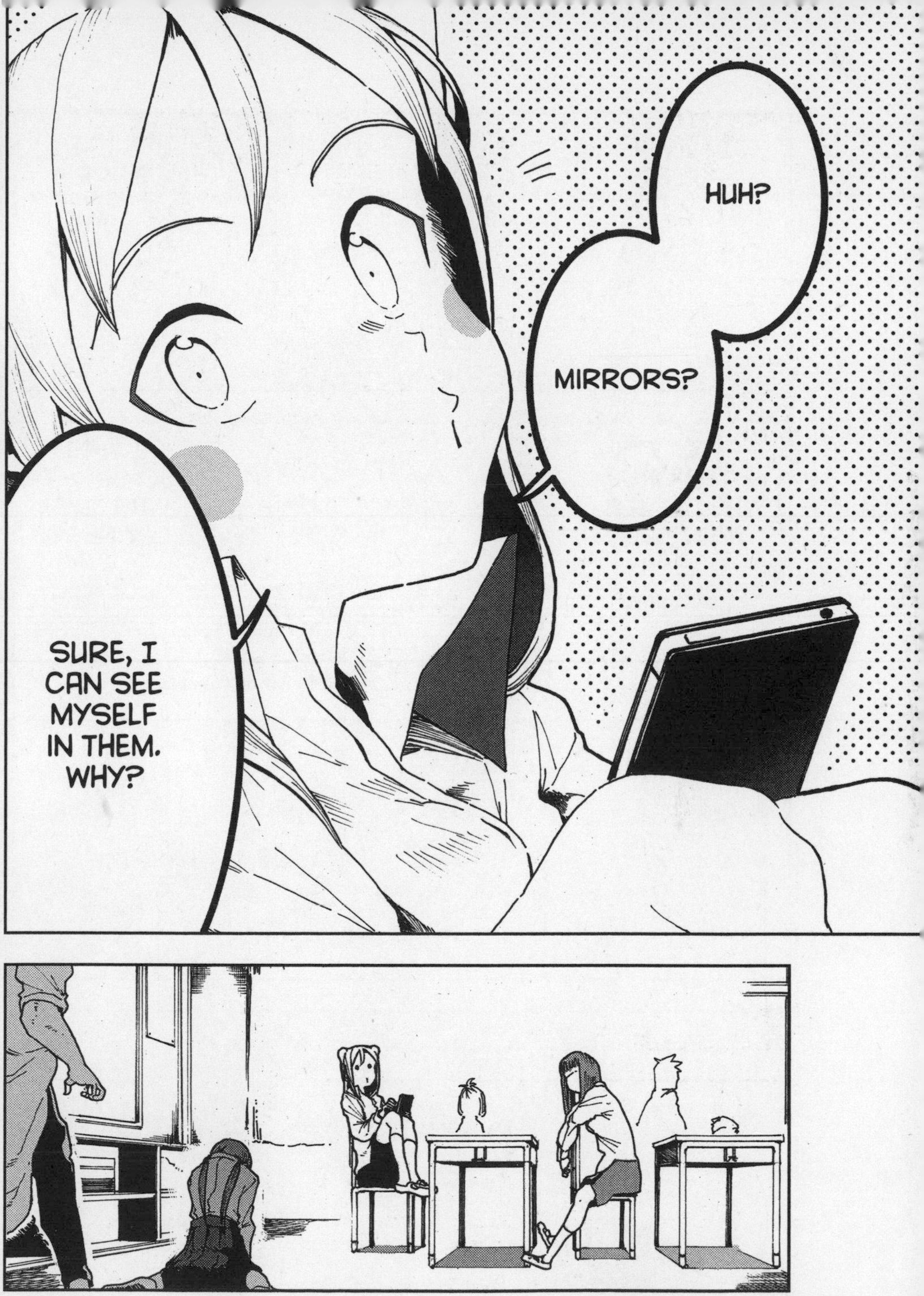
HUH?
MIRRORS?
SURE, I CAN SEE MYSELF IN THEM. WHY?

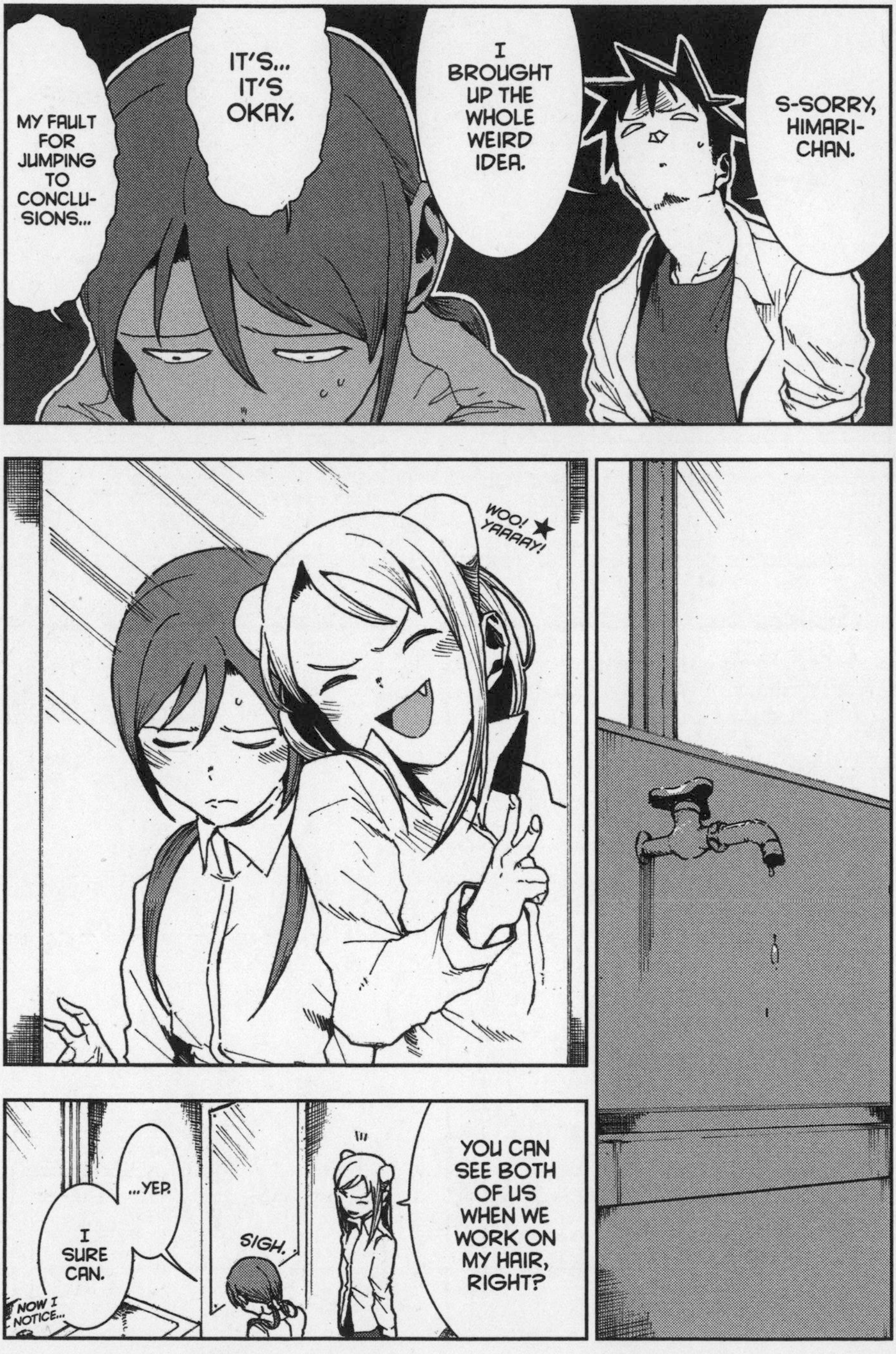
S-SORRY, HIMARI-CHAN.
I BROUGHT UP THE WHOLE WEIRD IDEA.
IT'S... IT'S OKAY.
MY FAULT FOR JUMPING TO CONCLUSIONS...
WOO! ★ YAAAAY!
YOU CAN SEE BOTH OF US WHEN WE WORK ON MY HAIR, RIGHT?
SIGH.
...YEP.
I SURE CAN.
NOW I NOTICE...

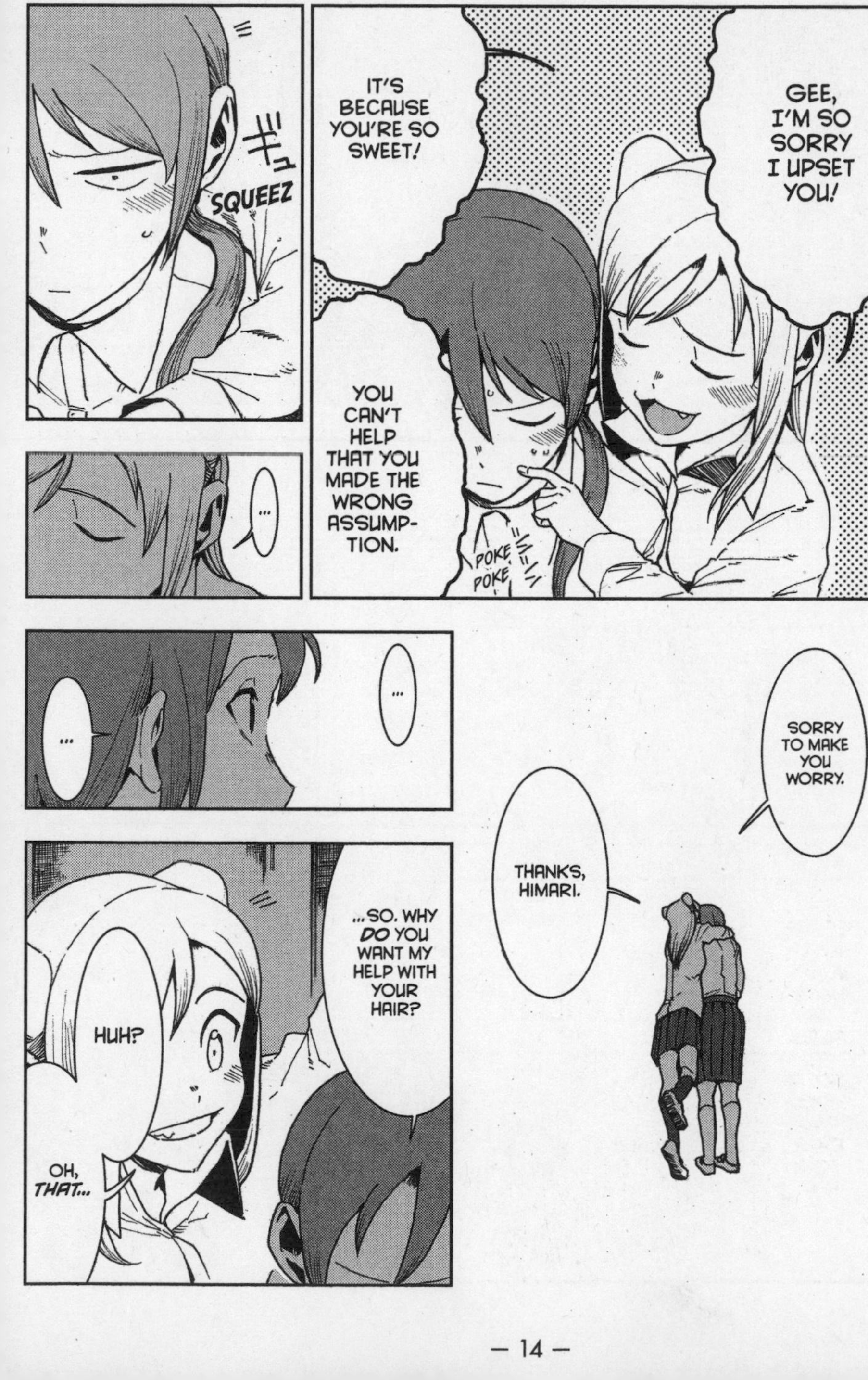
GEE, I'M SO SORRY I UPSET YOU!
IT'S BECAUSE YOU'RE SO SWEET!
YOU CAN'T HELP THAT YOU MADE THE WRONG ASSUMPTION.
POKE POKE
ギュ
SQUEEZ
...
SORRY TO MAKE YOU WORRY.
THANKS, HIMARI.
...
...
...SO. WHY *DO* YOU WANT MY HELP WITH YOUR HAIR?
HUH?
OH, *THAT*...

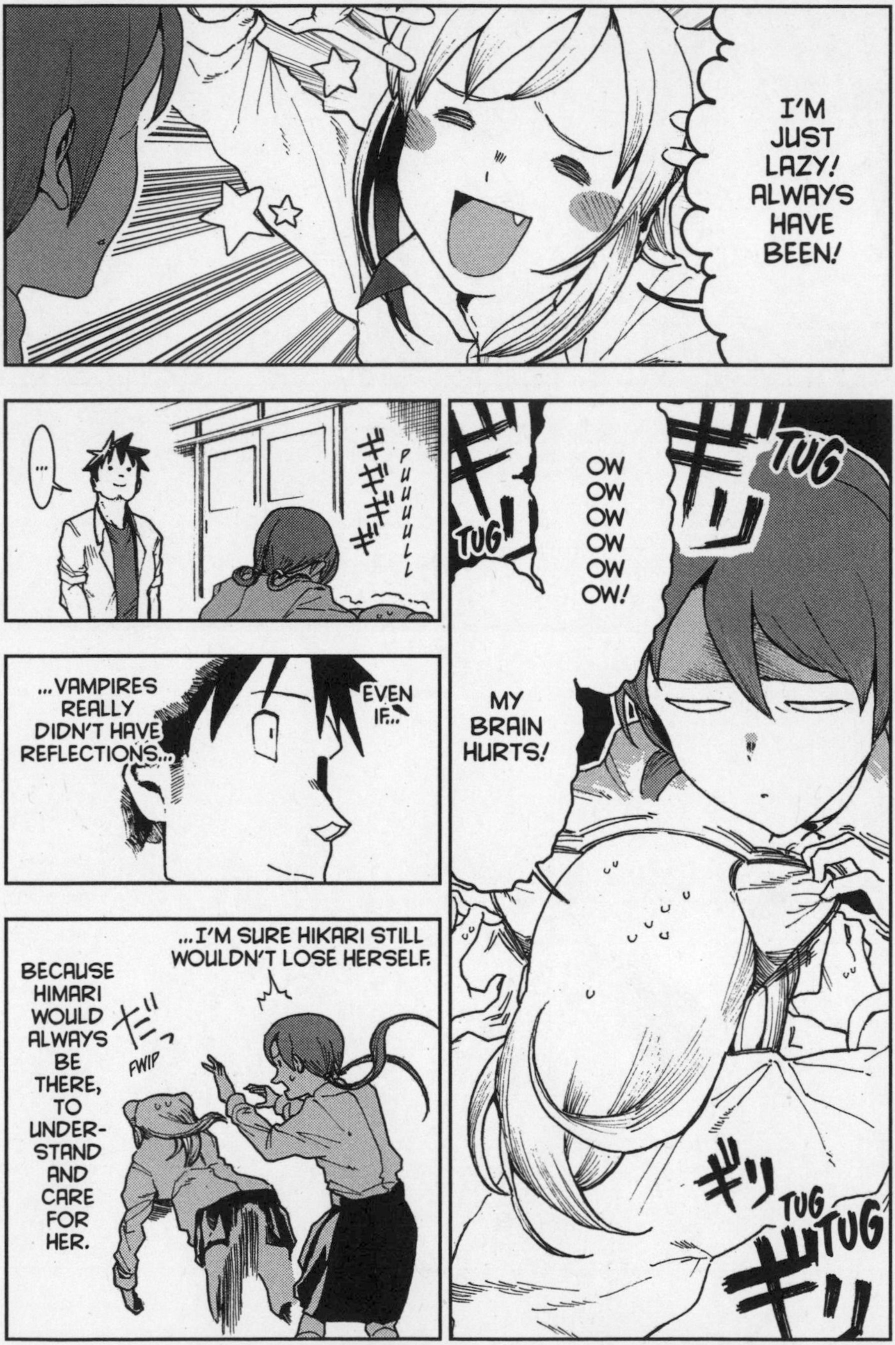

I'M JUST LAZY! ALWAYS HAVE BEEN!
TUG
OW OW OW OW OW OW!
TUG
MY BRAIN HURTS!
TUG TUG
...
PUUUULL
EVEN IF...
...VAMPIRES REALLY DIDN'T HAVE REFLECTIONS...
...I'M SURE HIKARI STILL WOULDN'T LOSE HERSELF.
BECAUSE HIMARI WOULD ALWAYS BE THERE, TO UNDER-STAND AND CARE FOR HER.
FWIP

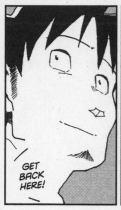

GET BACK HERE!

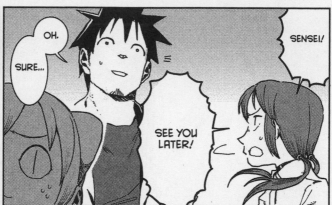

OH.

SURE...

SEE YOU LATER!

SENSEI!

SHE'S THE
MIRROR
IMAGE
OF HER
SISTER.

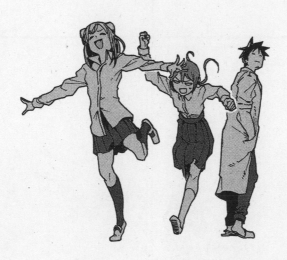

IF YOU QUIT DOING YOUR HAIR THAT WAY, MAYBE YOU WOULDN'T HAVE TO WORRY ABOUT BEING LATE TO SCHOOL.
WHA-AAT?
IF YOU *STARTED* DOING YOUR HAIR LIKE THIS, YOU WOULD BE LATE, TOO!
GRRR!
NOT MY POINT!
THE NEXT DAY
...
AND WITH TIME TO SPARE! YOU'RE SOME-THING, HIMARI!
HIMARI HAIR
UH-HUH...
THIS IS 800% MORE EMBAR-RASSING THAN BEING TARDY...

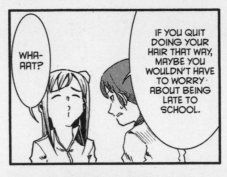

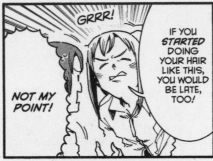

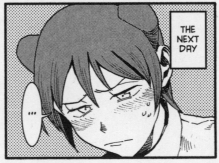

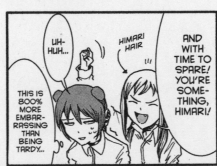

INTERVIEWS WITH MONSTER GIRLS

Chapter 25: Dullahans Transcend Space and Time (Part 1)

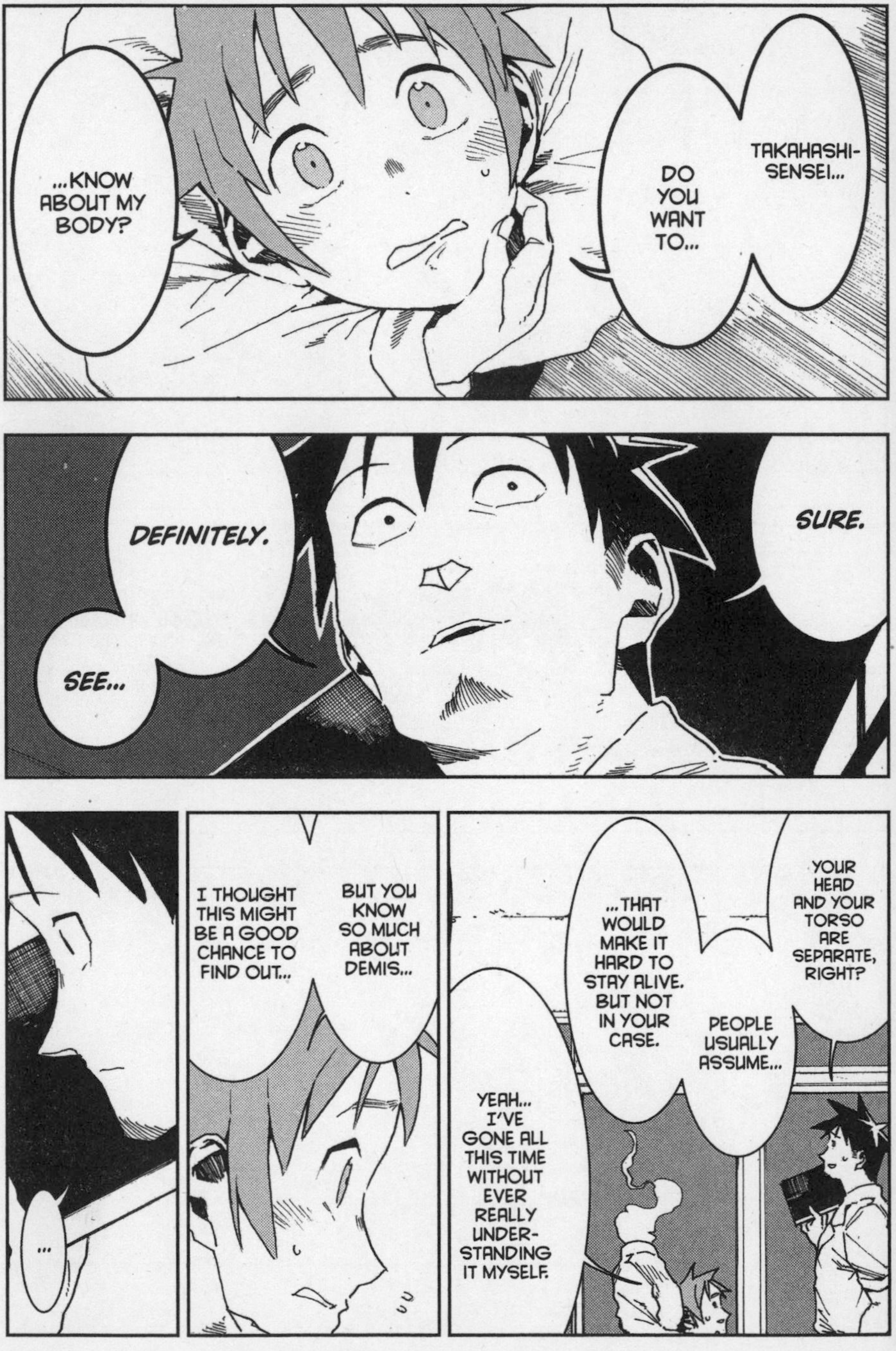
TAKAHASHI-SENSEI...
DO YOU WANT TO...
...KNOW ABOUT MY BODY?
SURE.
DEFINITELY.
SEE...
YOUR HEAD AND YOUR TORSO ARE SEPARATE, RIGHT?
PEOPLE USUALLY ASSUME...
...THAT WOULD MAKE IT HARD TO STAY ALIVE. BUT NOT IN YOUR CASE.
YEAH... I'VE GONE ALL THIS TIME WITHOUT EVER REALLY UNDER-STANDING IT MYSELF.
BUT YOU KNOW SO MUCH ABOUT DEMIS...
I THOUGHT THIS MIGHT BE A GOOD CHANCE TO FIND OUT...
...

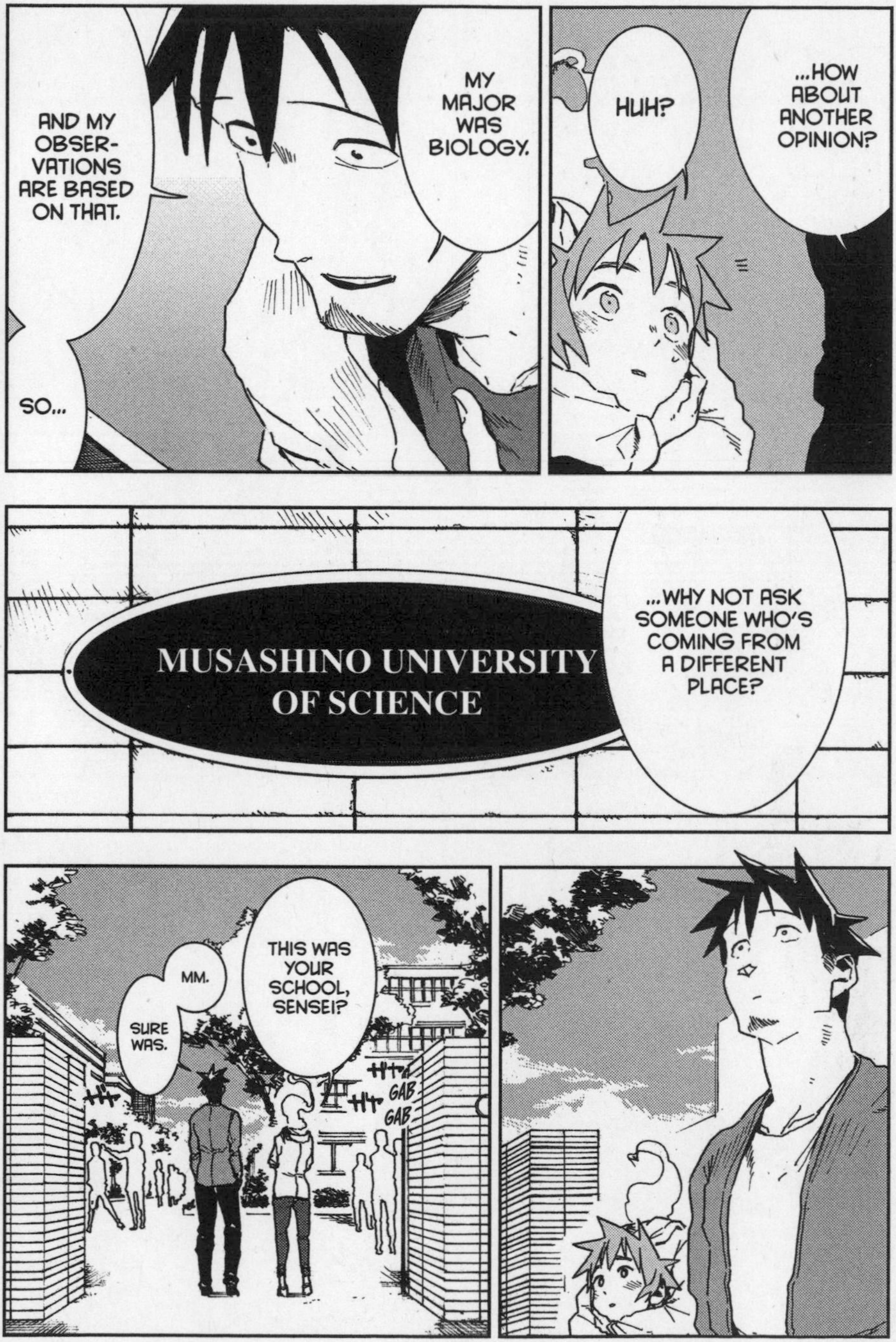
...HOW ABOUT ANOTHER OPINION?
HUH?
MY MAJOR WAS BIOLOGY.
AND MY OBSERVATIONS ARE BASED ON THAT.
SO...
...WHY NOT ASK SOMEONE WHO'S COMING FROM A DIFFERENT PLACE?
MUSASHINO UNIVERSITY OF SCIENCE
THIS WAS YOUR SCHOOL, SENSEI?
MM.
SURE WAS.
GAB GAB

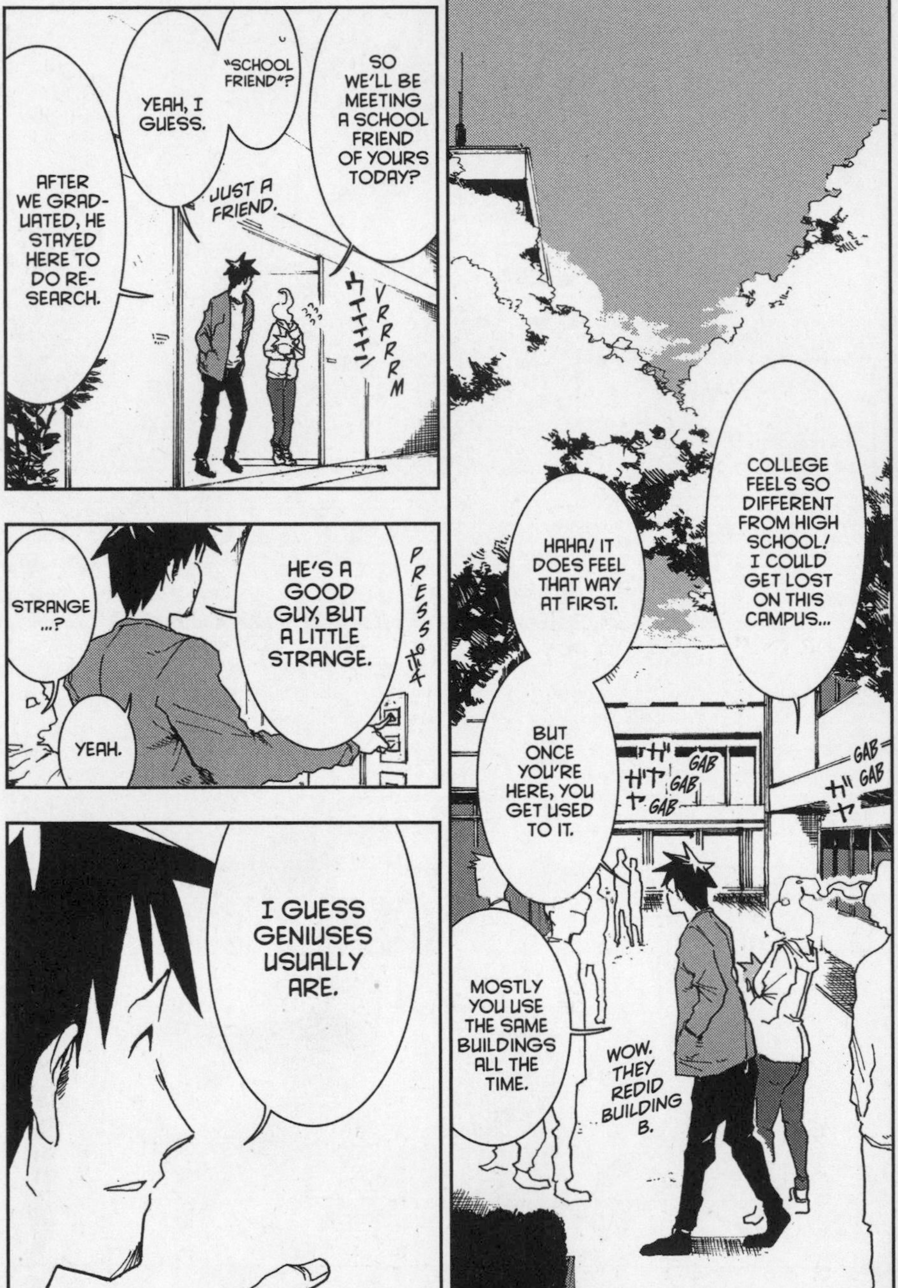
COLLEGE FEELS SO DIFFERENT FROM HIGH SCHOOL! I COULD GET LOST ON THIS CAMPUS...
HAHA! IT DOES FEEL THAT WAY AT FIRST.
BUT ONCE YOU'RE HERE, YOU GET USED TO IT.
ガヤ GAB GAB
ガヤガヤ GAB GAB GAB
MOSTLY YOU USE THE SAME BUILDINGS ALL THE TIME.
WOW. THEY REDID BUILDING B.
SO WE'LL BE MEETING A SCHOOL FRIEND OF YOURS TODAY?
"SCHOOL FRIEND"?
YEAH, I GUESS.
JUST A FRIEND.
AFTER WE GRADUATED, HE STAYED HERE TO DO RESEARCH.
ウィィィン VRRRRM
PRESS ポチ
HE'S A GOOD GUY, BUT A LITTLE STRANGE.
STRANGE ...?
YEAH.
I GUESS GENIUSES USUALLY ARE.

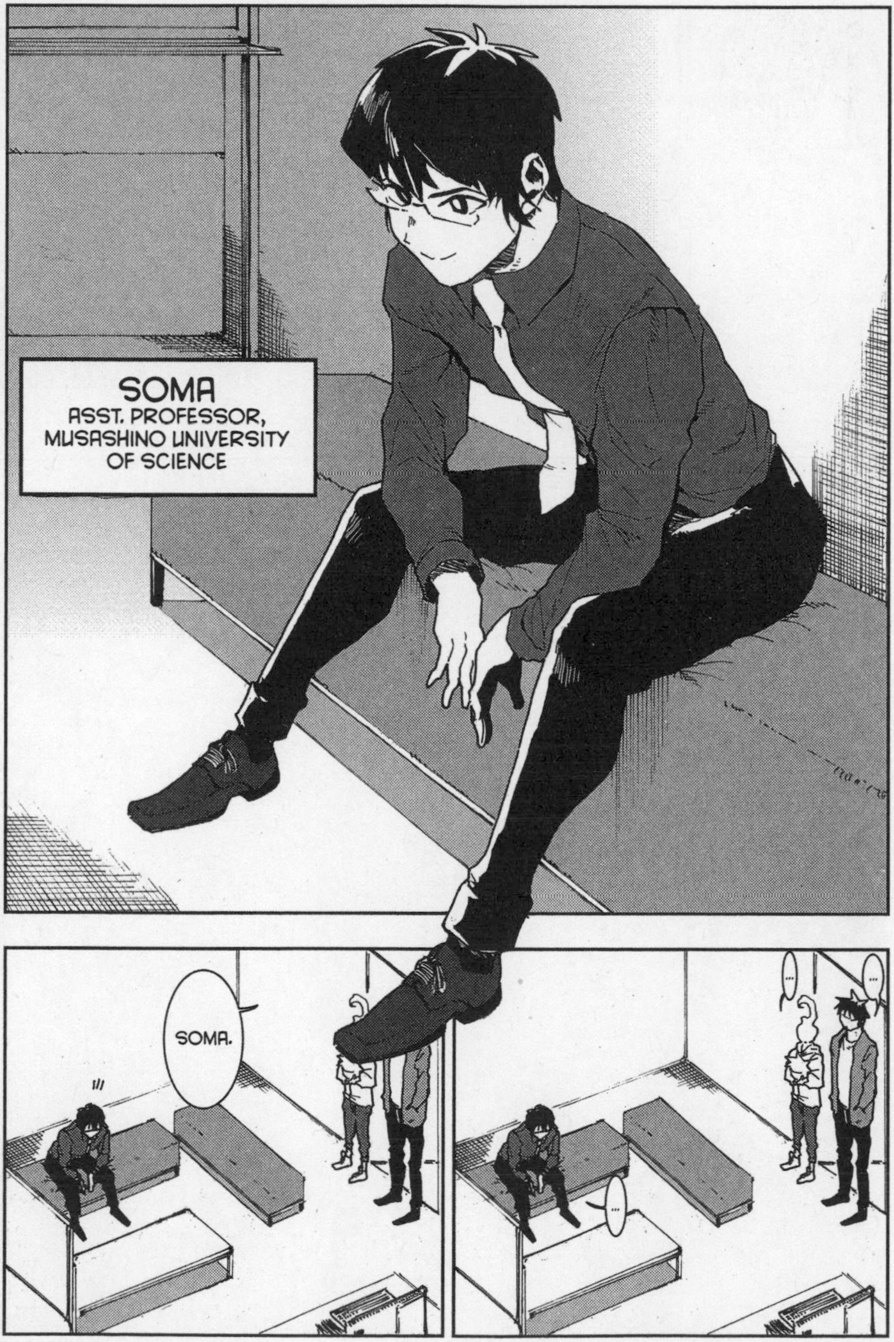
SOMA
ASST. PROFESSOR, MUSASHINO UNIVERSITY OF SCIENCE
...
...
...
SOMA.

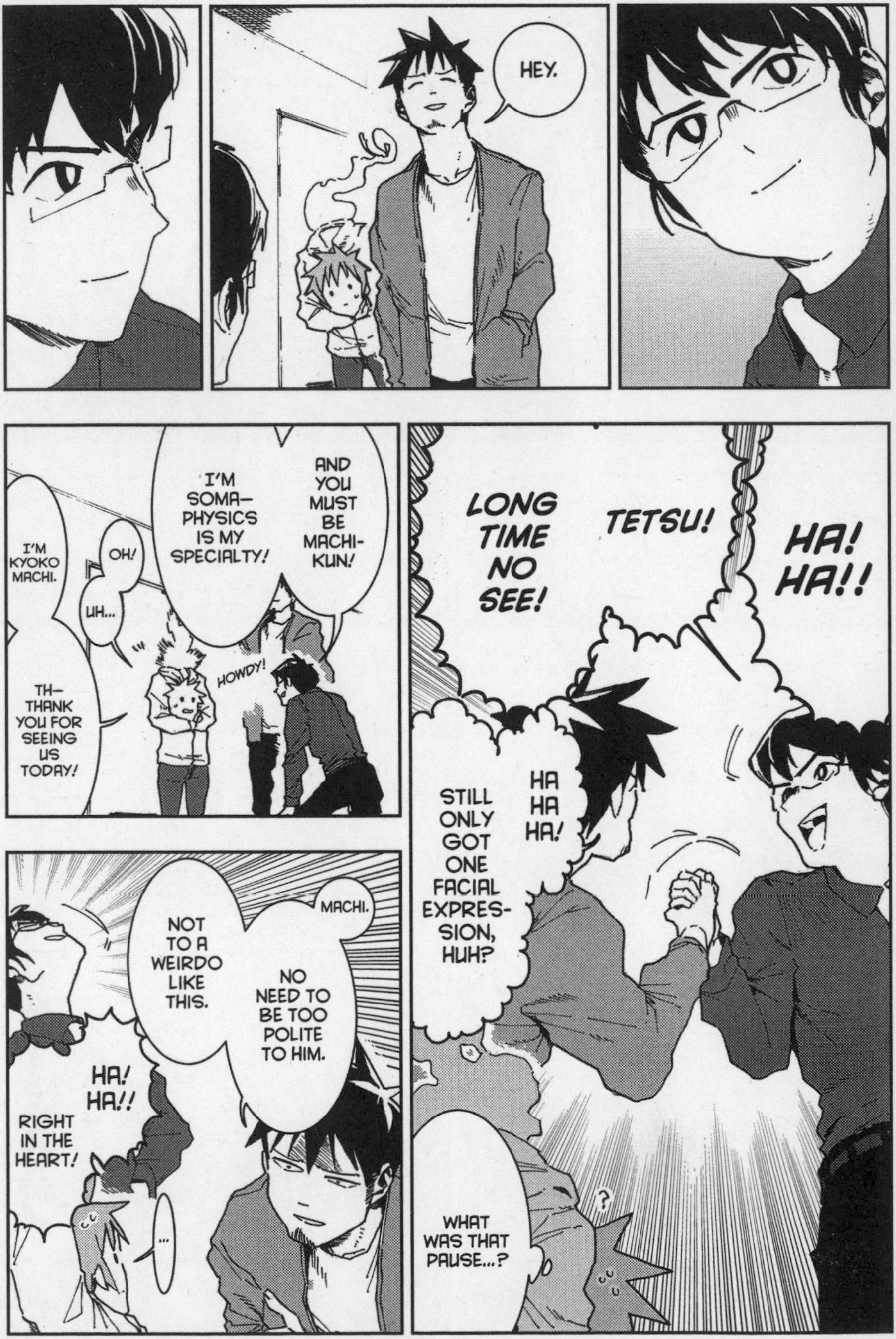
HEY.
HA! HA!!
TETSU!
LONG TIME NO SEE!
HA HA HA!
STILL ONLY GOT ONE FACIAL EXPRES-SION, HUH?
WHAT WAS THAT PAUSE...?
AND YOU MUST BE MACHI-KUN!
I'M SOMA— PHYSICS IS MY SPECIALTY!
HOWDY!
OH!
UH...
I'M KYOKO MACHI.
TH— THANK YOU FOR SEEING US TODAY!
MACHI.
NO NEED TO BE TOO POLITE TO HIM.
NOT TO A WEIRDO LIKE THIS.
HA! HA!!
RIGHT IN THE HEART!
...

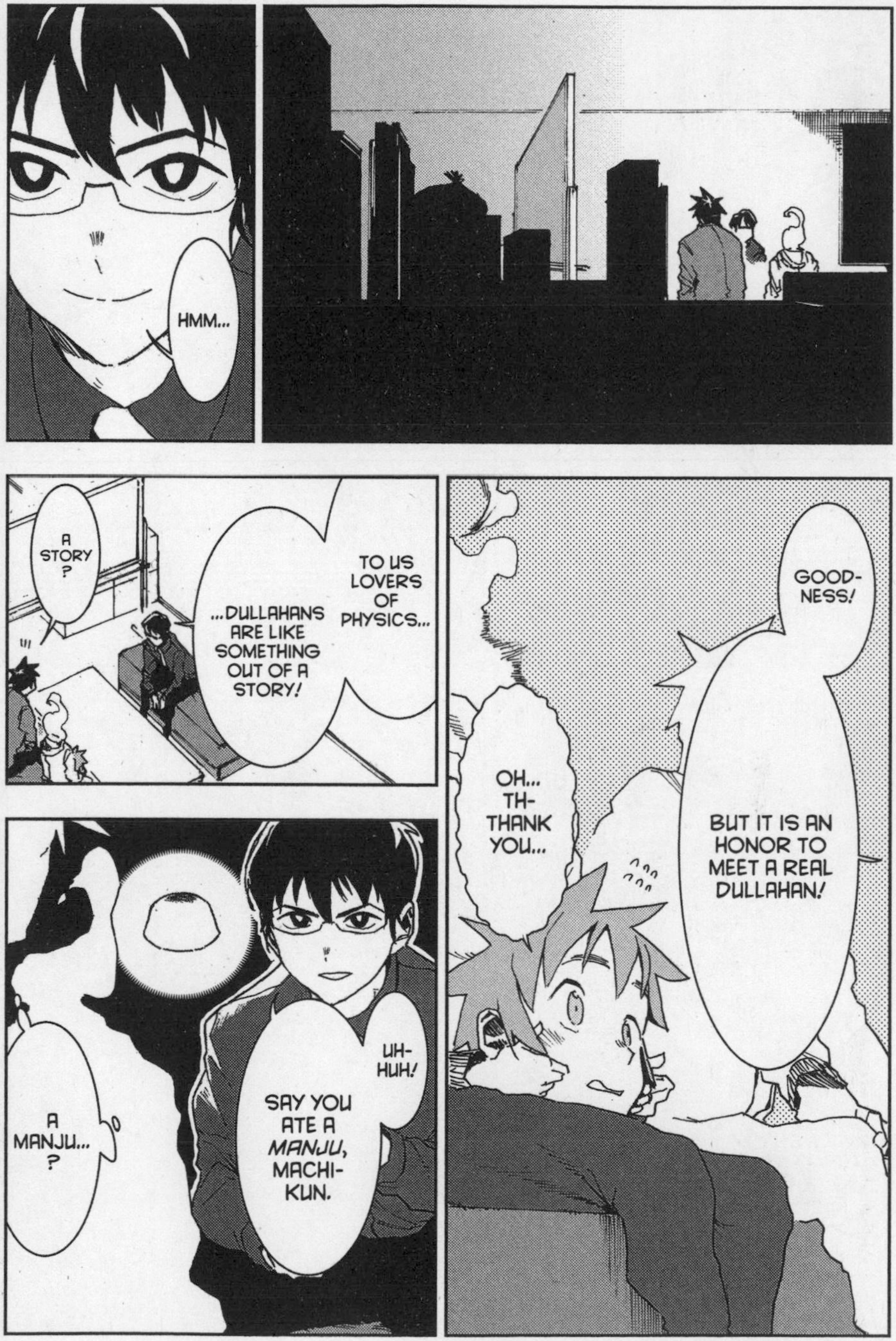
HMM...
GOOD-NESS!
BUT IT IS AN HONOR TO MEET A REAL DULLAHAN!
OH... TH-THANK YOU...
TO US LOVERS OF PHYSICS...
...DULLAHANS ARE LIKE SOMETHING OUT OF A STORY!
A STORY?
UH-HUH!
SAY YOU ATE A *MANJU*, MACHI-KUN.
A MANJU...?

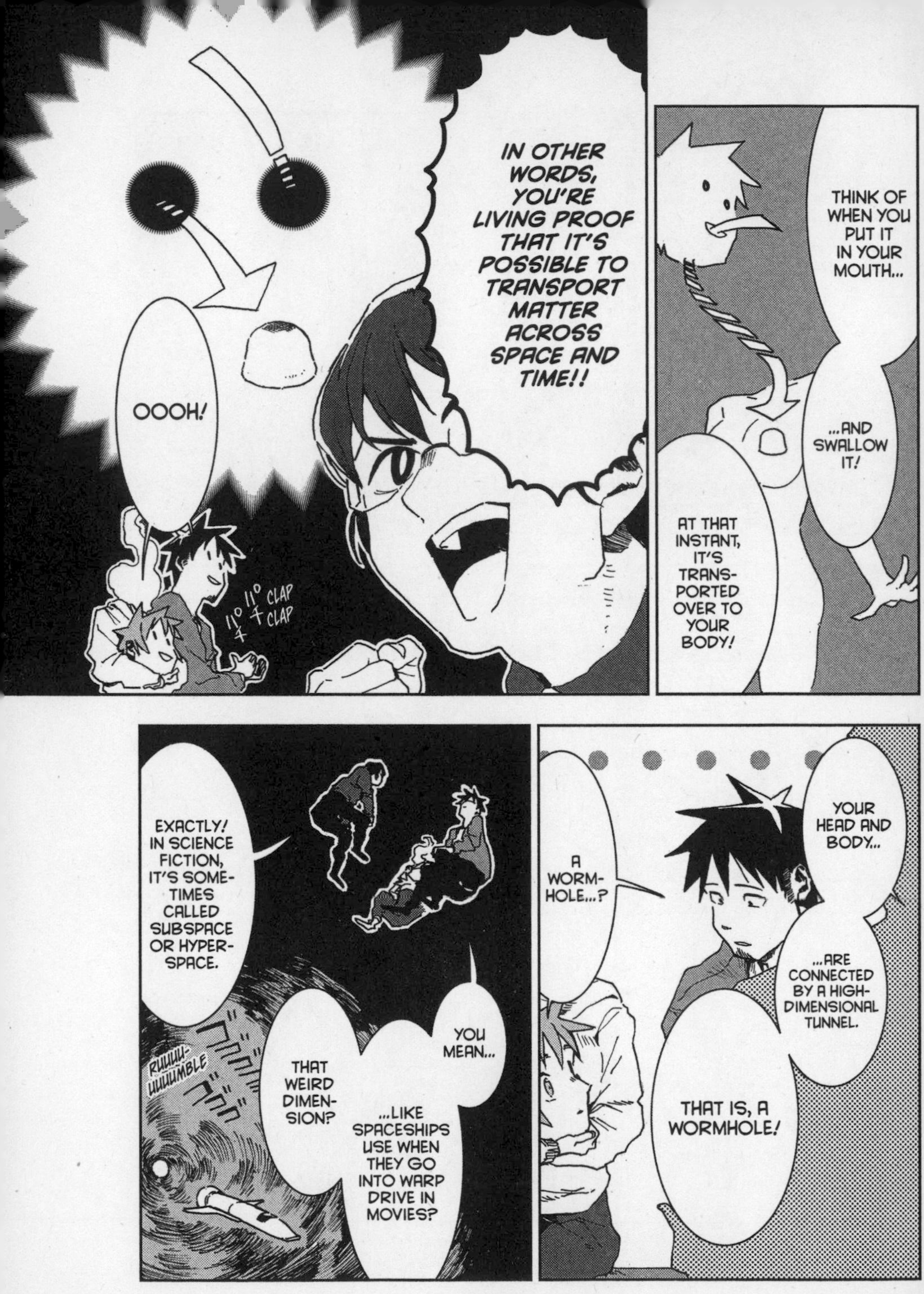
THINK OF WHEN YOU PUT IT IN YOUR MOUTH...
...AND SWALLOW IT!
AT THAT INSTANT, IT'S TRANS-PORTED OVER TO YOUR BODY!
IN OTHER WORDS, YOU'RE LIVING PROOF THAT IT'S POSSIBLE TO TRANSPORT MATTER ACROSS SPACE AND TIME!!
OOOH!
CLAP CLAP
YOUR HEAD AND BODY...
...ARE CONNECTED BY A HIGH-DIMENSIONAL TUNNEL.
THAT IS, A WORMHOLE!
A WORM-HOLE...?
YOU MEAN...
...LIKE SPACESHIPS USE WHEN THEY GO INTO WARP DRIVE IN MOVIES?
THAT WEIRD DIMEN-SION?
EXACTLY! IN SCIENCE FICTION, IT'S SOME-TIMES CALLED SUBSPACE OR HYPER-SPACE.
RUUUU-UUUUMBLE

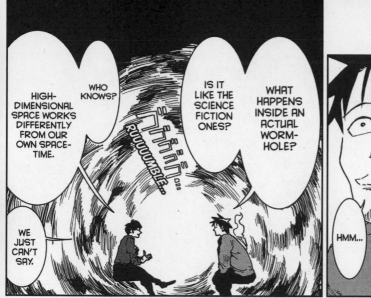

...
HMM...
WHAT HAPPENS INSIDE AN ACTUAL WORM-HOLE?
IS IT LIKE THE SCIENCE FICTION ONES?
RUUUUMBLE...
WHO KNOWS?
HIGH-DIMENSIONAL SPACE WORKS DIFFERENTLY FROM OUR OWN SPACE-TIME.
WE JUST CAN'T SAY.
BUT THIS WORM-HOLE THAT CONNECTS MACHI-KUN'S HEAD AND BODY...
...SEEMS TO BE A VERY STURDY ONE!
SCREEEEE
HER NERVES AND BLOOD VESSELS ALL SEEM TO BE CONNECTED THROUGH IT.
AND HER NECK PER-FORMS ALL ITS EXPECTED FUNCTIONS!
ITS... FUNC-TIONS...
I GUESS SO...
UH-HUH...
?
MEAN-ING ...?
MACHI'S— YOU KNOW.
NECK.
THE PART YOU'RE SAYING IS A WORM-HOLE.

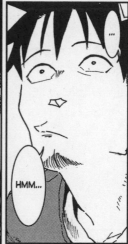

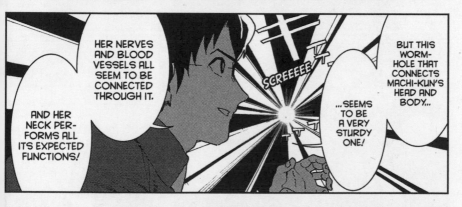

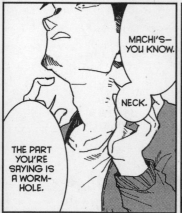

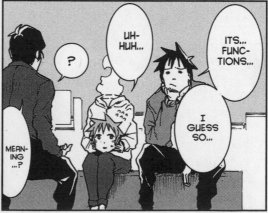

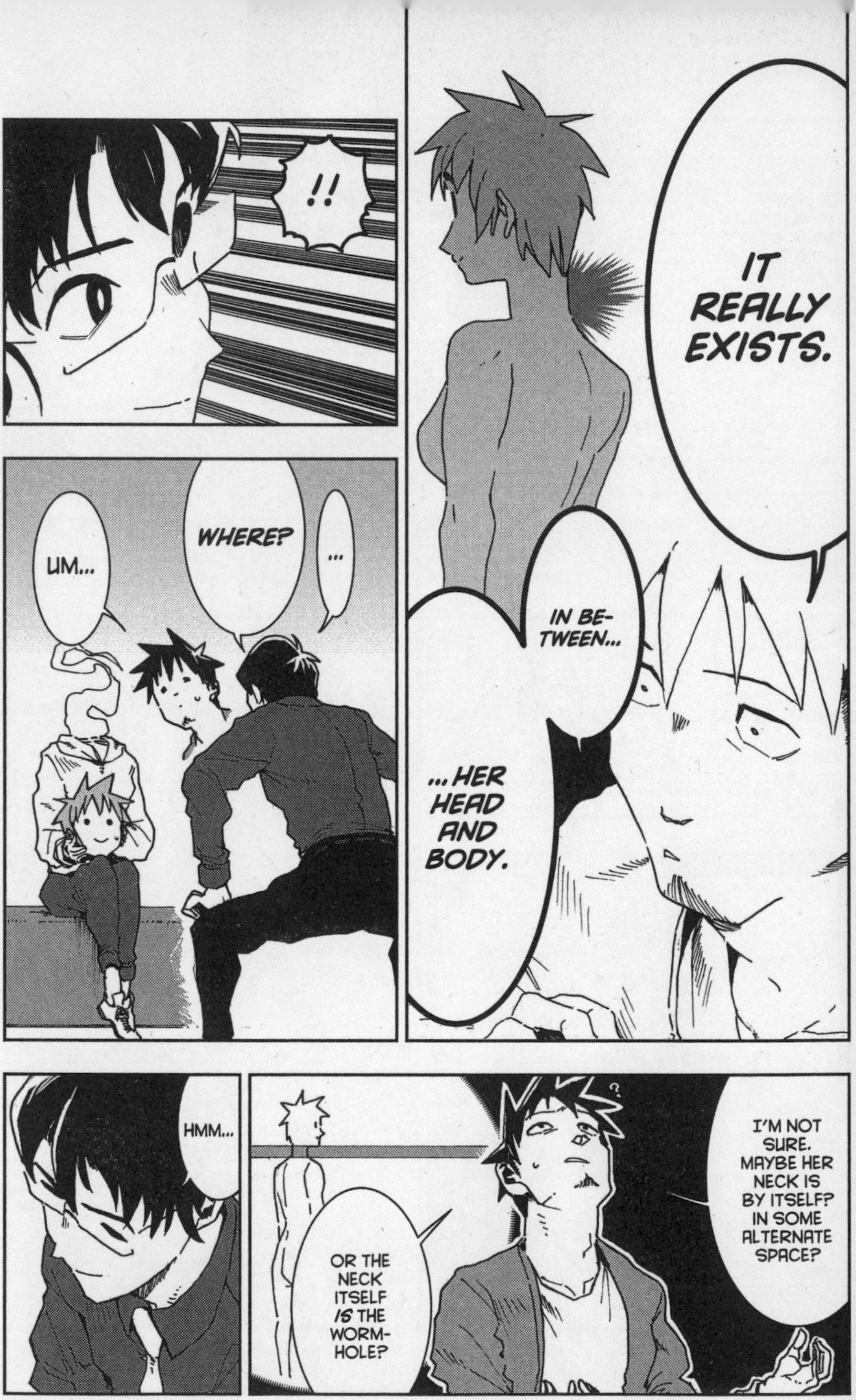
IT REALLY EXISTS.
IN BE-TWEEN...
...HER HEAD AND BODY.
!!
...
WHERE?
UM...
I'M NOT SURE. MAYBE HER NECK IS BY ITSELF? IN SOME ALTERNATE SPACE?
OR THE NECK ITSELF *IS* THE WORM-HOLE?
HMM...

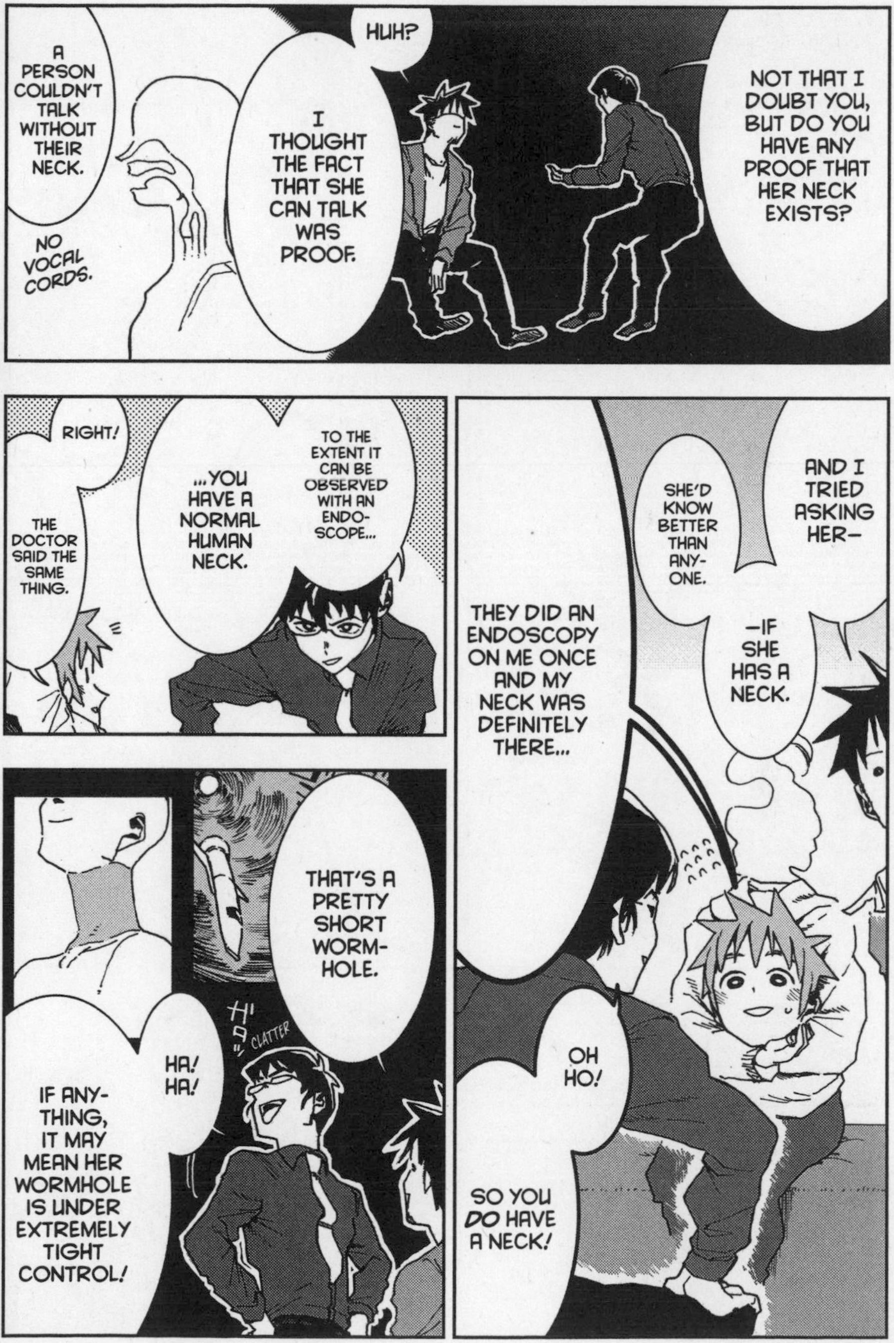
NOT THAT I DOUBT YOU, BUT DO YOU HAVE ANY PROOF THAT HER NECK EXISTS?
HUH?
I THOUGHT THE FACT THAT SHE CAN TALK WAS PROOF.
A PERSON COULDN'T TALK WITHOUT THEIR NECK.
NO VOCAL CORDS.
AND I TRIED ASKING HER—
SHE'D KNOW BETTER THAN ANYONE.
—IF SHE HAS A NECK.
THEY DID AN ENDOSCOPY ON ME ONCE AND MY NECK WAS DEFINITELY THERE...
OH HO!
SO YOU *DO* HAVE A NECK!
TO THE EXTENT IT CAN BE OBSERVED WITH AN ENDOSCOPE...
...YOU HAVE A NORMAL HUMAN NECK.
RIGHT!
THE DOCTOR SAID THE SAME THING.
THAT'S A PRETTY SHORT WORMHOLE.
HA! HA!
ガタ
CLATTER
IF ANYTHING, IT MAY MEAN HER WORMHOLE IS UNDER EXTREMELY TIGHT CONTROL!

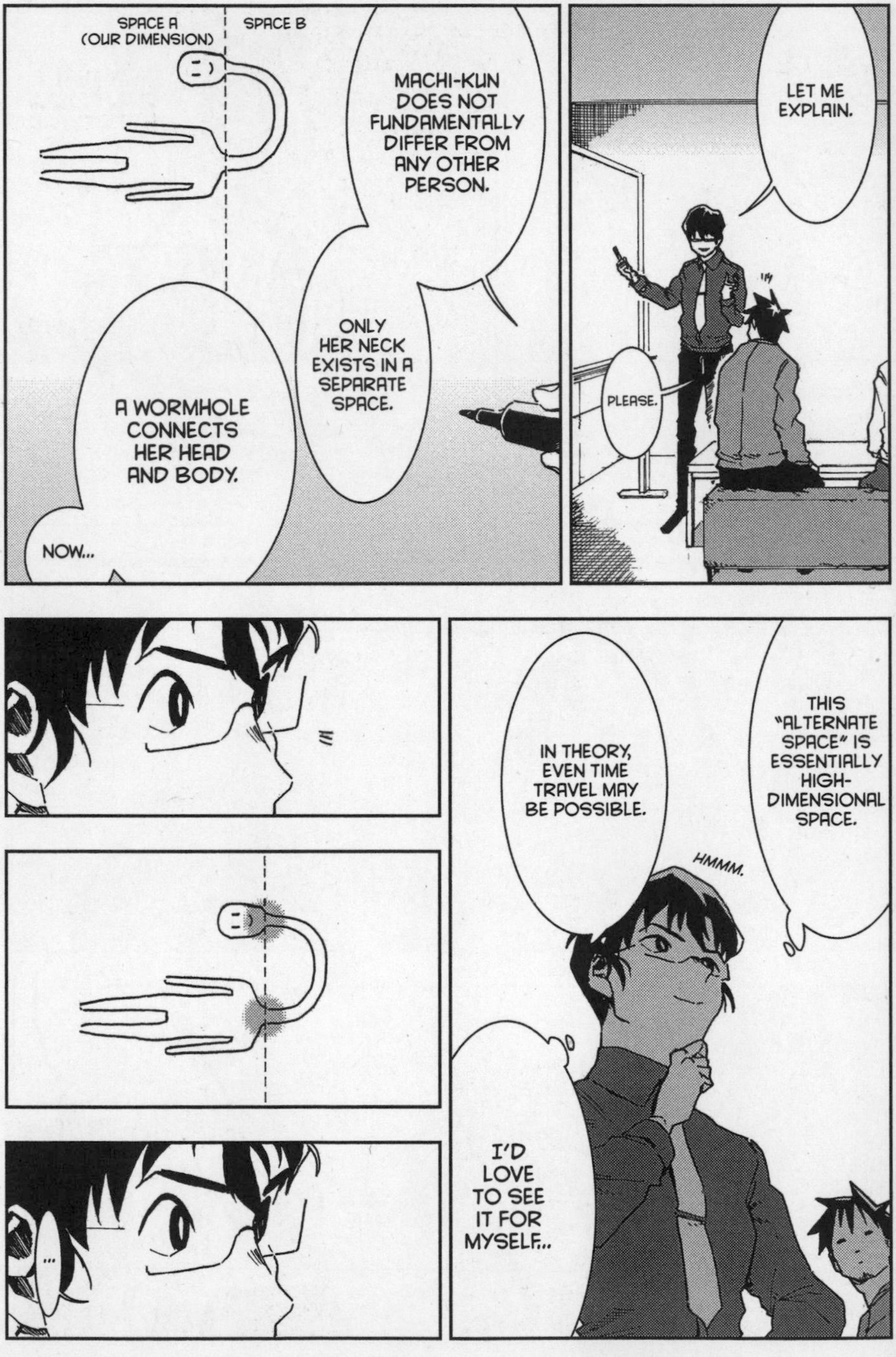
LET ME EXPLAIN.
PLEASE.
MACHI-KUN DOES NOT FUNDAMENTALLY DIFFER FROM ANY OTHER PERSON.
SPACE B
SPACE A (OUR DIMENSION)
ONLY HER NECK EXISTS IN A SEPARATE SPACE.
A WORMHOLE CONNECTS HER HEAD AND BODY.
NOW...
THIS "ALTERNATE SPACE" IS ESSENTIALLY HIGH-DIMENSIONAL SPACE.
IN THEORY, EVEN TIME TRAVEL MAY BE POSSIBLE.
HMMM.
I'D LOVE TO SEE IT FOR MYSELF...
...

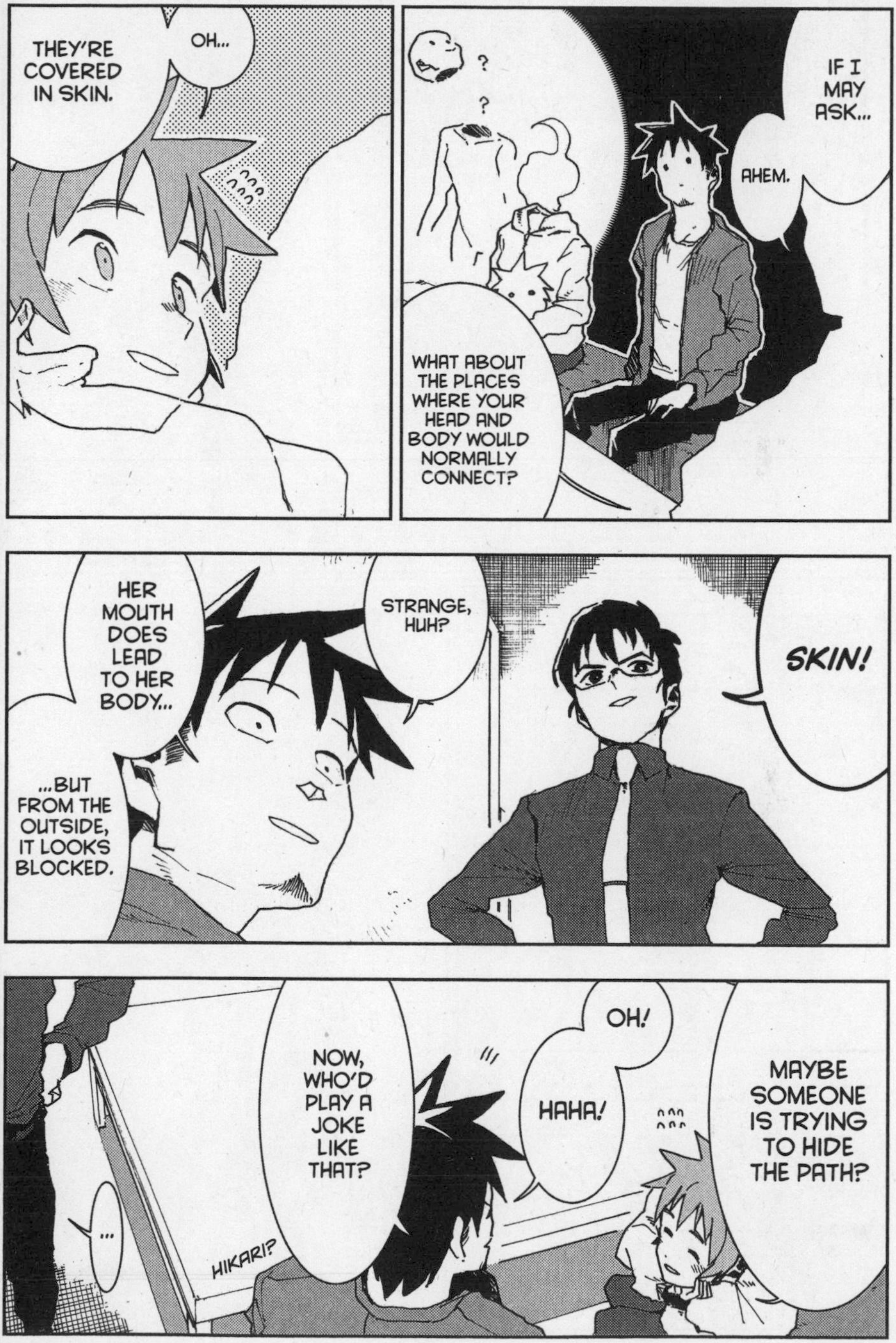
IF I MAY ASK...
AHEM.
?
?
WHAT ABOUT THE PLACES WHERE YOUR HEAD AND BODY WOULD NORMALLY CONNECT?
OH...
THEY'RE COVERED IN SKIN.
SKIN!
STRANGE, HUH?
HER MOUTH DOES LEAD TO HER BODY...
...BUT FROM THE OUTSIDE, IT LOOKS BLOCKED.
MAYBE SOMEONE IS TRYING TO HIDE THE PATH?
OH!
HAHA!
NOW, WHO'D PLAY A JOKE LIKE THAT?
HIKARI?
...

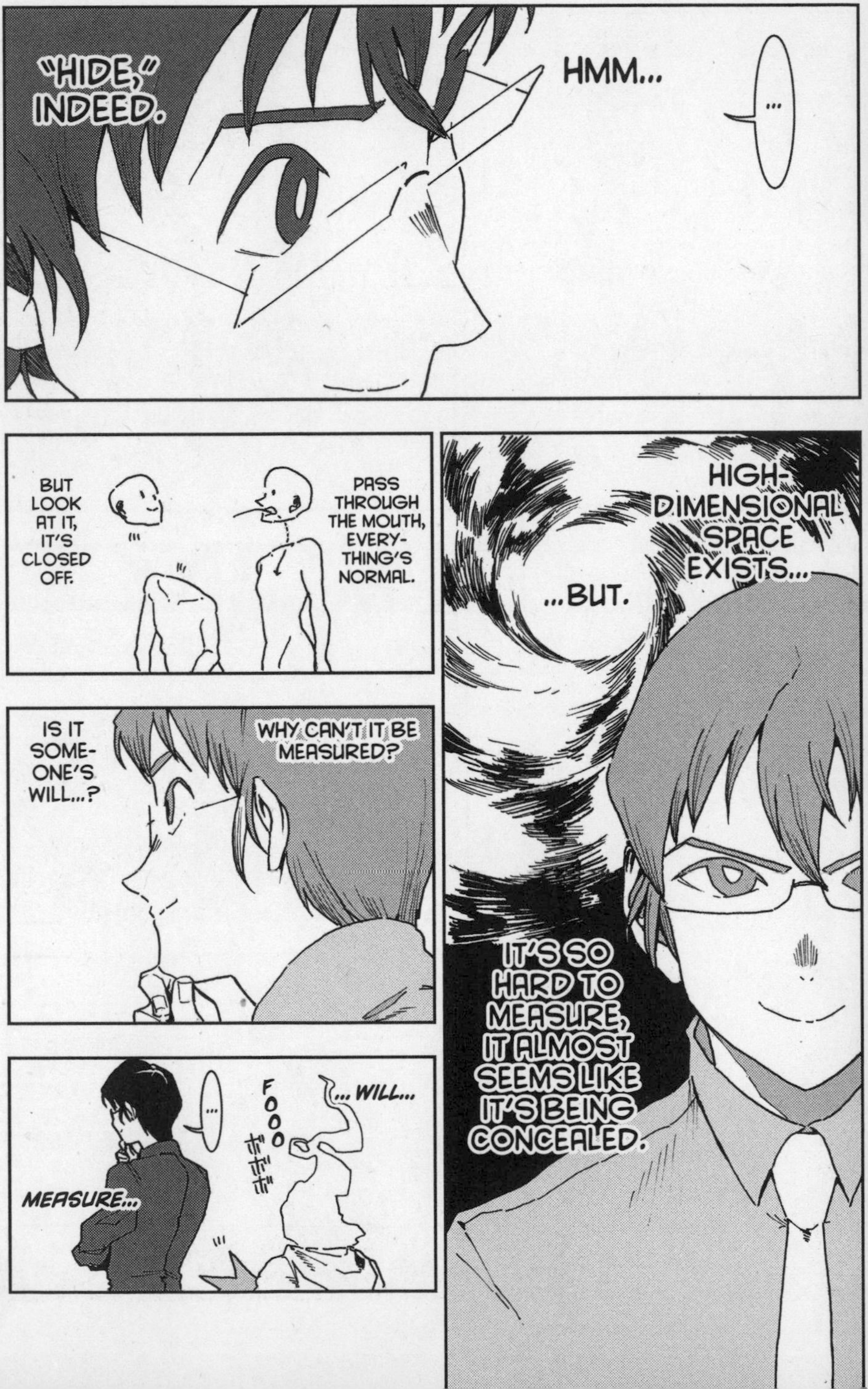
...
HMM...
"HIDE," INDEED.
HIGH-DIMENSIONAL SPACE EXISTS...
...BUT.
IT'S SO HARD TO MEASURE, IT ALMOST SEEMS LIKE IT'S BEING CONCEALED.
PASS THROUGH THE MOUTH, EVERY-THING'S NORMAL.
BUT LOOK AT IT, IT'S CLOSED OFF.
WHY CAN'T IT BE MEASURED?
IS IT SOME-ONE'S WILL...?
... WILL...
FOOOO
ボボボ
...
MEASURE...

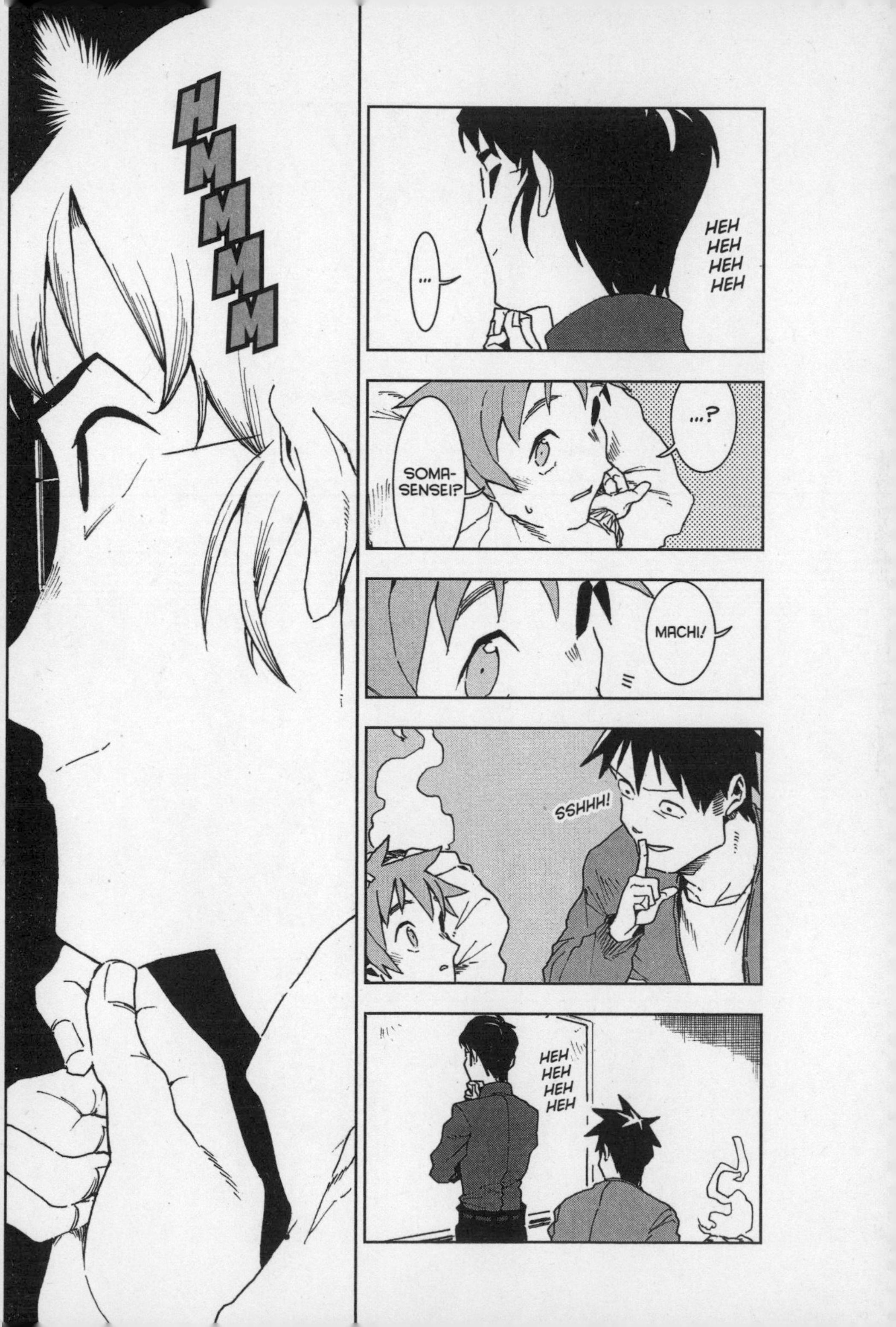
HEH HEH HEH HEH
...
...?
SOMA-SENSEI!?
MACHI!
SSHHH!
HEH HEH HEH HEH
HMMMM

IS SOMA-SENSEI... THINKING?
YEAH... HIS EXPRESSION NEVER CHANGES. IT'S LIKE TIME HAS STOPPED.
...
HE'S VERY STRANGE...
YEAH...
...
...
...
...
DEMI OR NOT...
WHAT'S STRANGE IS STRANGE.
YEAH...
...

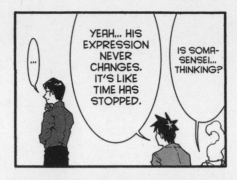

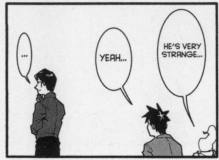

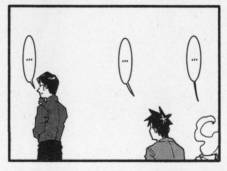

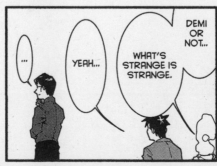

INTERVIEWS WITH MONSTER GIRLS

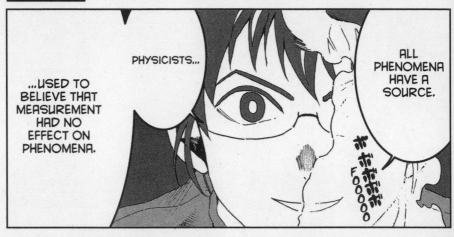

ALL PHENOMENA HAVE A SOURCE.
PHYSICISTS...
...USED TO BELIEVE THAT MEASUREMENT HAD NO EFFECT ON PHENOMENA.
FOOOOO
MEASURE-MENT?
STAAAARE
YES.
IN OTHER WORDS, WHETHER OR NOT HUMANS OBSERVE SOME-THING...
NOT LOOKING
LOOKING
...OR EVEN IF HUMANS DIDN'T EXIST...
PHENOMENON
...THE RESULT OF A PHENOMENON WOULD BE UNCHANGED.
THAT'S WHAT I MEAN.
PHENOMENON
HMM.
THAT SEEMS LIKE COMMON SENSE...
TRUE!
BUT IN FACT!

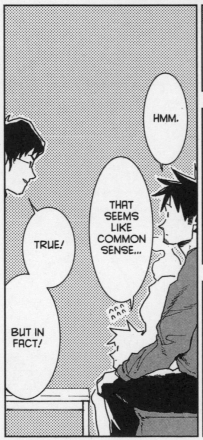

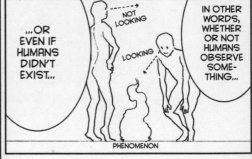

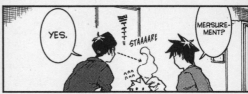

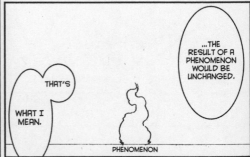

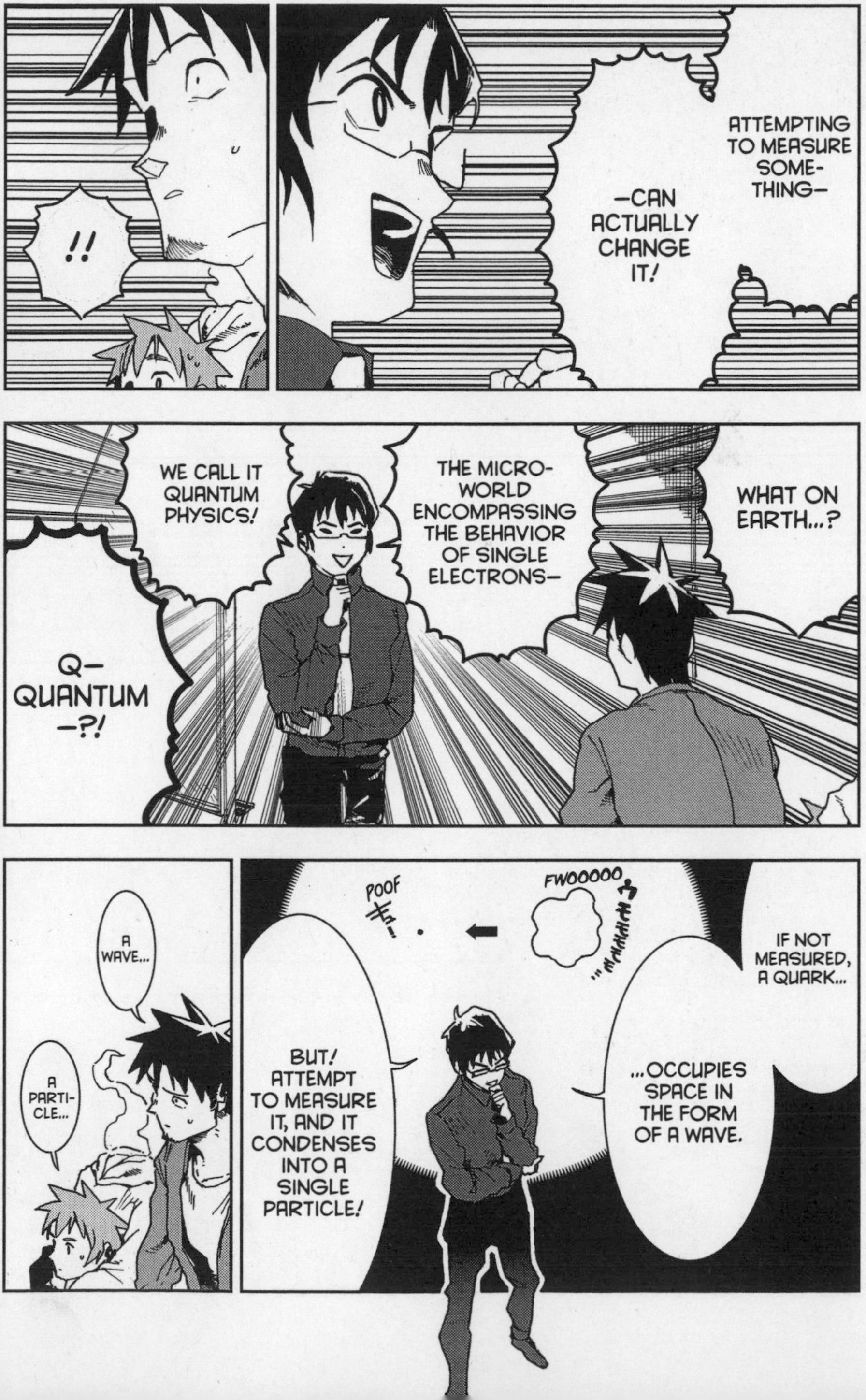
ATTEMPTING TO MEASURE SOME-THING—
—CAN ACTUALLY CHANGE IT!
!!
WHAT ON EARTH...?
THE MICRO-WORLD ENCOMPASSING THE BEHAVIOR OF SINGLE ELECTRONS—
WE CALL IT QUANTUM PHYSICS!
Q—QUANTUM—?!
IF NOT MEASURED, A QUARK...
FWOOOOO
...OCCUPIES SPACE IN THE FORM OF A WAVE.
POOF
BUT! ATTEMPT TO MEASURE IT, AND IT CONDENSES INTO A SINGLE PARTICLE!
A WAVE...
A PARTI-CLE...

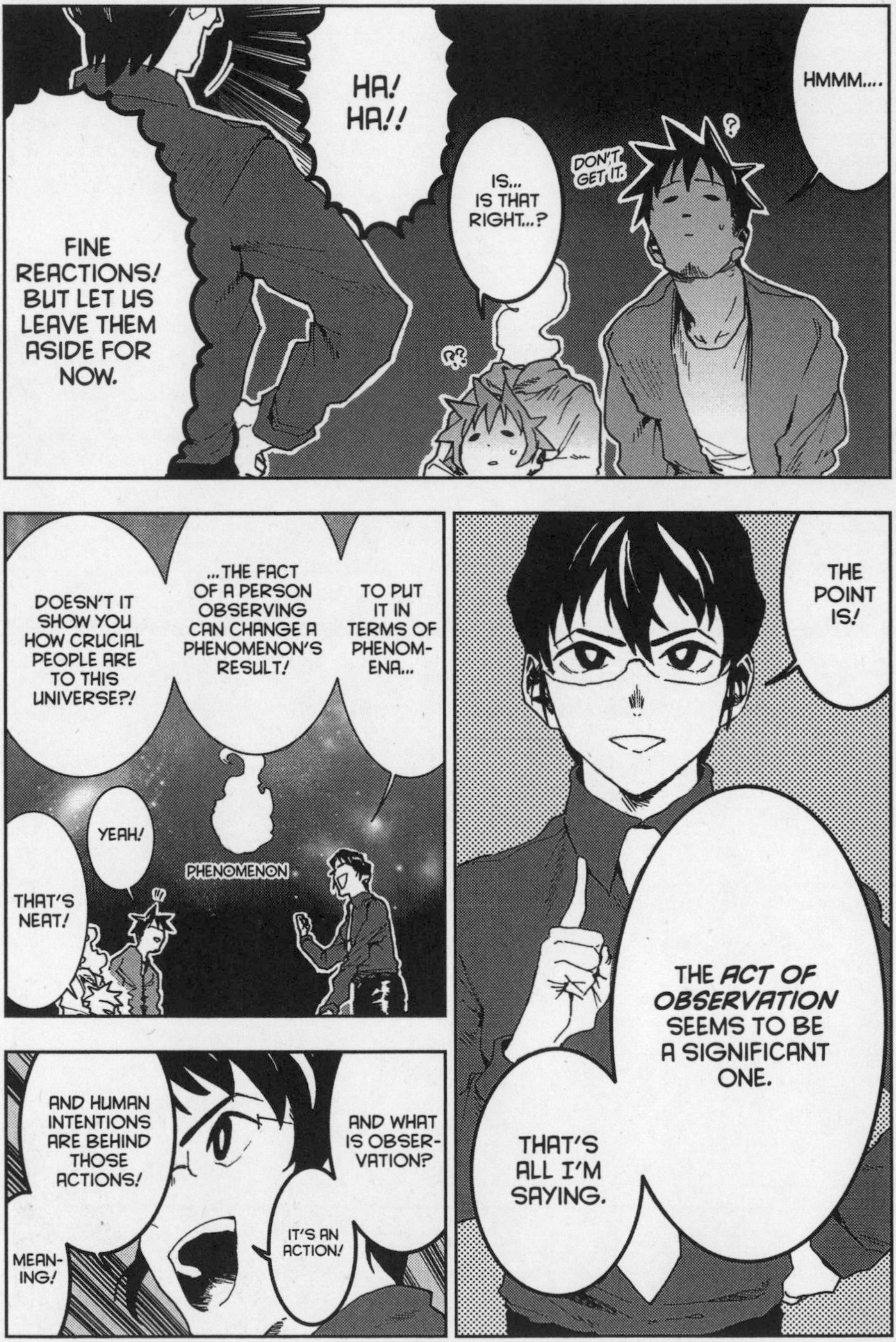
HMMM....
DON'T GET IT.
IS... IS THAT RIGHT...?
HA! HA!!
FINE REACTIONS! BUT LET US LEAVE THEM ASIDE FOR NOW.
THE POINT IS!
THE *ACT OF OBSERVATION* SEEMS TO BE A SIGNIFICANT ONE.
THAT'S ALL I'M SAYING.
TO PUT IT IN TERMS OF PHENOM-ENA...
...THE FACT OF A PERSON OBSERVING CAN CHANGE A PHENOMENON'S RESULT!
DOESN'T IT SHOW YOU HOW CRUCIAL PEOPLE ARE TO THIS UNIVERSE?!
PHENOMENON
YEAH!
THAT'S NEAT!
AND WHAT IS OBSER-VATION?
IT'S AN ACTION!
AND HUMAN INTENTIONS ARE BEHIND THOSE ACTIONS!
MEAN-ING!

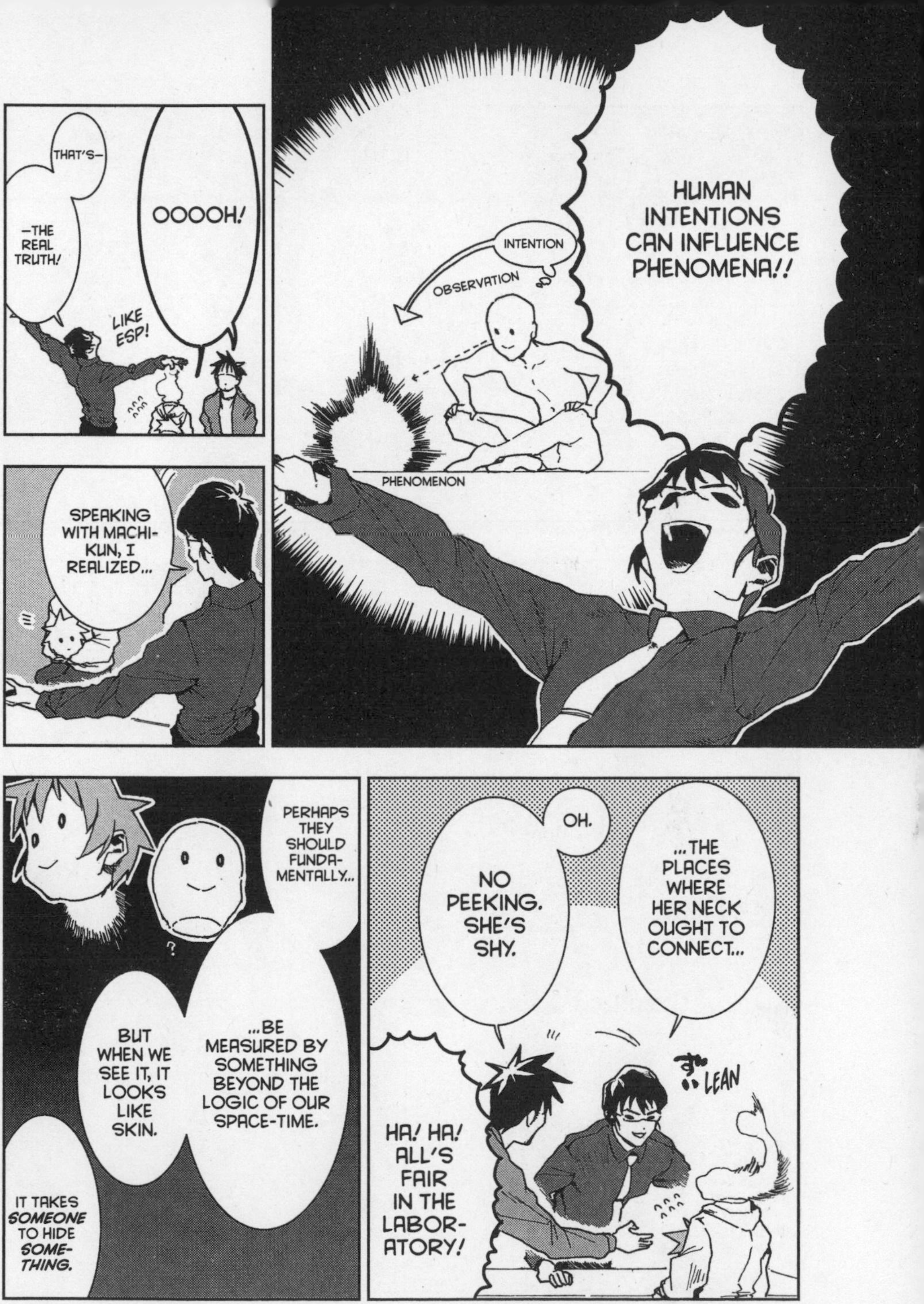
HUMAN INTENTIONS CAN INFLUENCE PHENOMENA!!
INTENTION
OBSERVATION
PHENOMENON
OOOOH!
THAT'S—
—THE REAL TRUTH!
LIKE ESP!
SPEAKING WITH MACHI-KUN, I REALIZED...
...THE PLACES WHERE HER NECK OUGHT TO CONNECT...
OH.
NO PEEKING. SHE'S SHY.
LEAN
HA! HA! ALL'S FAIR IN THE LABORATORY!
PERHAPS THEY SHOULD FUNDAMENTALLY...
...BE MEASURED BY SOMETHING BEYOND THE LOGIC OF OUR SPACE-TIME.
BUT WHEN WE SEE IT, IT LOOKS LIKE SKIN.
IT TAKES *SOMEONE* TO HIDE *SOMETHING.*

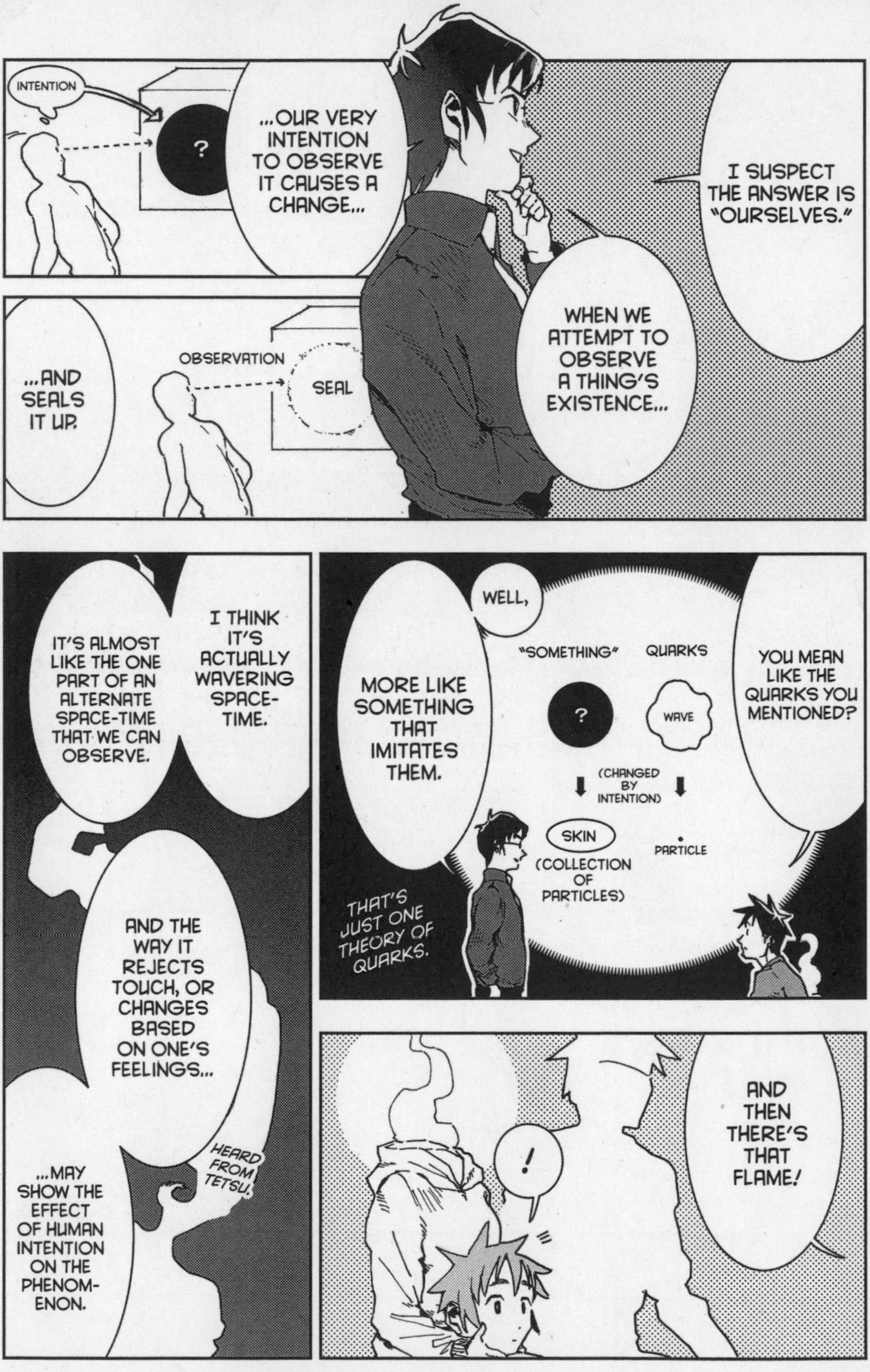
I SUSPECT THE ANSWER IS "OURSELVES."
WHEN WE ATTEMPT TO OBSERVE A THING'S EXISTENCE...
INTENTION
?
...OUR VERY INTENTION TO OBSERVE IT CAUSES A CHANGE...
OBSERVATION
SEAL
...AND SEALS IT UP.
YOU MEAN LIKE THE QUARKS YOU MENTIONED?
WELL,
"SOMETHING"
QUARKS
?
WAVE
(CHANGED BY INTENTION)
SKIN
(COLLECTION OF PARTICLES)
PARTICLE
MORE LIKE SOMETHING THAT IMITATES THEM.
THAT'S JUST ONE THEORY OF QUARKS.
!
AND THEN THERE'S THAT FLAME!
I THINK IT'S ACTUALLY WAVERING SPACE-TIME.
IT'S ALMOST LIKE THE ONE PART OF AN ALTERNATE SPACE-TIME THAT WE CAN OBSERVE.
AND THE WAY IT REJECTS TOUCH, OR CHANGES BASED ON ONE'S FEELINGS...
HEARD FROM TETSU.
...MAY SHOW THE EFFECT OF HUMAN INTENTION ON THE PHENOMENON.

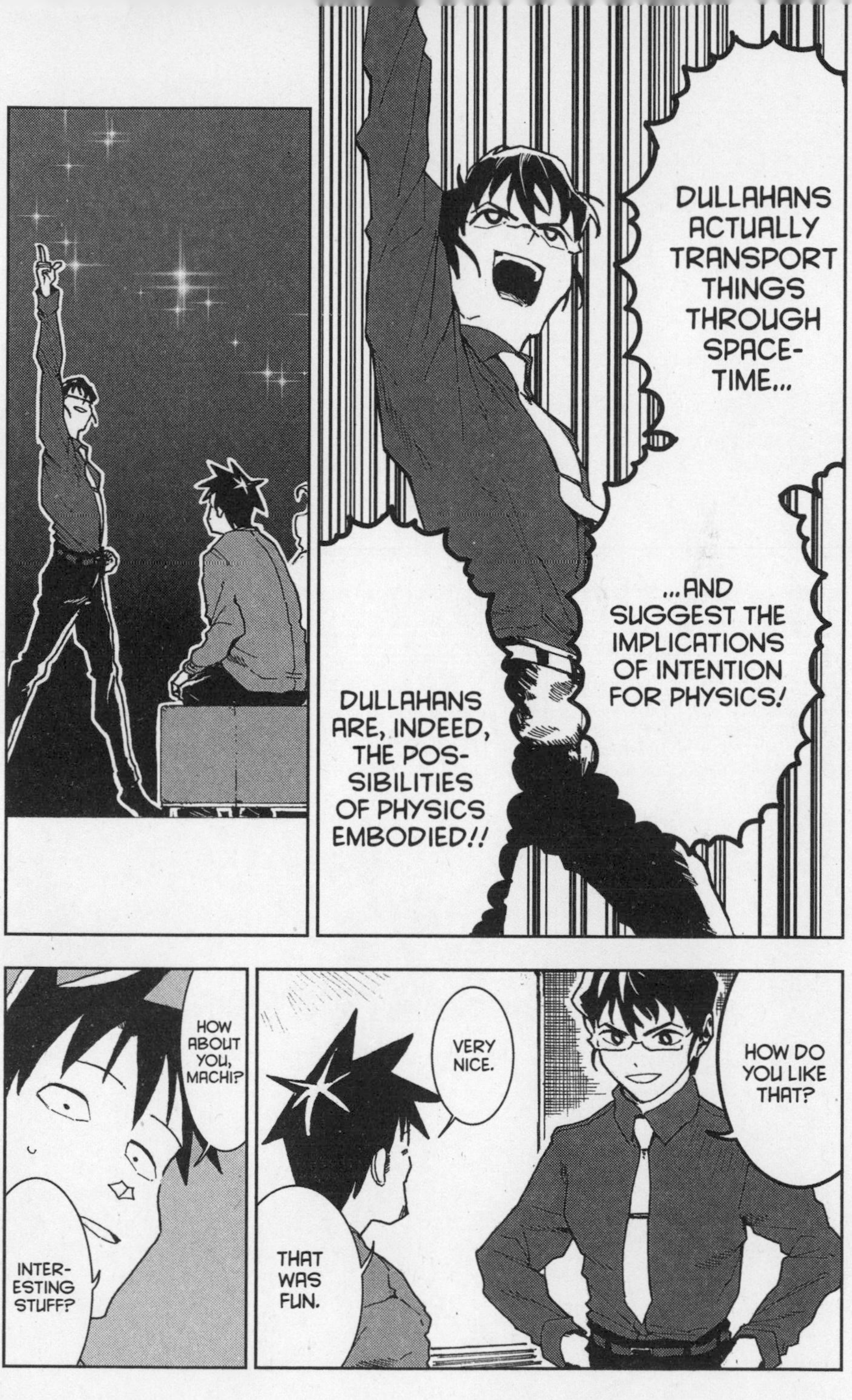
DULLAHANS ACTUALLY TRANSPORT THINGS THROUGH SPACE-TIME...
...AND SUGGEST THE IMPLICATIONS OF INTENTION FOR PHYSICS!
DULLAHANS ARE, INDEED, THE POS-SIBILITIES OF PHYSICS EMBODIED!!
HOW DO YOU LIKE THAT?
VERY NICE.
THAT WAS FUN.
HOW ABOUT YOU, MACHI?
INTER-ESTING STUFF?

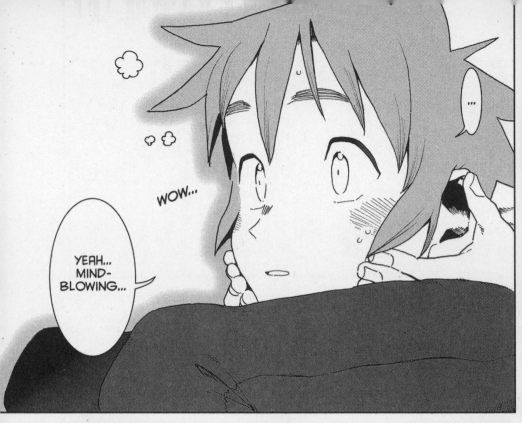

WOW...

YEAH...
MIND-
BLOWING...

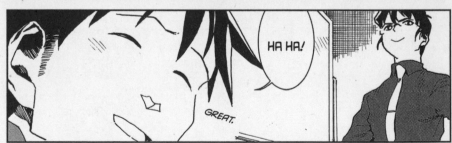

HA HA!

GREAT.

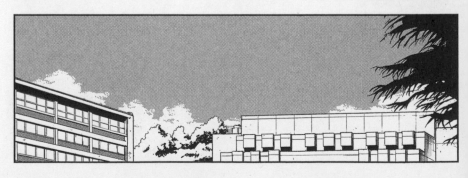

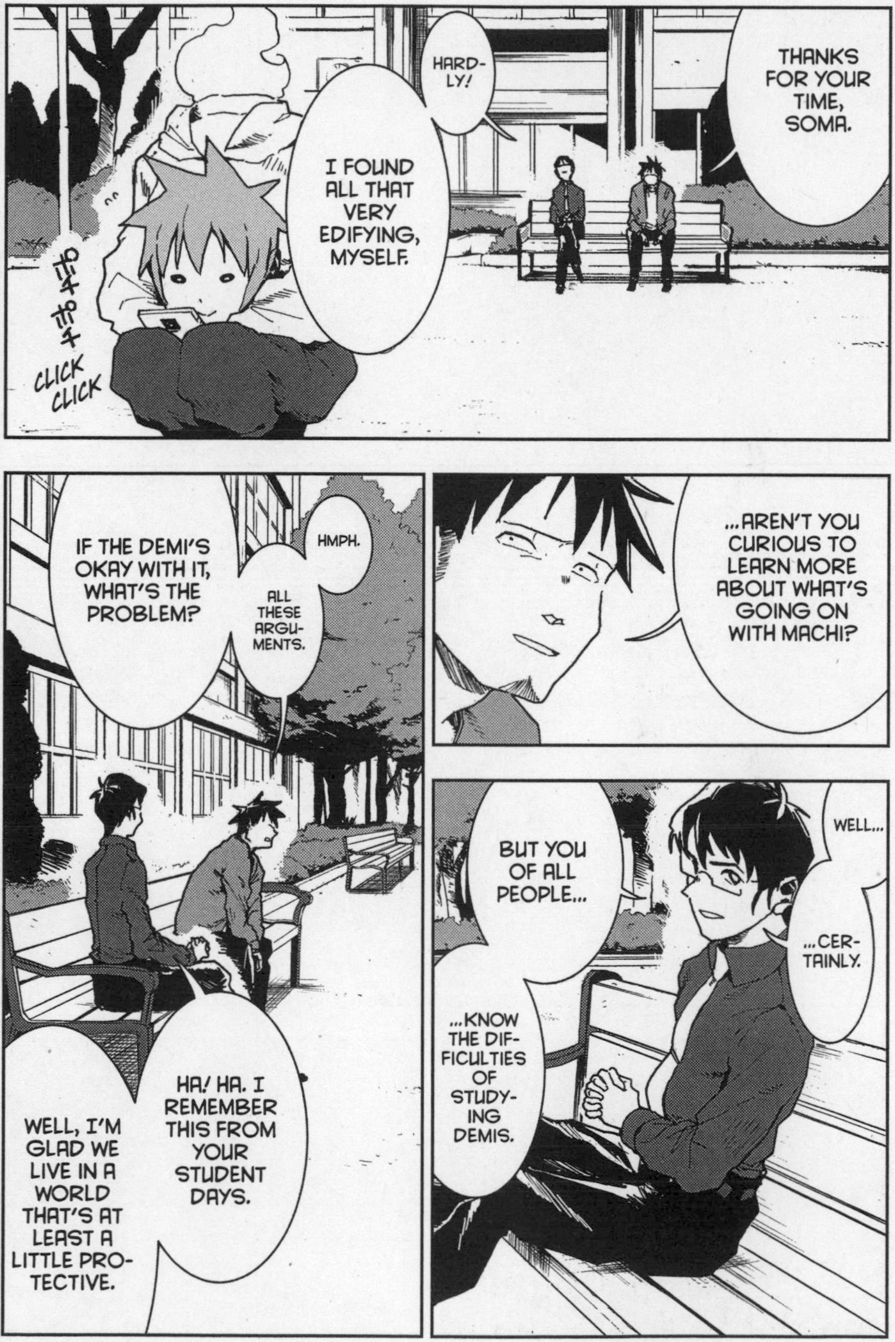
THANKS FOR YOUR TIME, SOMA.
HARD-LY!
I FOUND ALL THAT VERY EDIFYING, MYSELF.
ポチポチ
CLICK CLICK
...AREN'T YOU CURIOUS TO LEARN MORE ABOUT WHAT'S GOING ON WITH MACHI?
WELL...
...CER-TAINLY.
BUT YOU OF ALL PEOPLE...
...KNOW THE DIF-FICULTIES OF STUDY-ING DEMIS.
HMPH.
ALL THESE ARGU-MENTS.
IF THE DEMI'S OKAY WITH IT, WHAT'S THE PROBLEM?
HA! HA. I REMEMBER THIS FROM YOUR STUDENT DAYS.
WELL, I'M GLAD WE LIVE IN A WORLD THAT'S AT LEAST A LITTLE PRO-TECTIVE.

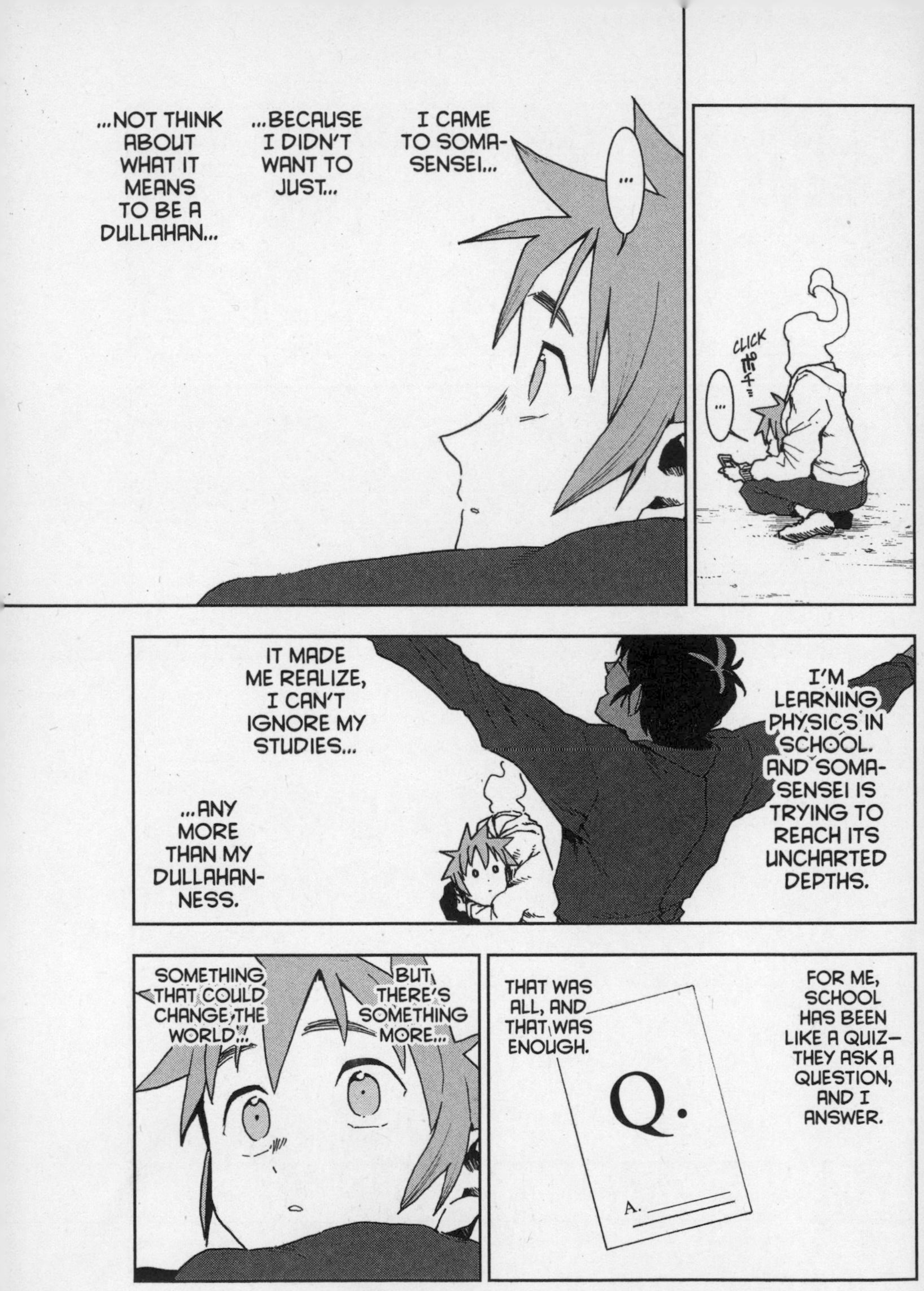
...
CLICK
ポチ
...
I CAME TO SOMA-SENSEI...
...BECAUSE I DIDN'T WANT TO JUST...
...NOT THINK ABOUT WHAT IT MEANS TO BE A DULLAHAN...
I'M LEARNING PHYSICS IN SCHOOL. AND SOMA-SENSEI IS TRYING TO REACH ITS UNCHARTED DEPTHS.
IT MADE ME REALIZE, I CAN'T IGNORE MY STUDIES...
...ANY MORE THAN MY DULLAHANNESS.
FOR ME, SCHOOL HAS BEEN LIKE A QUIZ—THEY ASK A QUESTION, AND I ANSWER.
Q.
A.
THAT WAS ALL, AND THAT WAS ENOUGH.
BUT THERE'S SOMETHING MORE...
SOMETHING THAT COULD CHANGE THE WORLD...

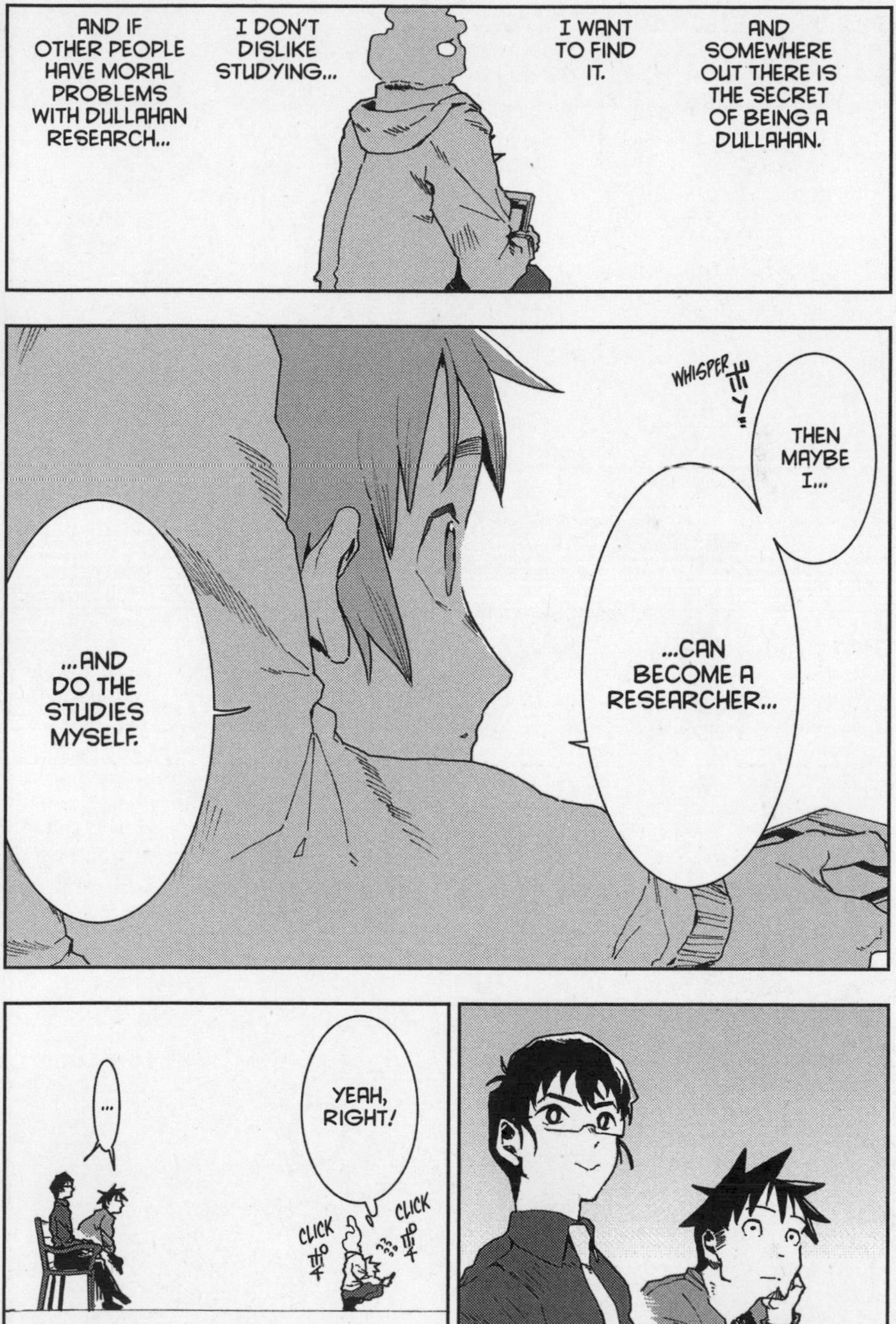
AND SOMEWHERE OUT THERE IS THE SECRET OF BEING A DULLAHAN.
I WANT TO FIND IT.
I DON'T DISLIKE STUDYING...
AND IF OTHER PEOPLE HAVE MORAL PROBLEMS WITH DULLAHAN RESEARCH...
WHISPER
THEN MAYBE I...
...CAN BECOME A RESEARCHER...
...AND DO THE STUDIES MYSELF.
CLICK
YEAH, RIGHT!
CLICK
...

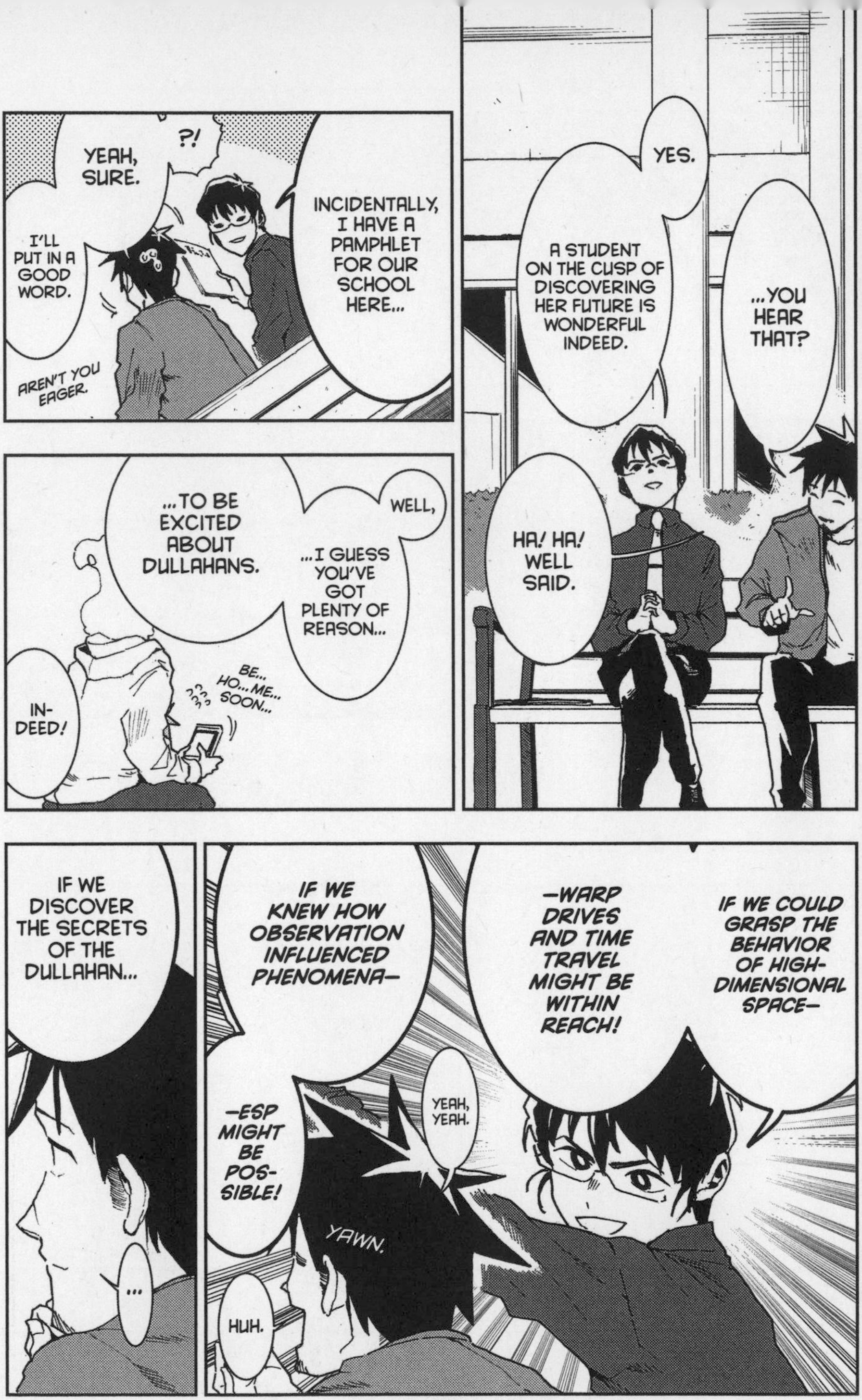
YES.
A STUDENT ON THE CUSP OF DISCOVERING HER FUTURE IS WONDERFUL INDEED.
...YOU HEAR THAT?
HA! HA! WELL SAID.
INCIDENTALLY, I HAVE A PAMPHLET FOR OUR SCHOOL HERE...
?!
YEAH, SURE.
I'LL PUT IN A GOOD WORD.
AREN'T YOU EAGER.
WELL,
...I GUESS YOU'VE GOT PLENTY OF REASON...
...TO BE EXCITED ABOUT DULLAHANS.
BE... HO...ME... SOON...
IN-DEED!
IF WE COULD GRASP THE BEHAVIOR OF HIGH-DIMENSIONAL SPACE—
—WARP DRIVES AND TIME TRAVEL MIGHT BE WITHIN REACH!
IF WE KNEW HOW OBSERVATION INFLUENCED PHENOMENA—
YEAH, YEAH.
—ESP MIGHT BE POS-SIBLE!
YAWN.
HUH.
IF WE DISCOVER THE SECRETS OF THE DULLAHAN...
...

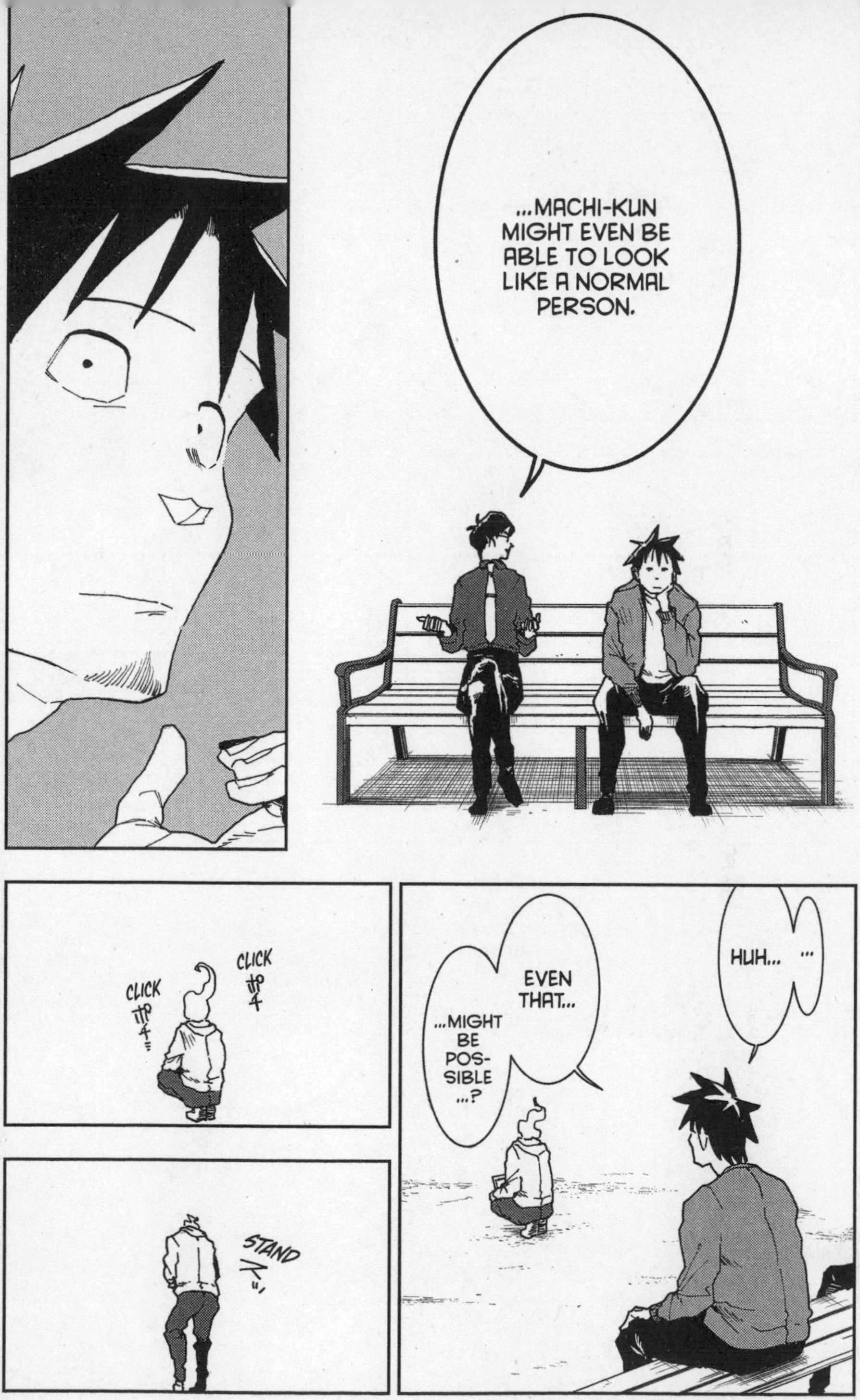
...MACHI-KUN MIGHT EVEN BE ABLE TO LOOK LIKE A NORMAL PERSON.
HUH... ...
EVEN THAT... ...MIGHT BE POS-SIBLE ...?
CLICK
CLICK
STAND

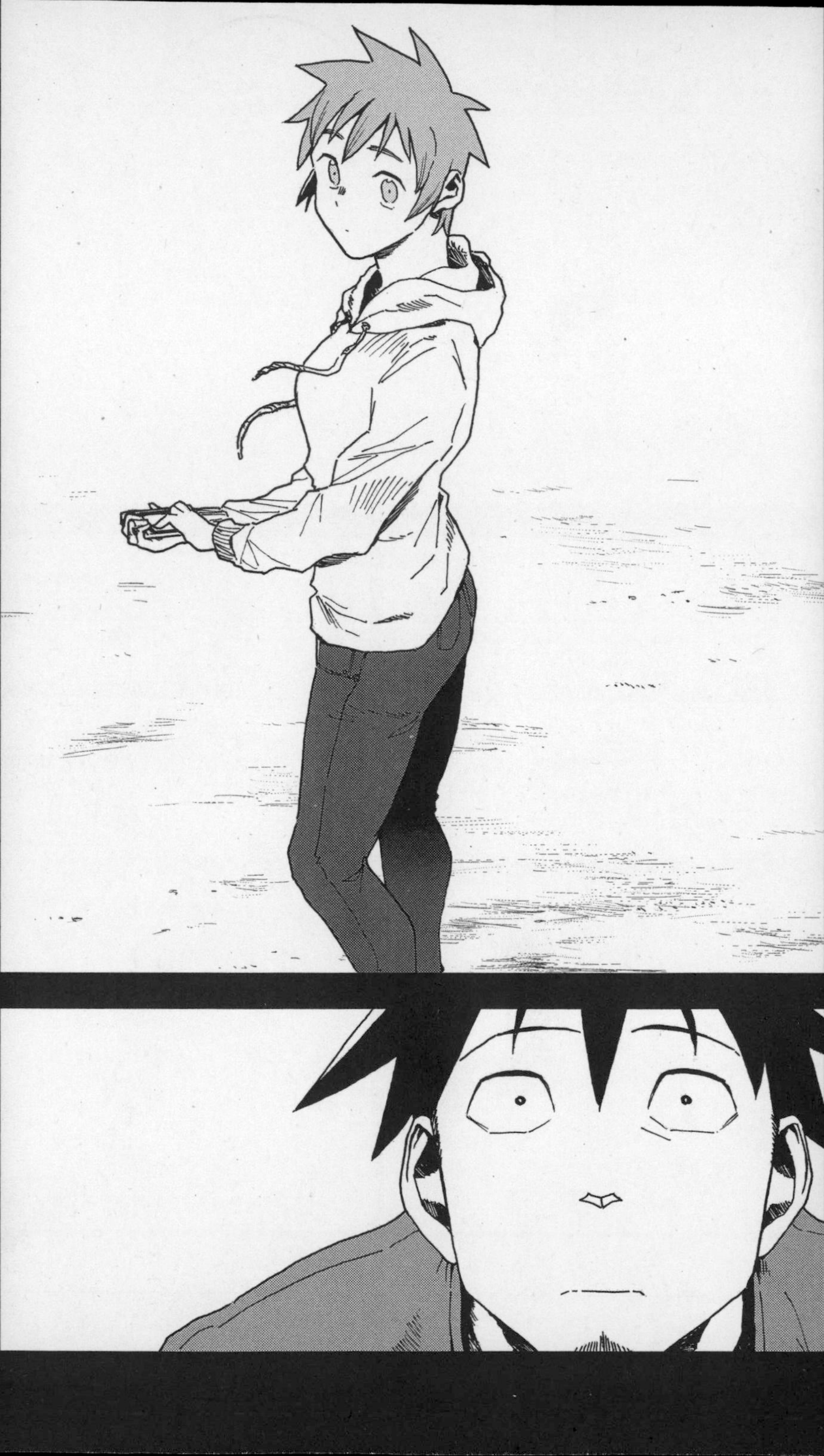

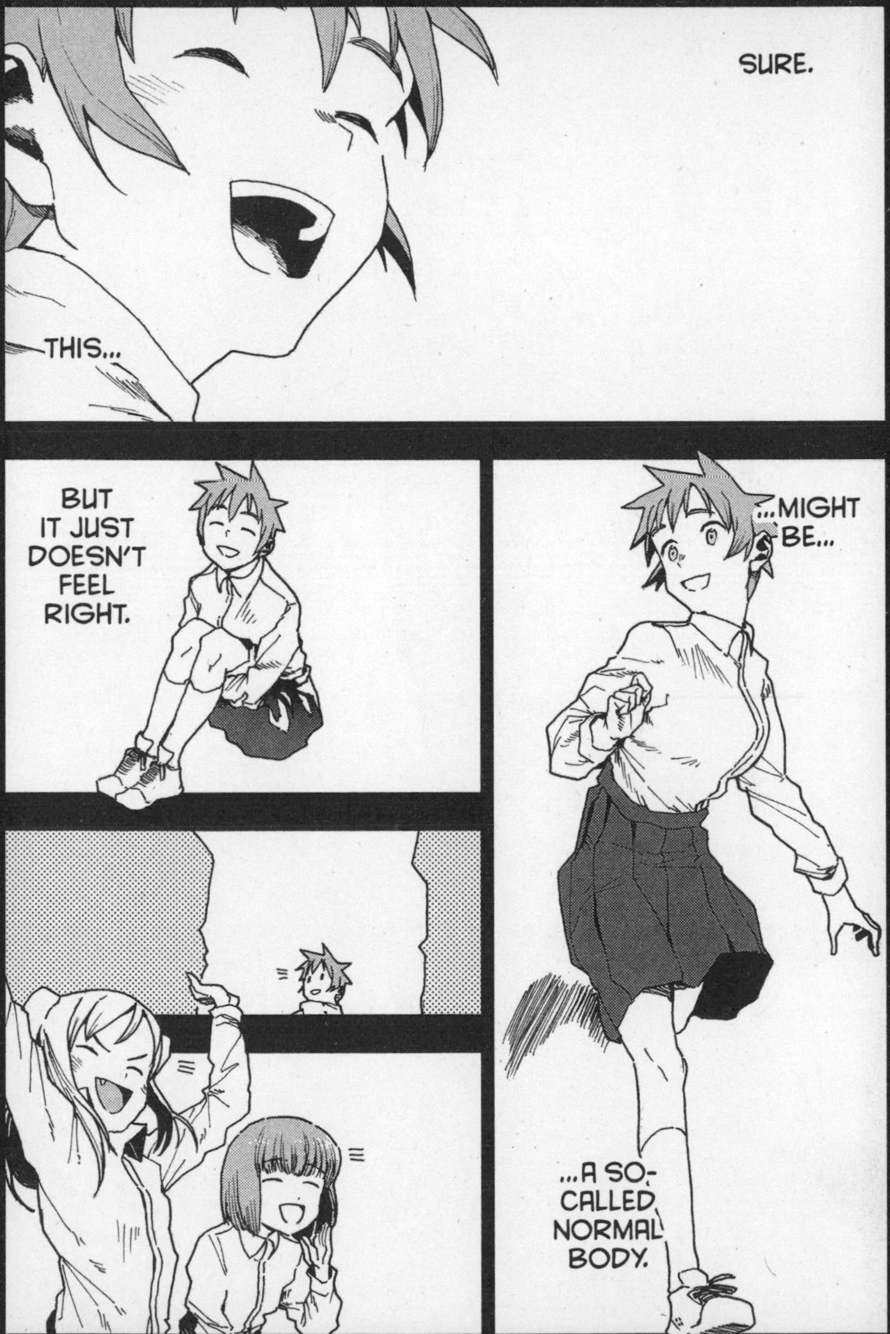
SURE.
THIS...
...MIGHT BE...
...A SO-CALLED NORMAL BODY.
BUT IT JUST DOESN'T FEEL RIGHT.

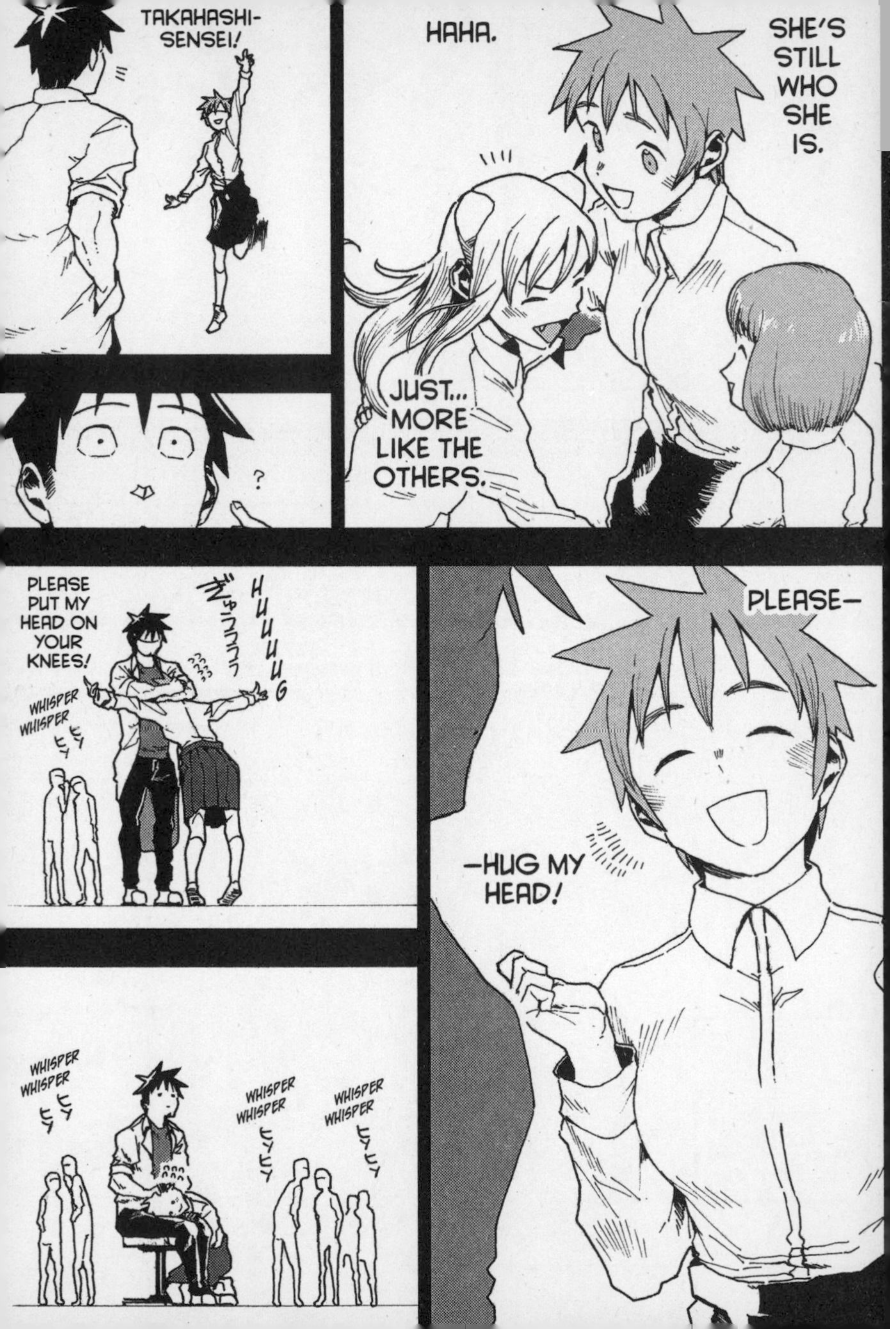
HAHA.
SHE'S STILL WHO SHE IS.
JUST... MORE LIKE THE OTHERS.
TAKAHASHI-SENSEI!
?
PLEASE—
—HUG MY HEAD!
PLEASE PUT MY HEAD ON YOUR KNEES!
HUUUUUG
WHISPER WHISPER
WHISPER WHISPER
WHISPER WHISPER
WHISPER WHISPER

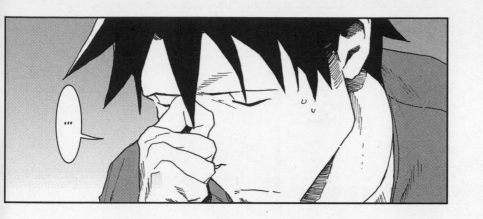

...
SUDDENLY THOSE ETHICAL QUESTIONS SEEM MORE IMPORTANT...
OH HO, TETSU! COME AROUND, HAVE YOU?
?
AN ADULT TRYING TO RESPECT SOCIAL BOUNDARIES IS WONDERFUL, TOO.

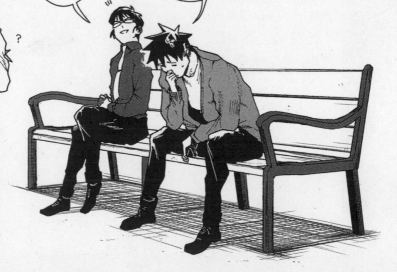

HOW DID YOU TWO MEET EACH OTHER?
IN CLASS.
OUR SEATS WERE NEXT TO EACH OTHER.
TAKA-HASHI
SOMA
MM!
HE HASN'T CHANGED A BIT.
A ROMANTICIST.
HE WANTS TO TAKE THE FICTION OUT OF SCIENCE FICTION.
HA! HA. A FINE TURN!
YOU *HAVE* CHANGED, TETSU!
REALLY?
EVERY TIME I SEE YOU, YOU ARE BRAWNIER!
...
...YOU MEANT MY LOOKS.
SO ADULTS GET THIS WAY WITH THEIR FRIENDS, TOO.
BLAH
BLAH

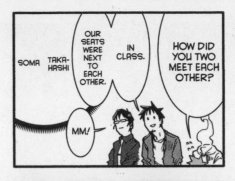

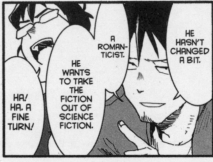

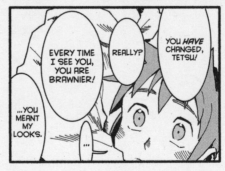

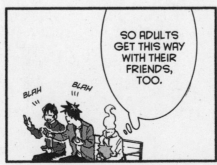

INTERVIEWS WITH MONSTER GIRLS

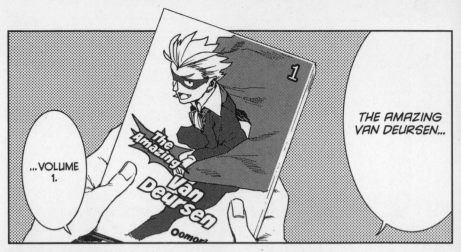

THE AMAZING VAN DEURSEN...
1
The Amazing Van Deursen
Oomori
...VOLUME 1.
THIS TAKES ME BACK...
A COMEDY *MANGA* ABOUT A VAMPIRE ROBIN HOOD.
MY DAD WAS A FAN WHEN I WAS YOUNG.
...
BUT WHAT'S IT DOING IN THE HALL-WAY?
?
SOMEONE MUST'VE DROPPED IT, BUT MOST KIDS DON'T READ COMICS THIS OLD...
SATO-SENSEI?

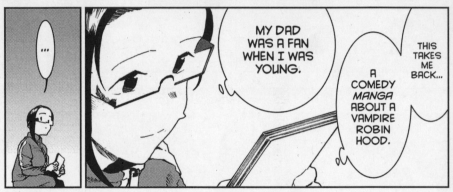

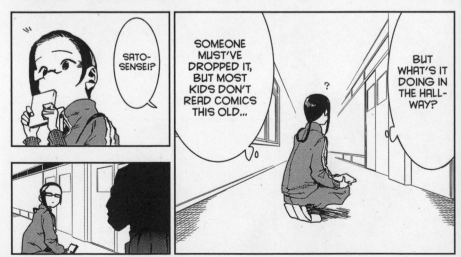

Chapter 27: Stranger Than Fiction

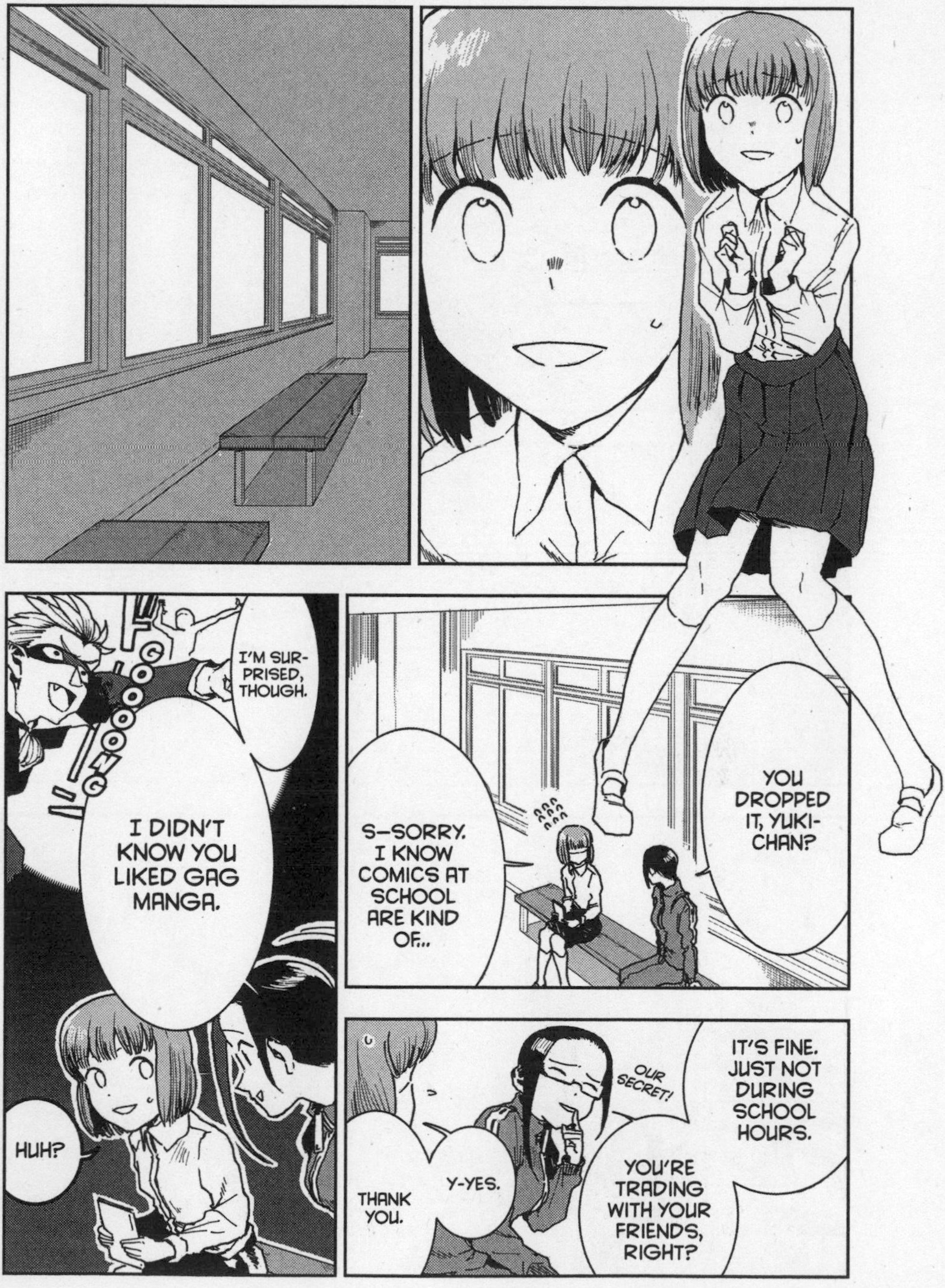
YOU DROPPED IT, YUKI-CHAN?
S-SORRY. I KNOW COMICS AT SCHOOL ARE KIND OF...
IT'S FINE. JUST NOT DURING SCHOOL HOURS.
OUR SECRET!
YOU'RE TRADING WITH YOUR FRIENDS, RIGHT?
Y-YES.
THANK YOU.
I'M SURPRISED, THOUGH.
FGOOOOOONG!
I DIDN'T KNOW YOU LIKED GAG MANGA.
HUH?

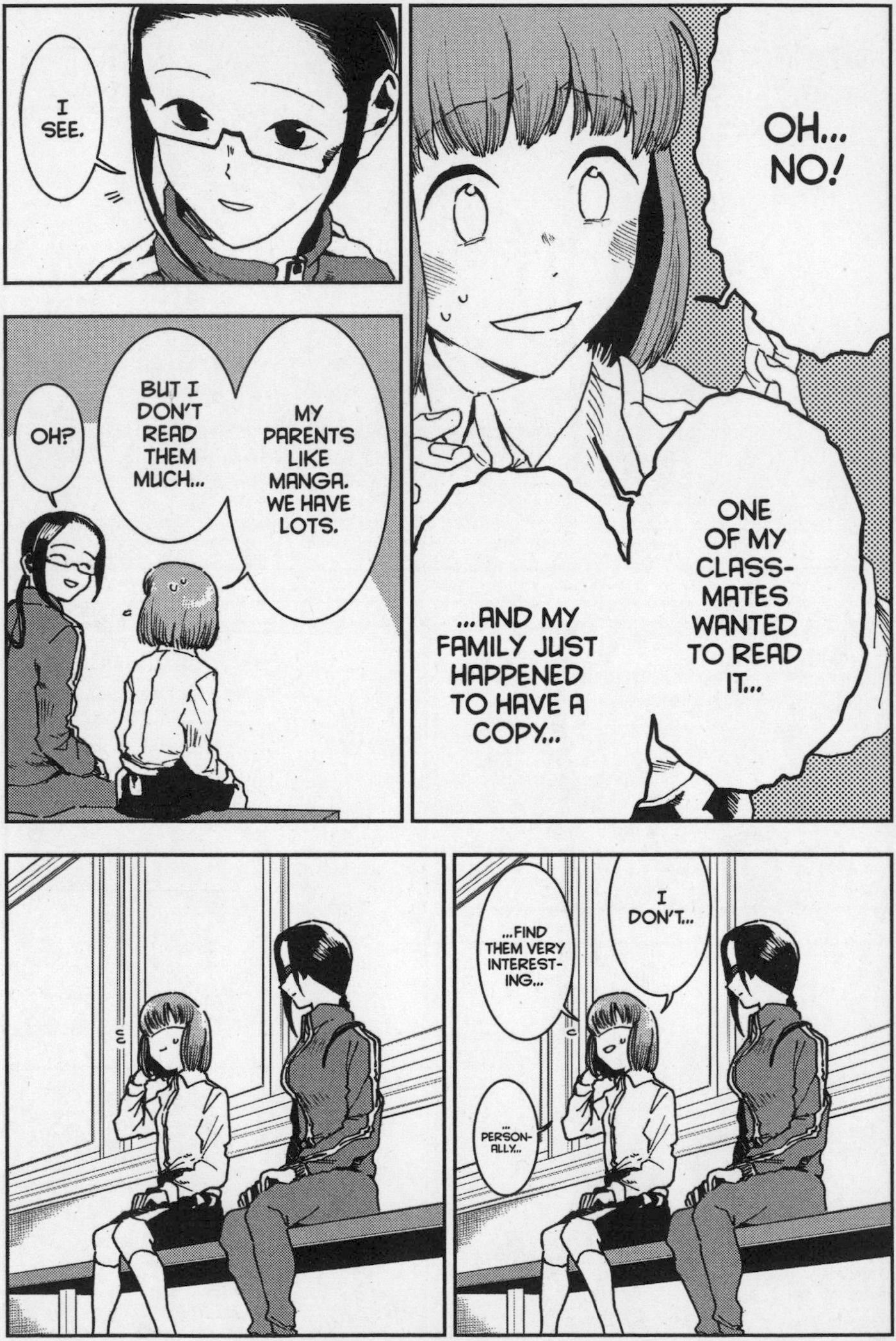
OH... NO!
ONE OF MY CLASS-MATES WANTED TO READ IT...
...AND MY FAMILY JUST HAPPENED TO HAVE A COPY...
I SEE.
MY PARENTS LIKE MANGA. WE HAVE LOTS.
BUT I DON'T READ THEM MUCH...
OH?
I DON'T...
...FIND THEM VERY INTEREST-ING...
... PERSON-ALLY...

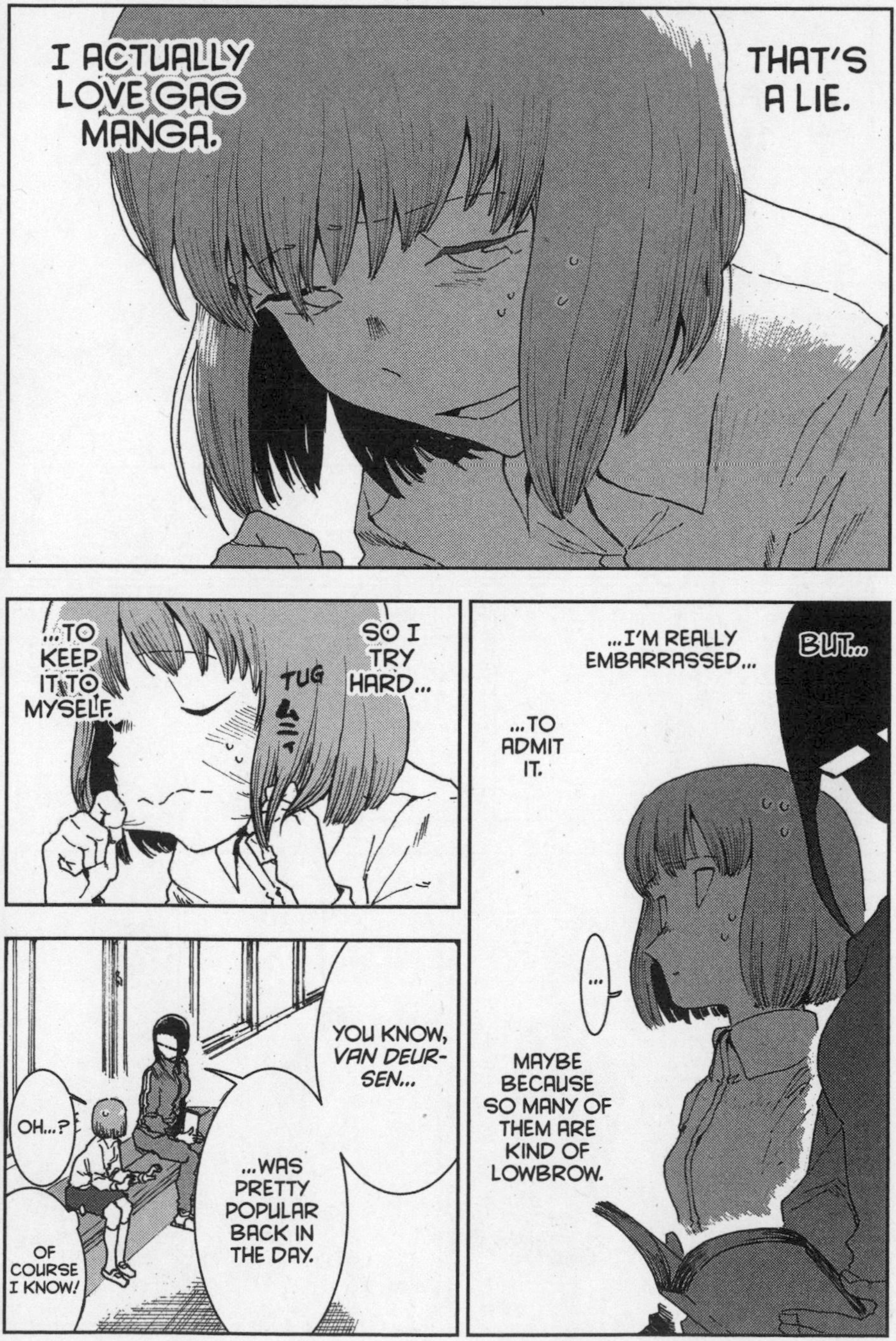
THAT'S A LIE.
I ACTUALLY LOVE GAG MANGA.
BUT...
...I'M REALLY EMBARRASSED...
...TO ADMIT IT.
...
MAYBE BECAUSE SO MANY OF THEM ARE KIND OF LOWBROW.
SO I TRY HARD...
TUG
...TO KEEP IT TO MYSELF.
YOU KNOW, *VAN DEURSEN*...
...WAS PRETTY POPULAR BACK IN THE DAY.
OH...?
OF COURSE I KNOW!

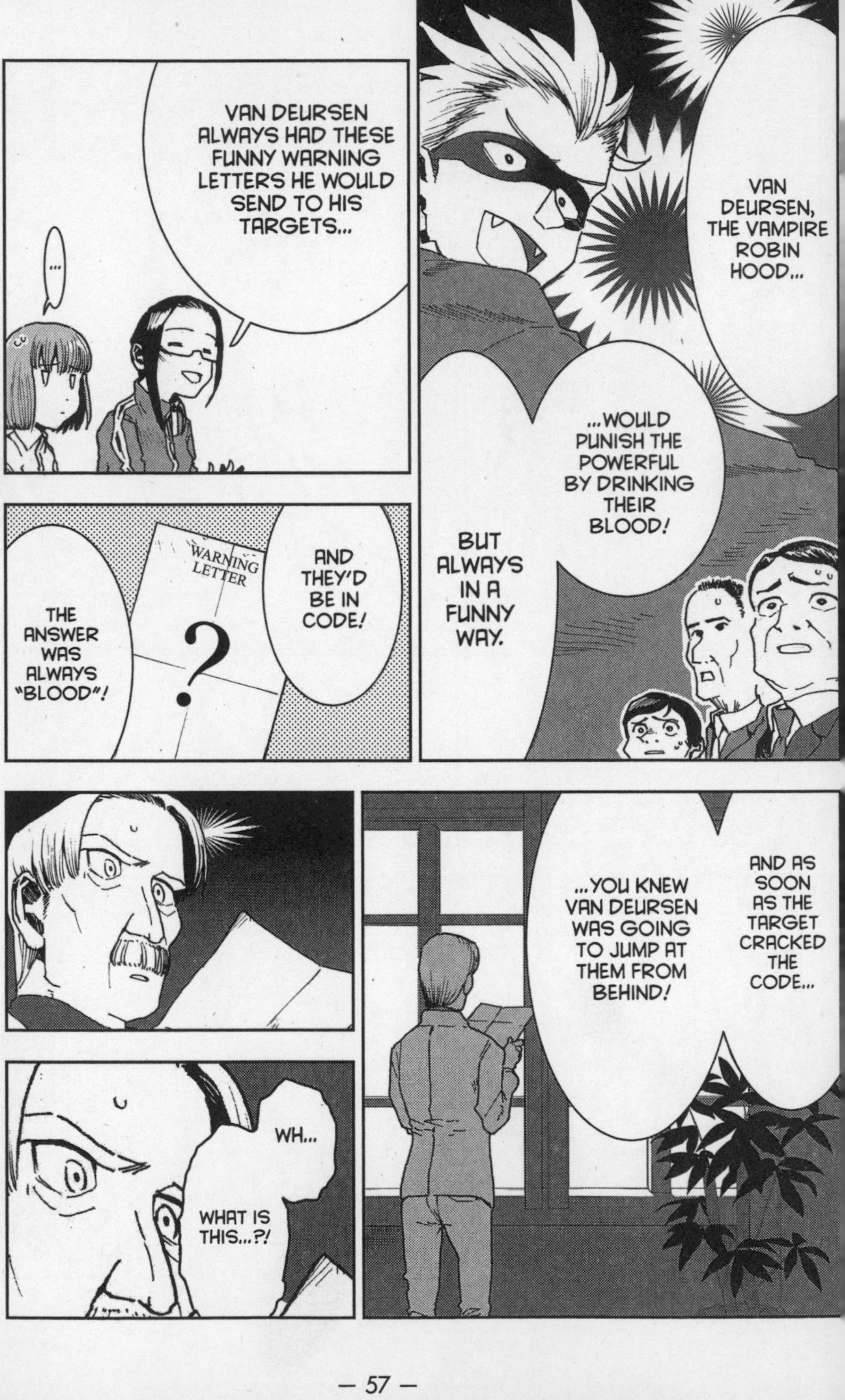
VAN DEURSEN, THE VAMPIRE ROBIN HOOD...
...WOULD PUNISH THE POWERFUL BY DRINKING THEIR BLOOD!
BUT ALWAYS IN A FUNNY WAY.
VAN DEURSEN ALWAYS HAD THESE FUNNY WARNING LETTERS HE WOULD SEND TO HIS TARGETS...
...
AND THEY'D BE IN CODE!
WARNING LETTER
?
THE ANSWER WAS ALWAYS "BLOOD"!
AND AS SOON AS THE TARGET CRACKED THE CODE...
...YOU KNEW VAN DEURSEN WAS GOING TO JUMP AT THEM FROM BEHIND!
WH...
WHAT IS THIS...?!

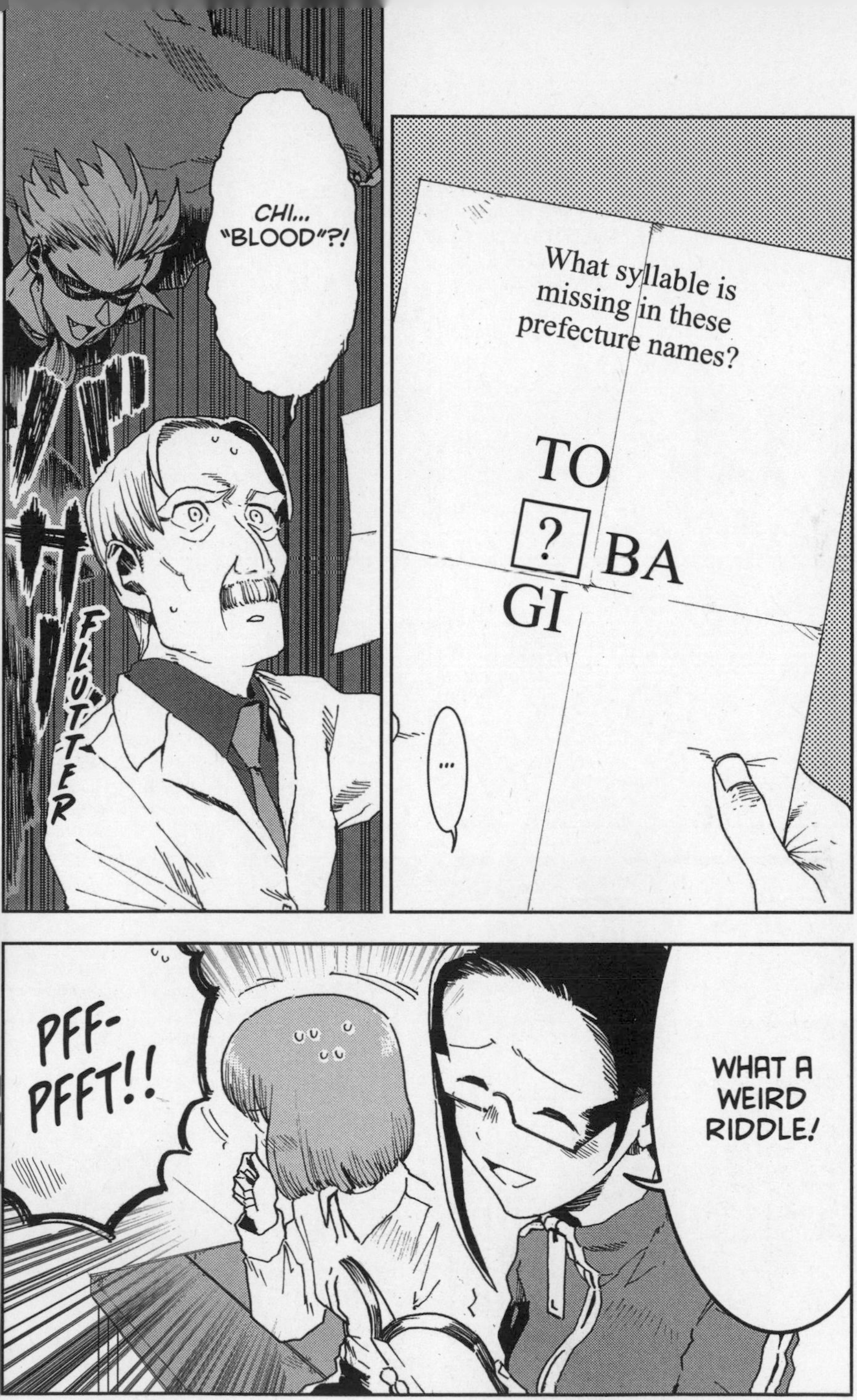
What syllable is missing in these prefecture names?
TO
?
BA
GI
...
CHI... "BLOOD"?!
FLUTTER
WHAT A WEIRD RIDDLE!
PFF-PFFT!!

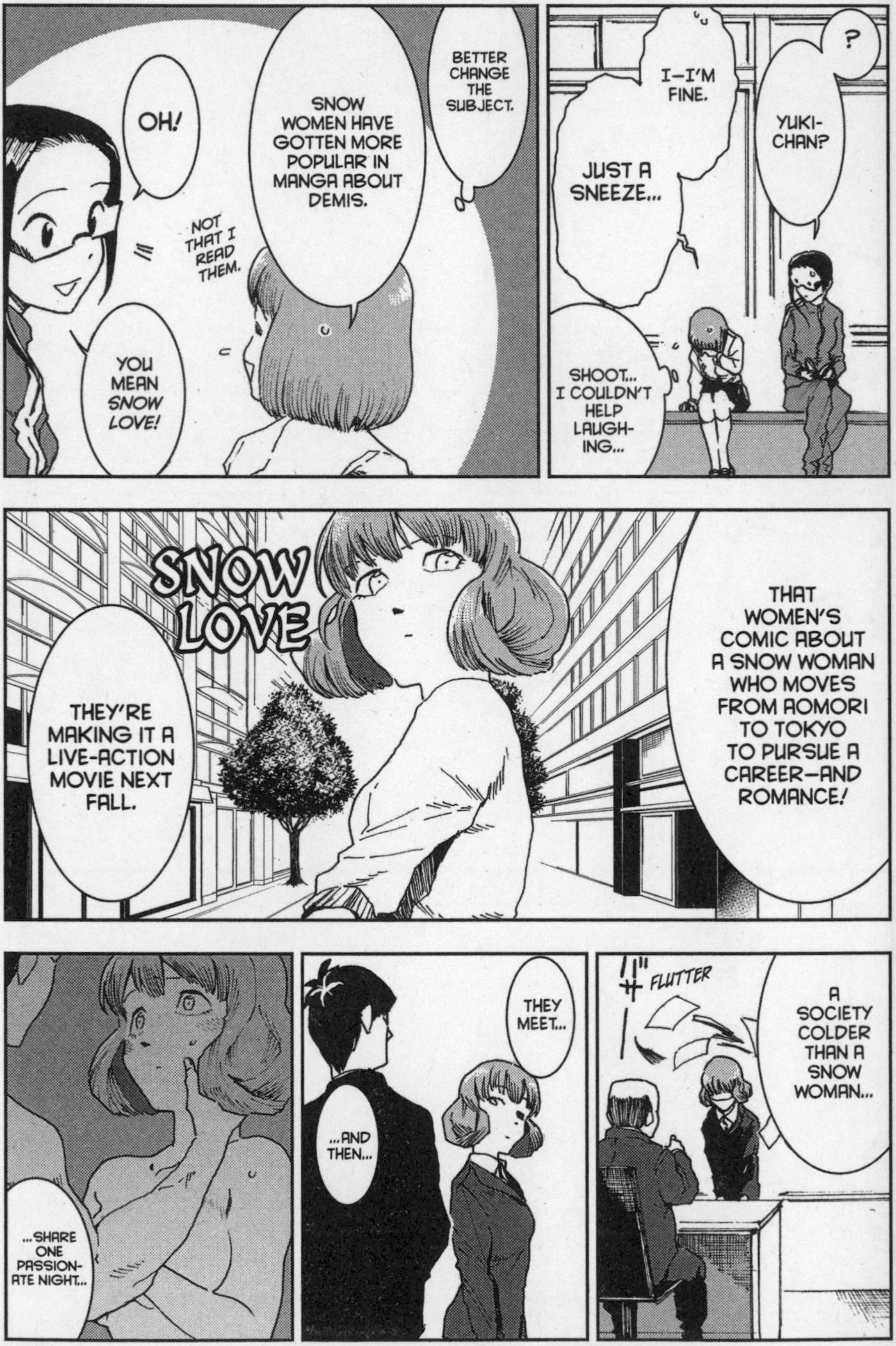
?
YUKI-CHAN?
I—I'M FINE.
JUST A SNEEZE...
SHOOT... I COULDN'T HELP LAUGHING...
BETTER CHANGE THE SUBJECT.
SNOW WOMEN HAVE GOTTEN MORE POPULAR IN MANGA ABOUT DEMIS.
NOT THAT I READ THEM.
OH!
YOU MEAN *SNOW LOVE*!
THAT WOMEN'S COMIC ABOUT A SNOW WOMAN WHO MOVES FROM AOMORI TO TOKYO TO PURSUE A CAREER—AND ROMANCE!
SNOW LOVE
THEY'RE MAKING IT A LIVE-ACTION MOVIE NEXT FALL.
FLUTTER
A SOCIETY COLDER THAN A SNOW WOMAN...
THEY MEET...
...AND THEN...
...SHARE ONE PASSIONATE NIGHT...

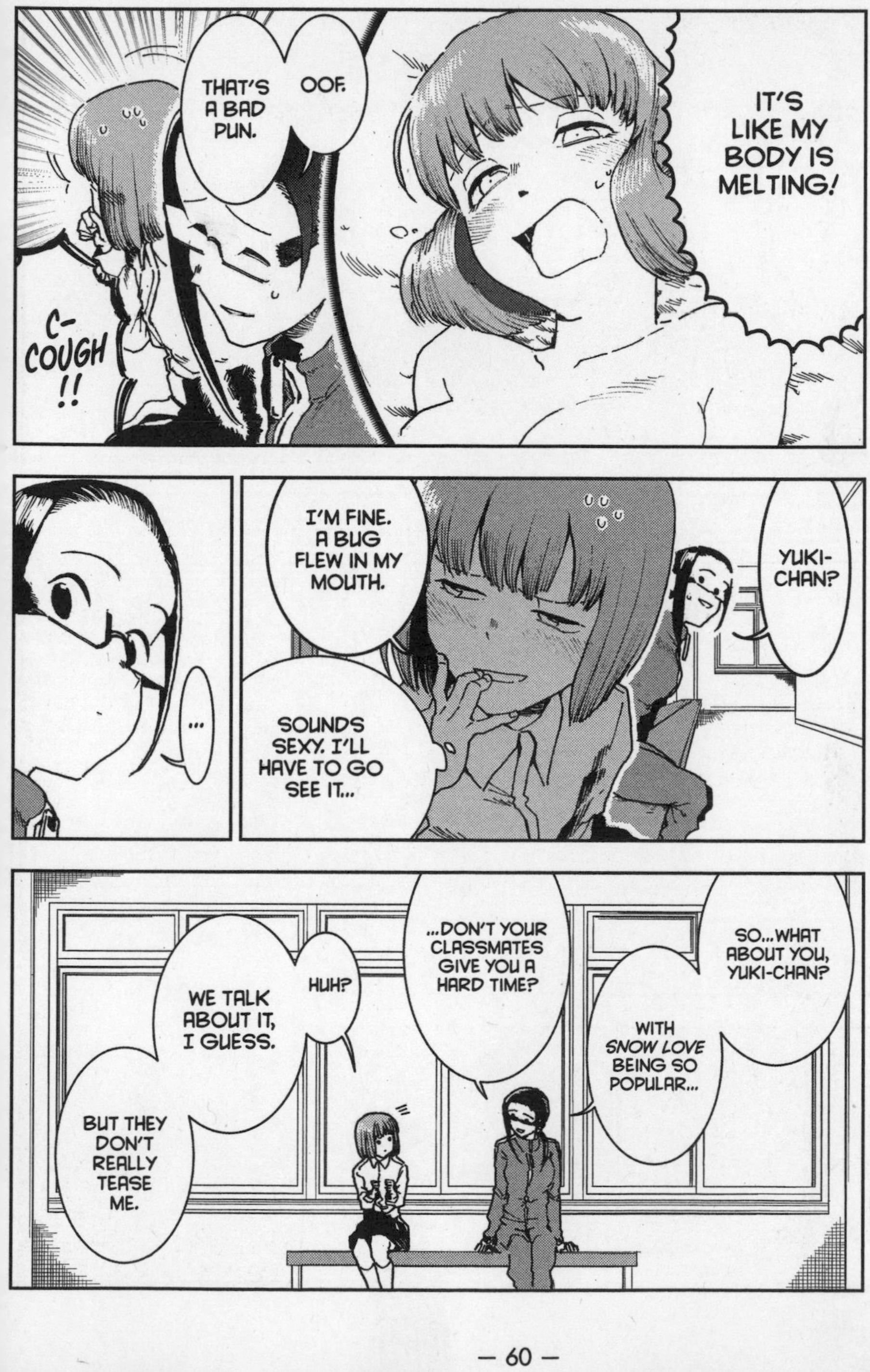
IT'S LIKE MY BODY IS MELTING!
OOF.
THAT'S A BAD PUN.
C-COUGH!!
YUKI-CHAN?
I'M FINE. A BUG FLEW IN MY MOUTH.
SOUNDS SEXY. I'LL HAVE TO GO SEE IT...
...
SO...WHAT ABOUT YOU, YUKI-CHAN?
WITH *SNOW LOVE* BEING SO POPULAR...
...DON'T YOUR CLASSMATES GIVE YOU A HARD TIME?
HUH?
WE TALK ABOUT IT, I GUESS.
BUT THEY DON'T REALLY TEASE ME.

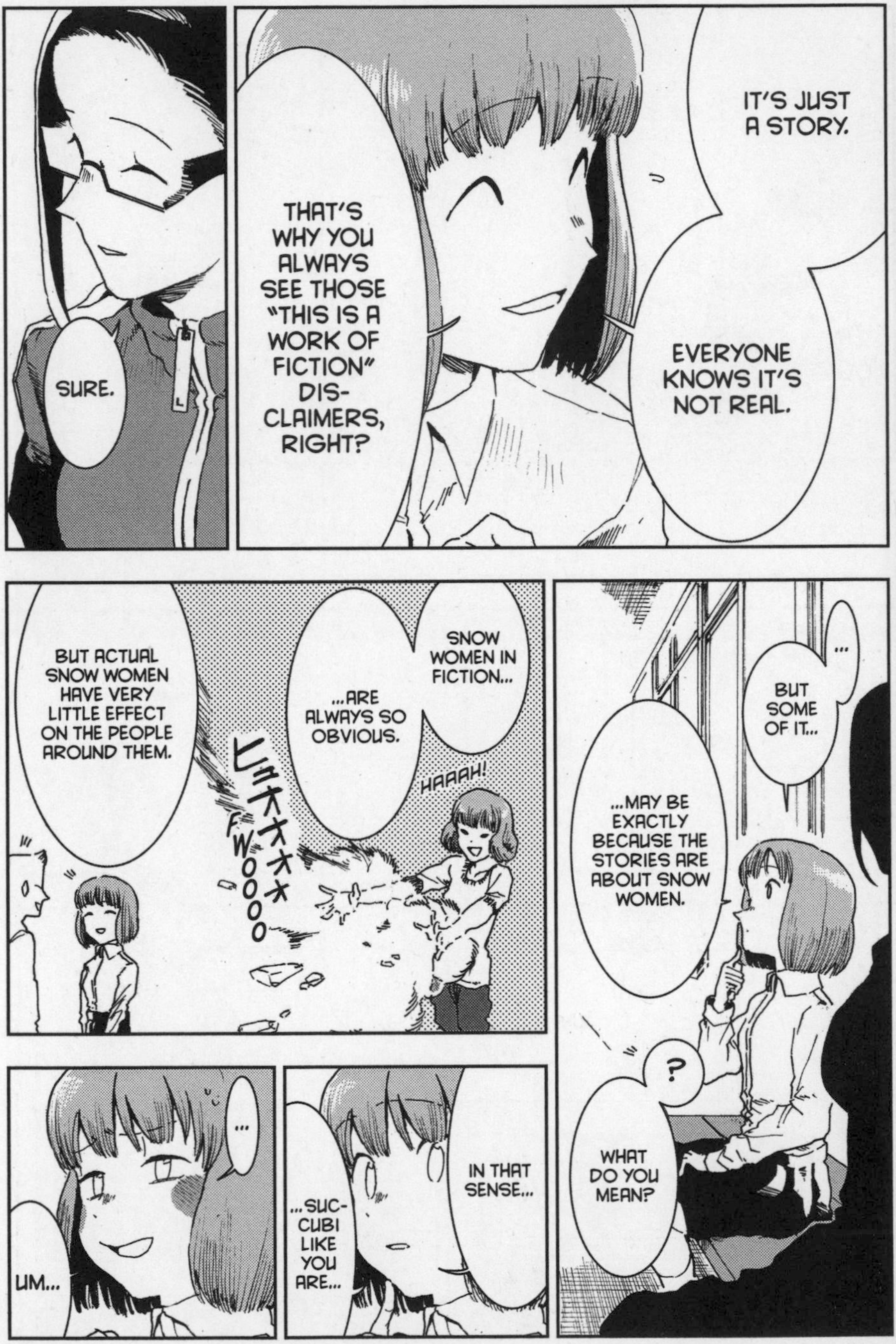
IT'S JUST A STORY.
EVERYONE KNOWS IT'S NOT REAL.
THAT'S WHY YOU ALWAYS SEE THOSE "THIS IS A WORK OF FICTION" DIS-CLAIMERS, RIGHT?
SURE.
...
BUT SOME OF IT...
...MAY BE EXACTLY BECAUSE THE STORIES ARE ABOUT SNOW WOMEN.
?
WHAT DO YOU MEAN?
SNOW WOMEN IN FICTION...
...ARE ALWAYS SO OBVIOUS.
HAAAH!
ヒュオオオオ
FWOOOO
BUT ACTUAL SNOW WOMEN HAVE VERY LITTLE EFFECT ON THE PEOPLE AROUND THEM.
IN THAT SENSE...
...SUC-CUBI LIKE YOU ARE...
...
UM...

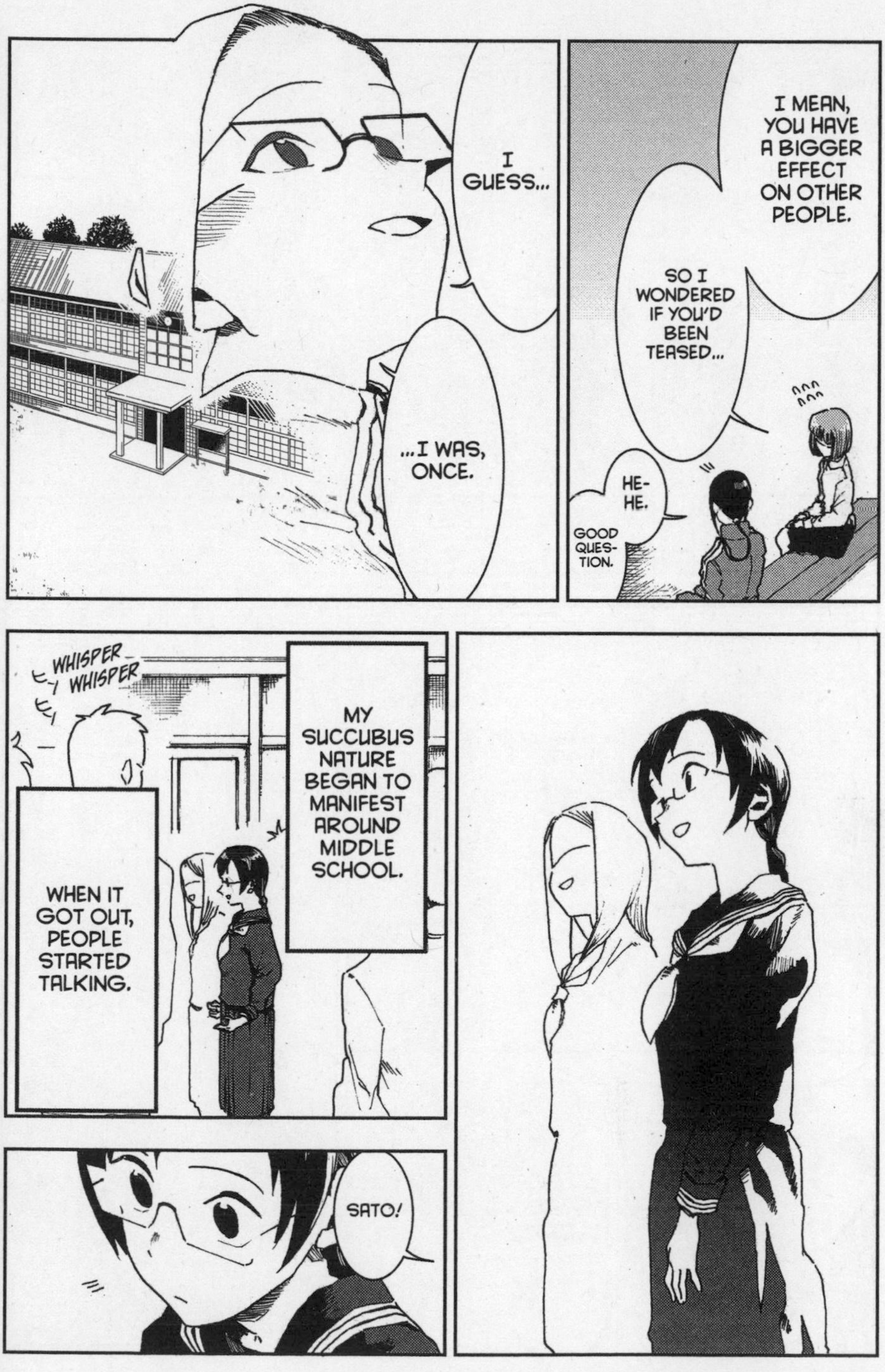
I MEAN, YOU HAVE A BIGGER EFFECT ON OTHER PEOPLE.
SO I WONDERED IF YOU'D BEEN TEASED...
HE-HE.
GOOD QUES-TION.
I GUESS...
...I WAS, ONCE.
MY SUCCUBUS NATURE BEGAN TO MANIFEST AROUND MIDDLE SCHOOL.
WHISPER WHISPER
WHEN IT GOT OUT, PEOPLE STARTED TALKING.
SATO!

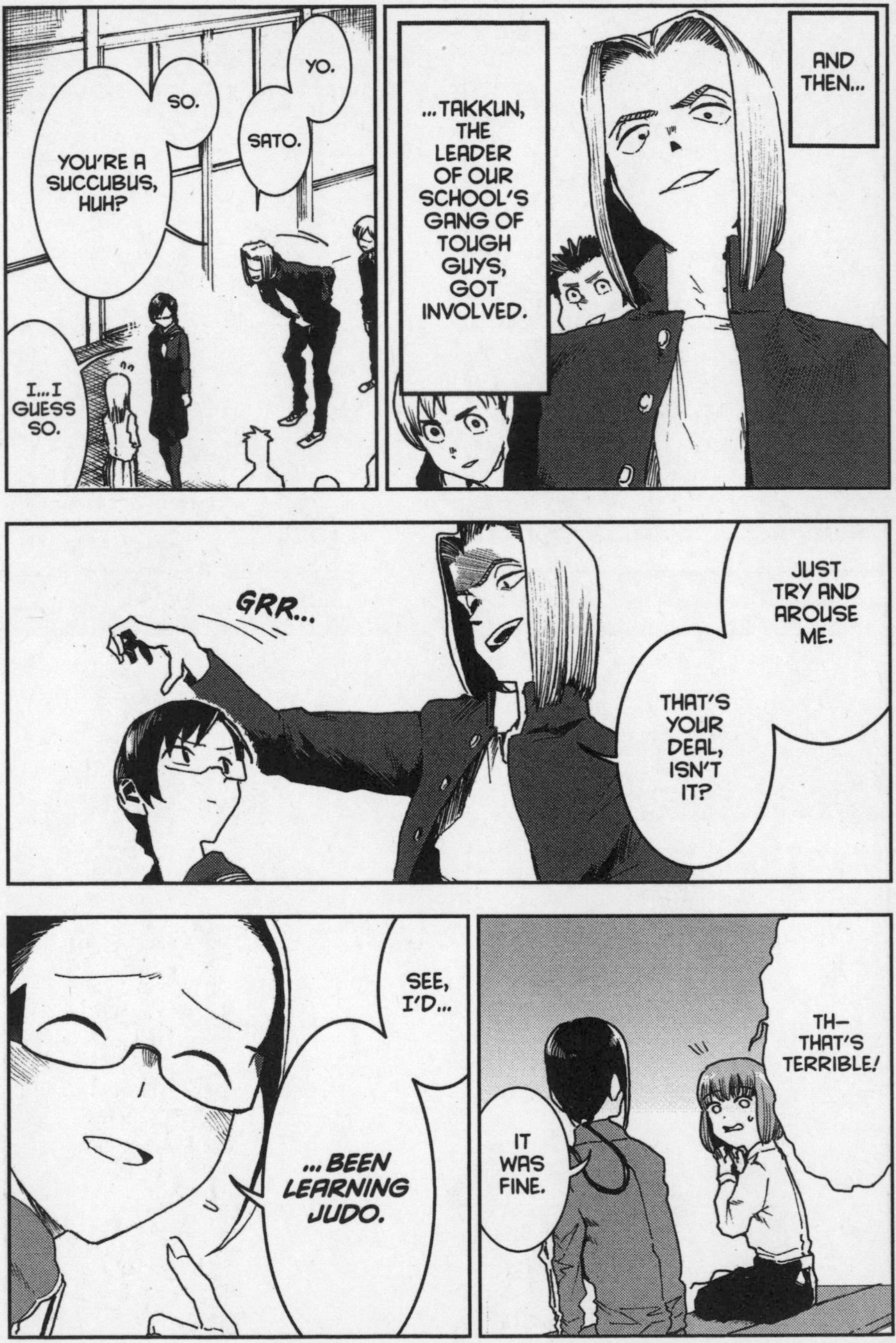
AND THEN...
...TAKKUN, THE LEADER OF OUR SCHOOL'S GANG OF TOUGH GUYS, GOT INVOLVED.
YO.
SATO.
SO.
YOU'RE A SUCCUBUS, HUH?
I...I GUESS SO.
JUST TRY AND AROUSE ME.
THAT'S YOUR DEAL, ISN'T IT?
GRR...
TH—THAT'S TERRIBLE!
IT WAS FINE.
SEE, I'D...
...BEEN LEARNING JUDO.

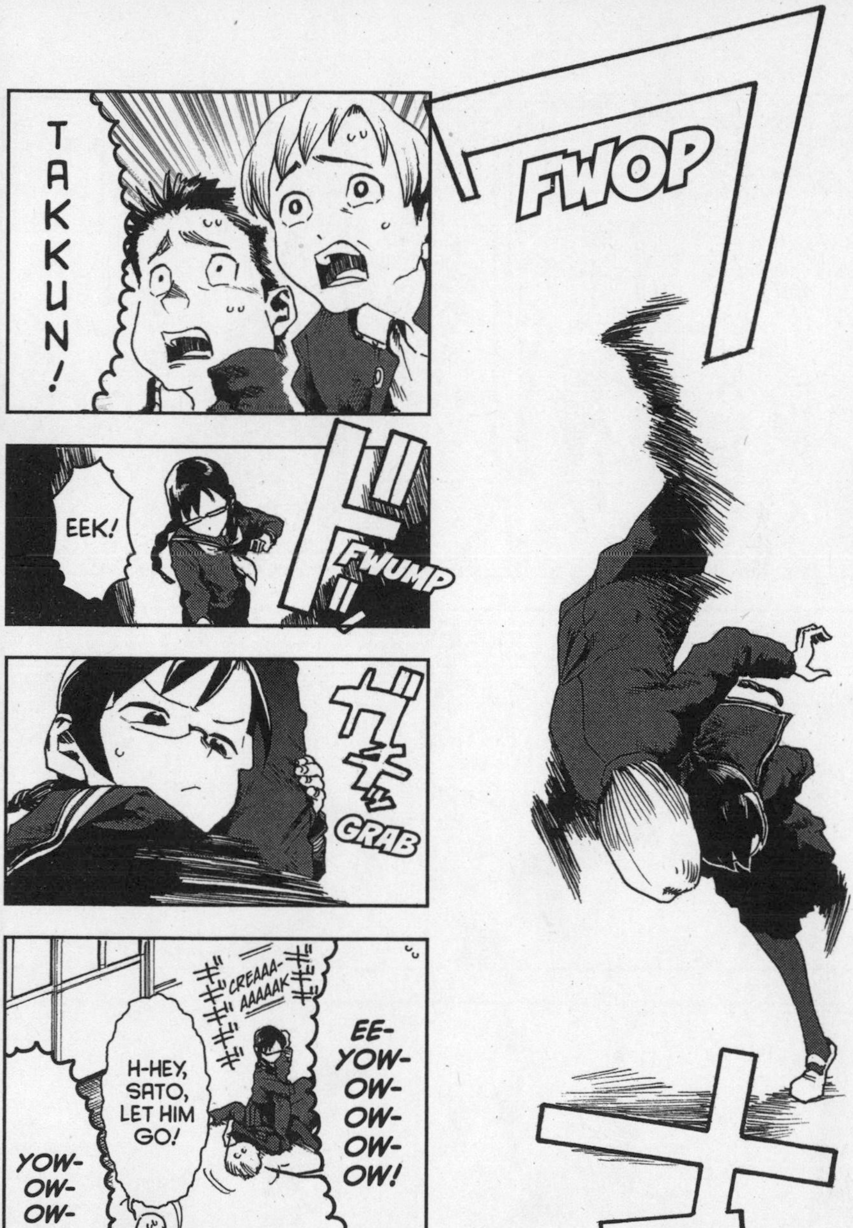
FWOP
TAKKUN!
EEK!
FWUMP
GRAB
EE-YOW-OW-OW-OW-OW!
CREAAA-AAAAAK
H-HEY, SATO, LET HIM GO!
TAK-KUN!
YOW-OW-OW-OW-OW! ST-ST-ST-

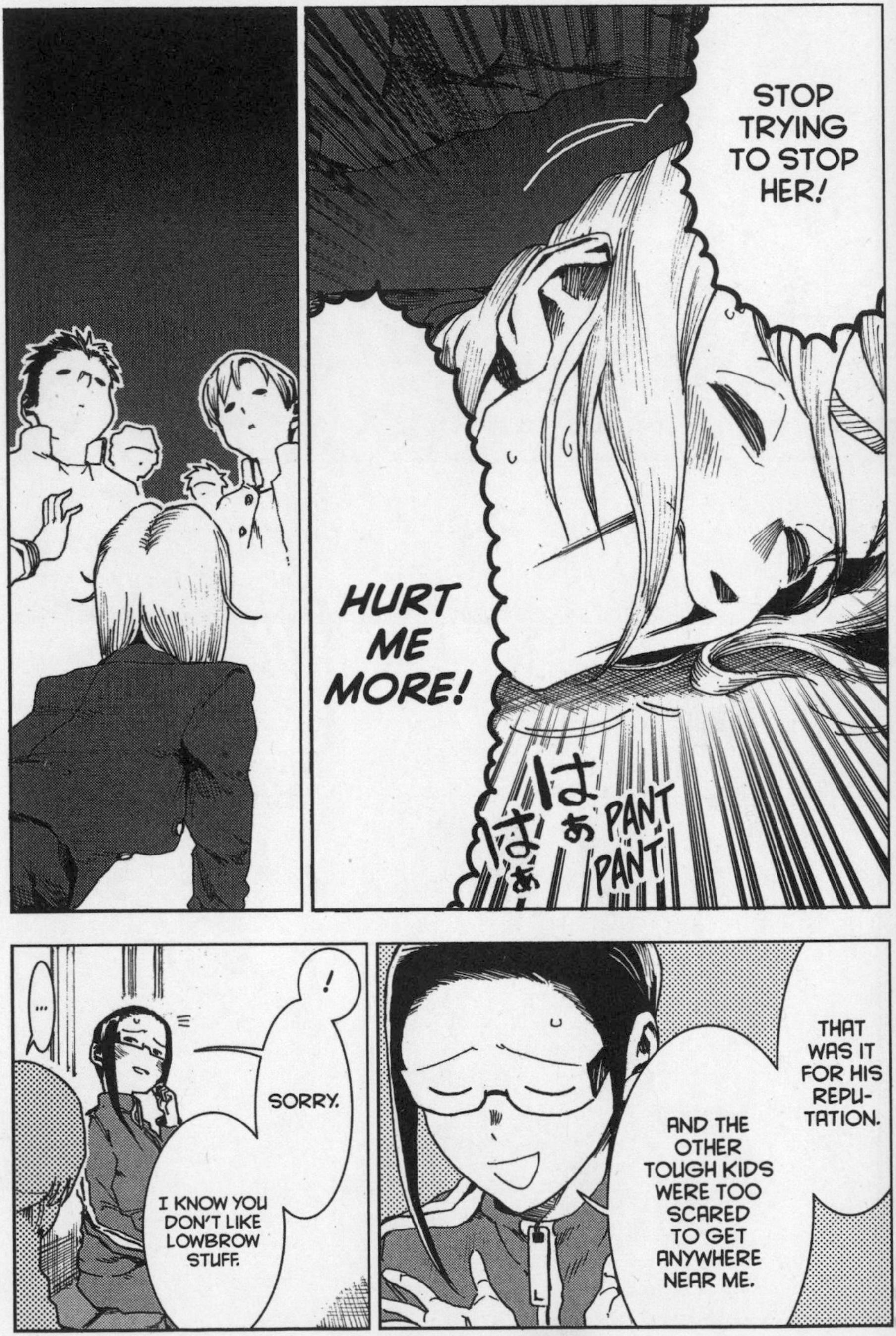
STOP TRYING TO STOP HER!
HURT ME MORE!
はぁ はぁ
PANT PANT
THAT WAS IT FOR HIS REPU-TATION.
AND THE OTHER TOUGH KIDS WERE TOO SCARED TO GET ANYWHERE NEAR ME.
...
!
SORRY.
I KNOW YOU DON'T LIKE LOWBROW STUFF.

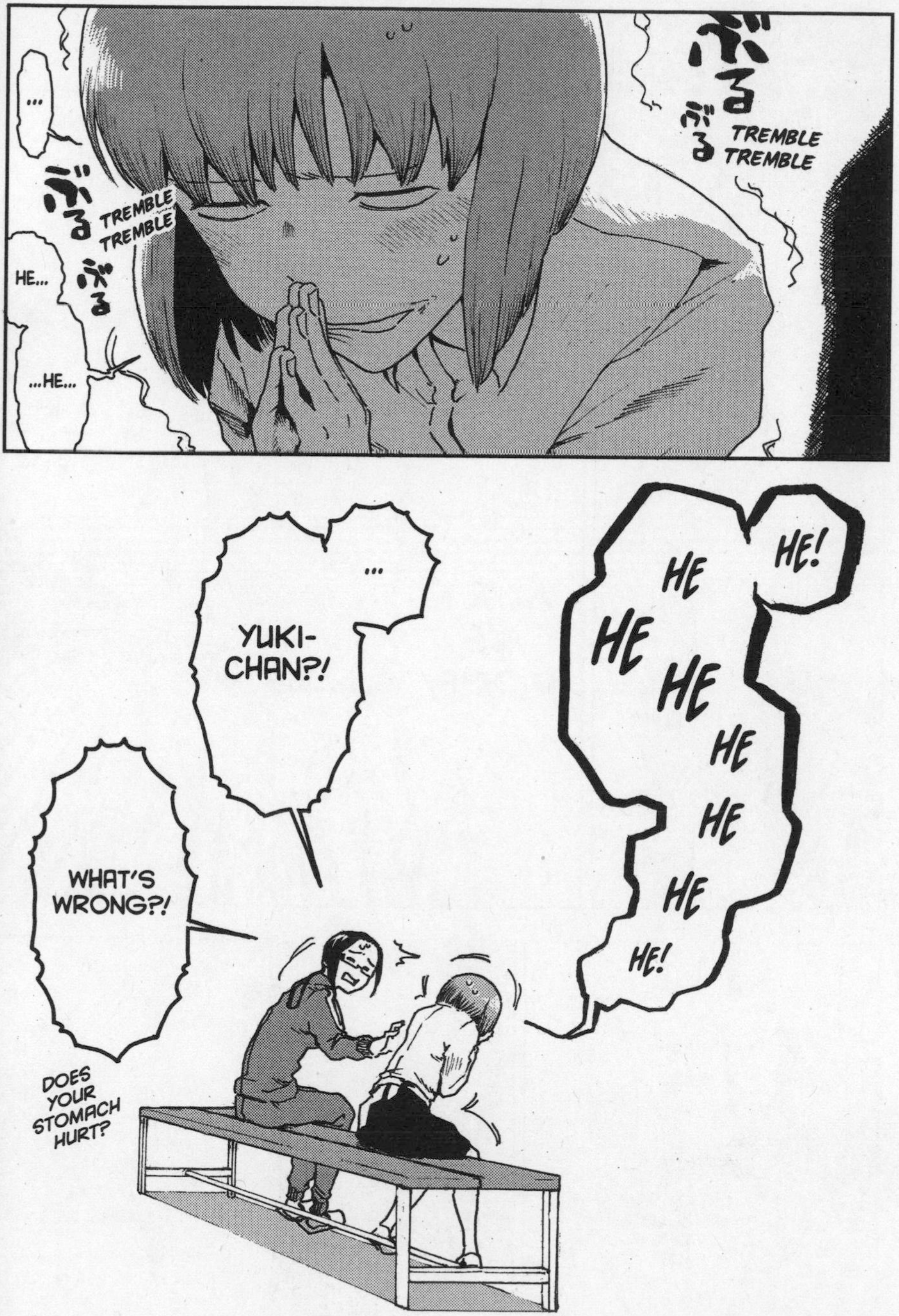
ぶる ぶる
TREMBLE TREMBLE
...
ぶる ぶる
TREMBLE TREMBLE
HE...
...HE...
HE! HE HE HE HE HE HE HE!
... YUKI-CHAN?!
WHAT'S WRONG?!
DOES YOUR STOMACH HURT?

FROM CH. 20, "DEMIS WANT TO BITE"
I THINK MY TEETH'D GET STUCK.
THAT'S NEVER LEAVING THIS ROOM, RIGHT?
...
...
...
TRYING NOT TO LAUGH.

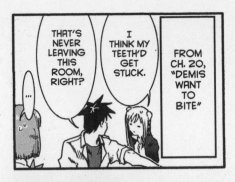

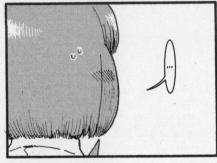

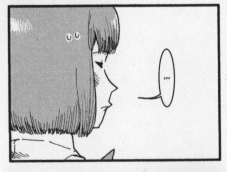

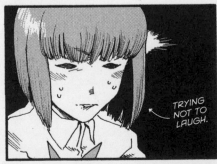

INTERVIEWS WITH
MONSTER GIRLS

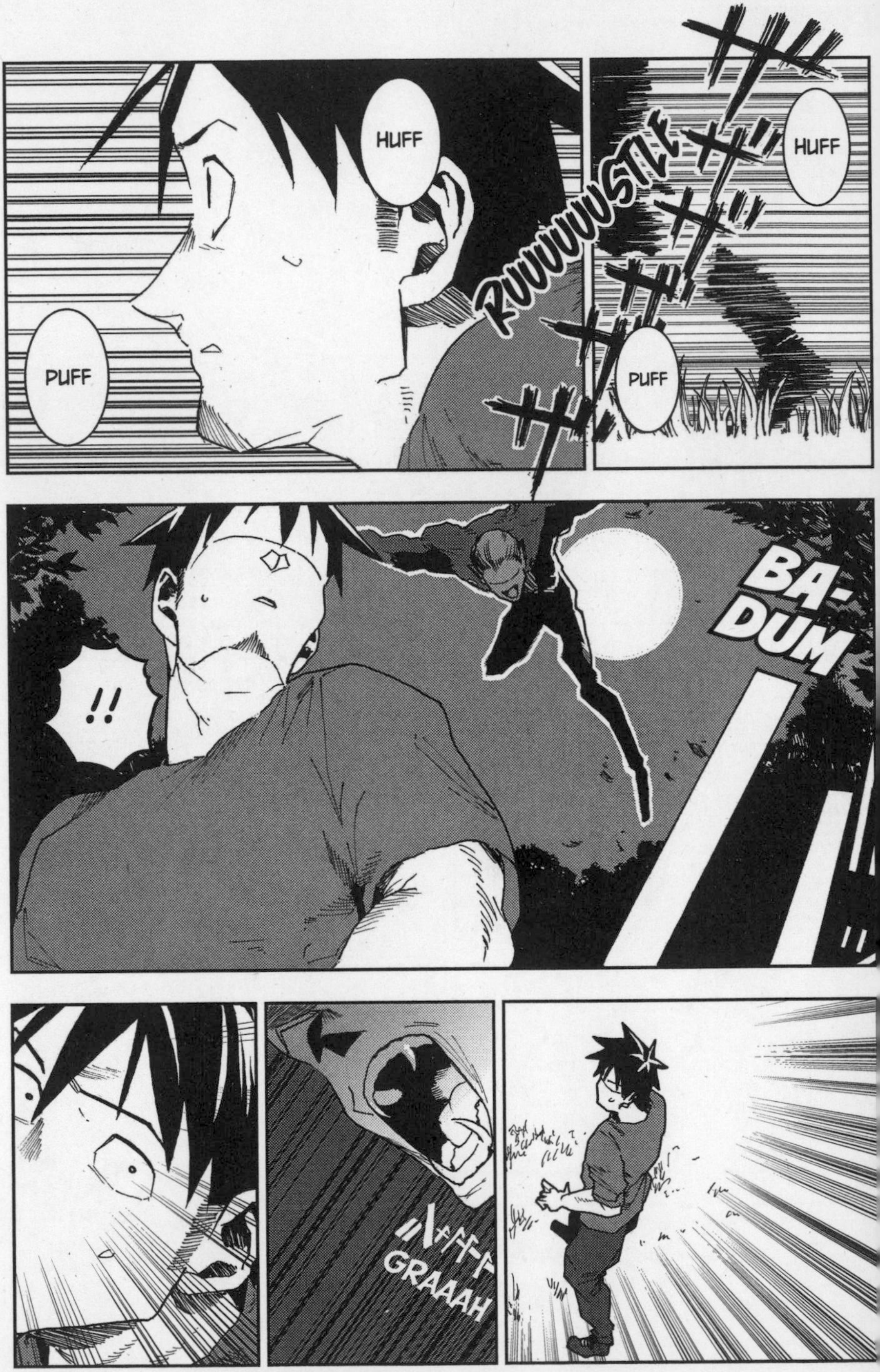
HUFF
PUFF
RUUUUUUSTLE
HUFF
PUFF
!!
BA-DUM
GRAAAH

Chapter 28: Vampires Among Us

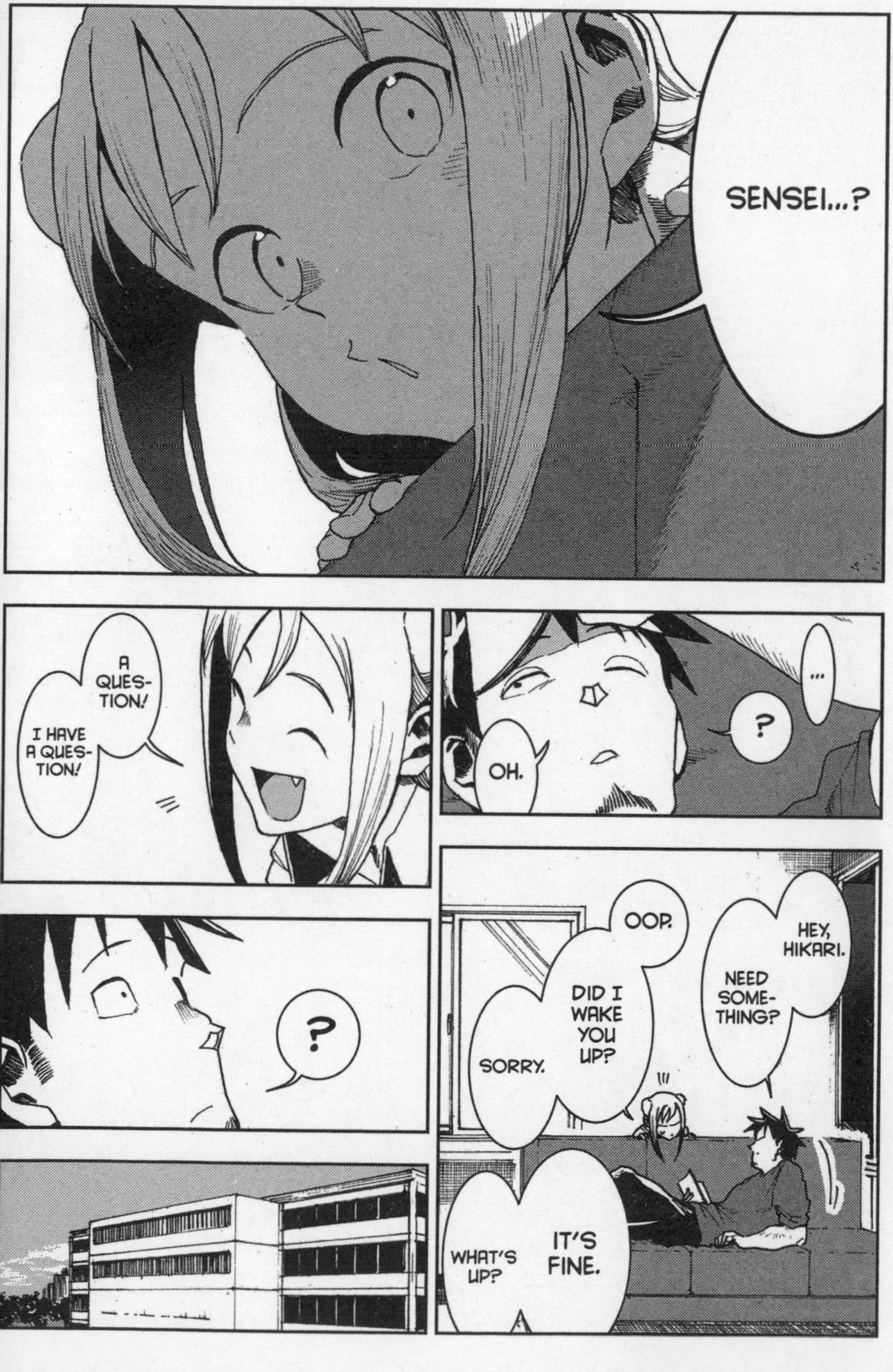
SENSEI...?
...
?
OH.
A QUESTION!
I HAVE A QUESTION!
HEY, HIKARI.
NEED SOMETHING?
OOP.
DID I WAKE YOU UP?
SORRY.
IT'S FINE.
WHAT'S UP?
?

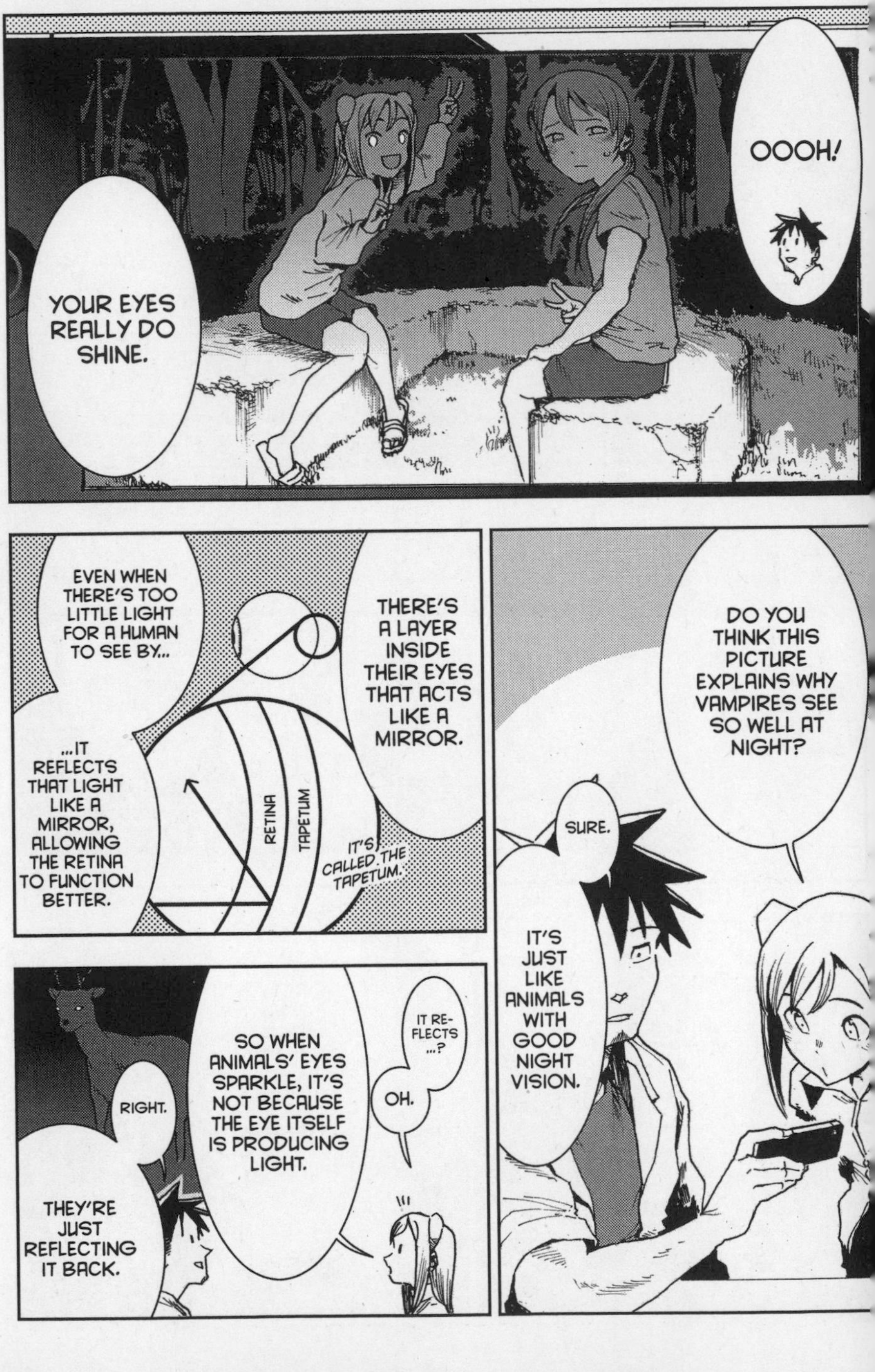
OOOH!
YOUR EYES REALLY DO SHINE.
DO YOU THINK THIS PICTURE EXPLAINS WHY VAMPIRES SEE SO WELL AT NIGHT?
SURE.
IT'S JUST LIKE ANIMALS WITH GOOD NIGHT VISION.
THERE'S A LAYER INSIDE THEIR EYES THAT ACTS LIKE A MIRROR.
EVEN WHEN THERE'S TOO LITTLE LIGHT FOR A HUMAN TO SEE BY...
...IT REFLECTS THAT LIGHT LIKE A MIRROR, ALLOWING THE RETINA TO FUNCTION BETTER.
RETINA
TAPETUM
IT'S CALLED THE TAPETUM.
IT RE-FLECTS ...?
OH.
SO WHEN ANIMALS' EYES SPARKLE, IT'S NOT BECAUSE THE EYE ITSELF IS PRODUCING LIGHT.
RIGHT.
THEY'RE JUST REFLECTING IT BACK.

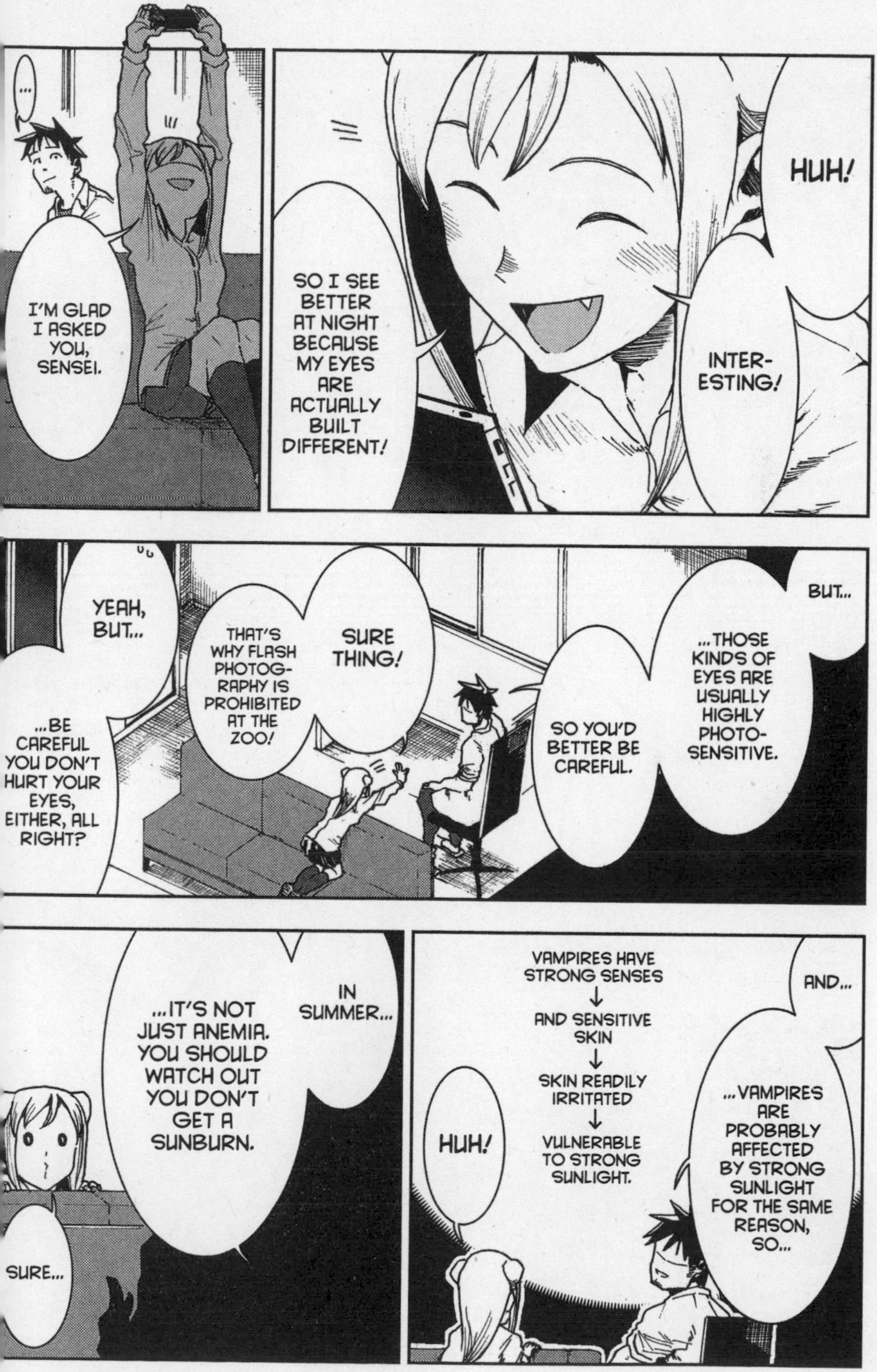
HUH!
INTER-ESTING!
SO I SEE BETTER AT NIGHT BECAUSE MY EYES ARE ACTUALLY BUILT DIFFERENT!
...
I'M GLAD I ASKED YOU, SENSEI.
BUT...
...THOSE KINDS OF EYES ARE USUALLY HIGHLY PHOTO-SENSITIVE.
SO YOU'D BETTER BE CAREFUL.
SURE THING!
THAT'S WHY FLASH PHOTOG-RAPHY IS PROHIBITED AT THE ZOO!
YEAH, BUT...
...BE CAREFUL YOU DON'T HURT YOUR EYES, EITHER, ALL RIGHT?
AND...
...VAMPIRES ARE PROBABLY AFFECTED BY STRONG SUNLIGHT FOR THE SAME REASON, SO...
VAMPIRES HAVE STRONG SENSES ↓ AND SENSITIVE SKIN ↓ SKIN READILY IRRITATED ↓ VULNERABLE TO STRONG SUNLIGHT.
HUH!
IN SUMMER...
...IT'S NOT JUST ANEMIA. YOU SHOULD WATCH OUT YOU DON'T GET A SUNBURN.
SURE...

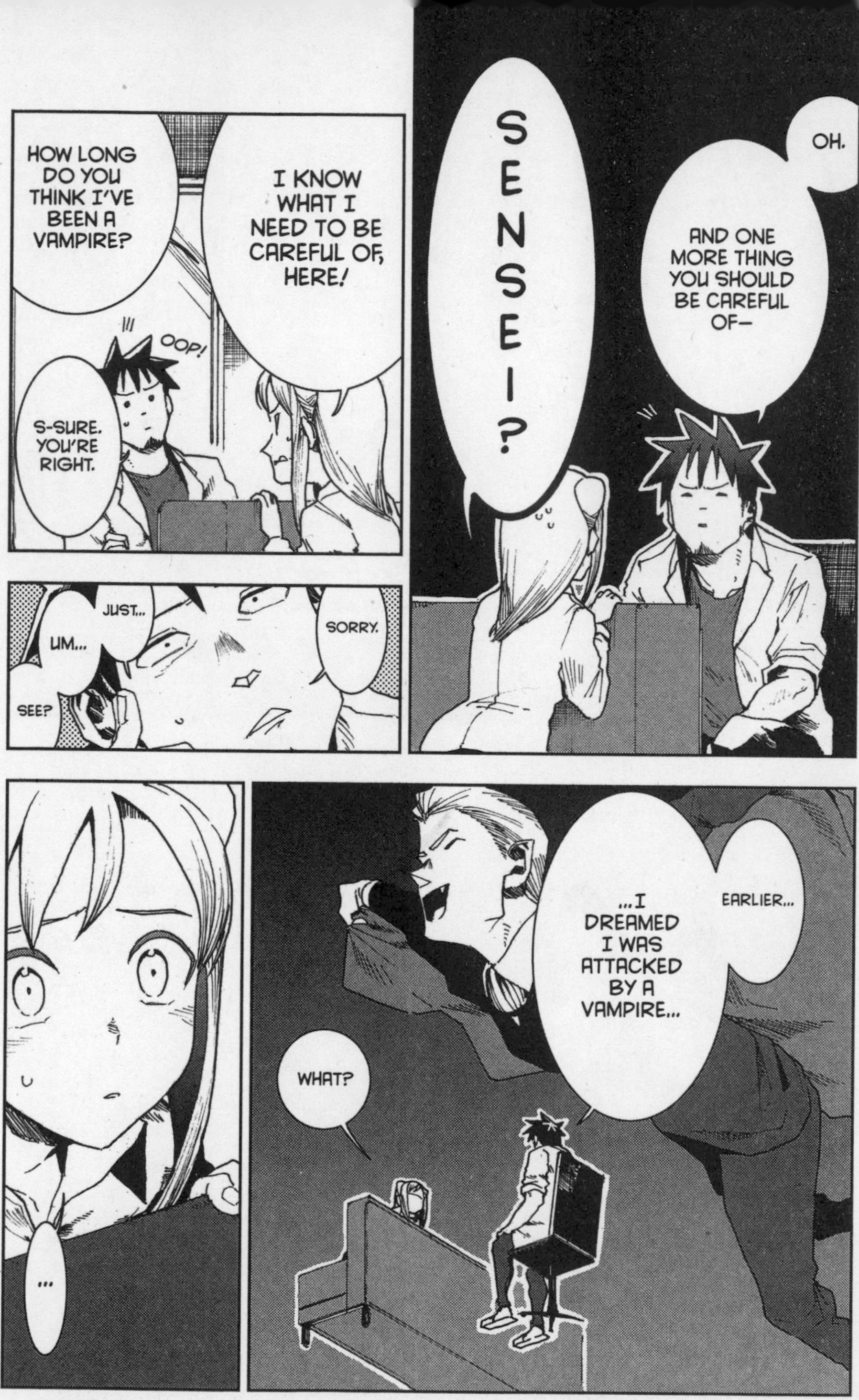
OH.
AND ONE MORE THING YOU SHOULD BE CAREFUL OF—
SENSEI?
I KNOW WHAT I NEED TO BE CAREFUL OF, HERE!
HOW LONG DO YOU THINK I'VE BEEN A VAMPIRE?
OOP!
S-SURE. YOU'RE RIGHT.
SORRY.
JUST...
UM...
SEE?
EARLIER...
...I DREAMED I WAS ATTACKED BY A VAMPIRE...
WHAT?
...

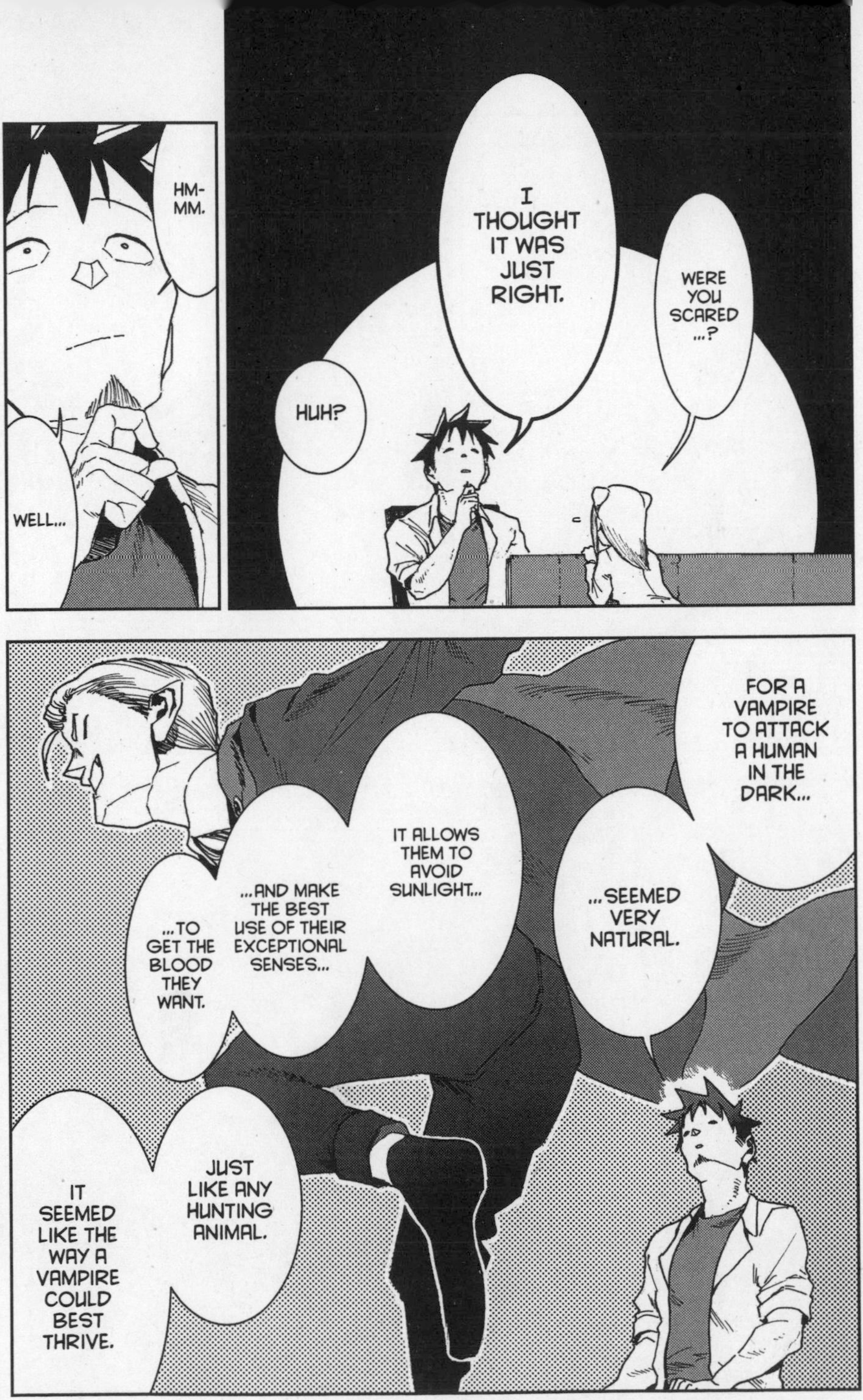
WERE YOU SCARED ...?
HUH?
I THOUGHT IT WAS JUST RIGHT.
HM-MM.
WELL...
FOR A VAMPIRE TO ATTACK A HUMAN IN THE DARK...
...SEEMED VERY NATURAL.
IT ALLOWS THEM TO AVOID SUNLIGHT...
...AND MAKE THE BEST USE OF THEIR EXCEPTIONAL SENSES...
...TO GET THE BLOOD THEY WANT.
JUST LIKE ANY HUNTING ANIMAL.
IT SEEMED LIKE THE WAY A VAMPIRE COULD BEST THRIVE.

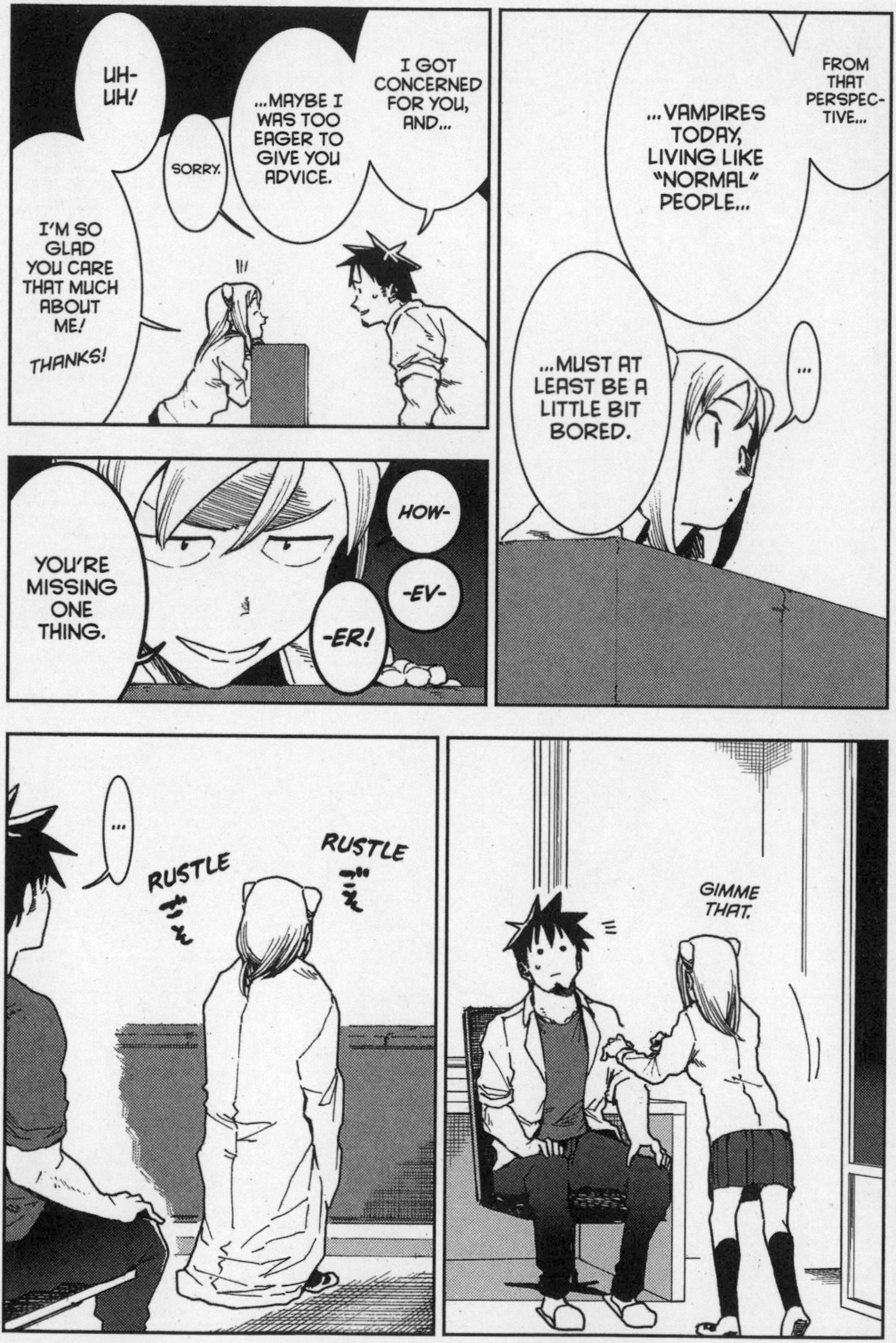
FROM THAT PERSPECTIVE...
...VAMPIRES TODAY, LIVING LIKE "NORMAL" PEOPLE...
...
...MUST AT LEAST BE A LITTLE BIT BORED.
I GOT CONCERNED FOR YOU, AND...
...MAYBE I WAS TOO EAGER TO GIVE YOU ADVICE.
SORRY.
UH-UH!
I'M SO GLAD YOU CARE THAT MUCH ABOUT ME!
THANKS!
HOW-
-EV-
-ER!
YOU'RE MISSING ONE THING.
GIMME THAT.
RUSTLE
RUSTLE
...

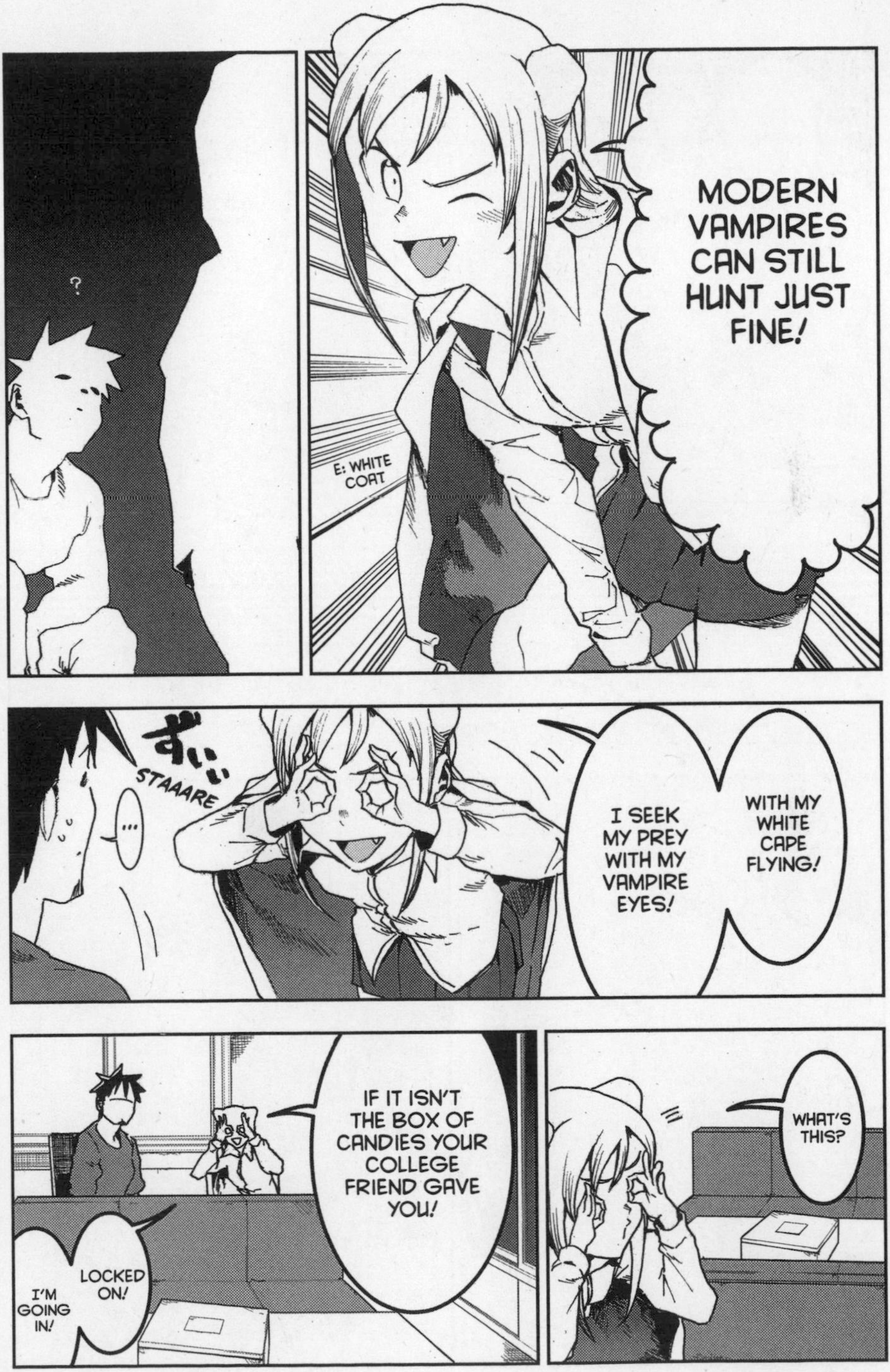
MODERN VAMPIRES CAN STILL HUNT JUST FINE!
E: WHITE COAT
?
WITH MY WHITE CAPE FLYING!
I SEEK MY PREY WITH MY VAMPIRE EYES!
ずいぃ
STAAARE
...
WHAT'S THIS?
IF IT ISN'T THE BOX OF CANDIES YOUR COLLEGE FRIEND GAVE YOU!
LOCKED ON!
I'M GOING IN!

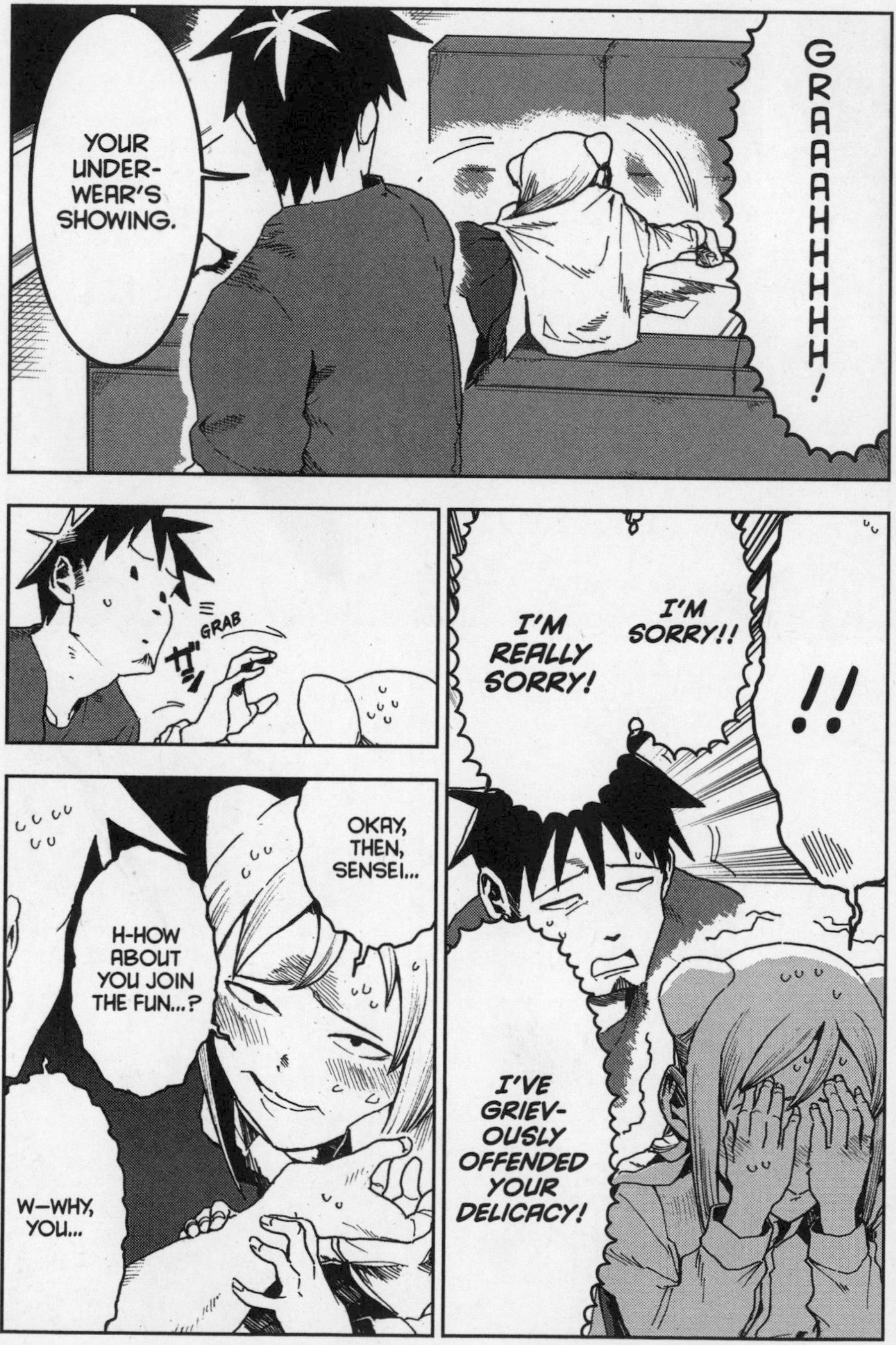
GRAAAHHHHHH!
YOUR UNDER-WEAR'S SHOWING.
I'M SORRY!!
I'M REALLY SORRY!
!!
I'VE GRIEV-OUSLY OFFENDED YOUR DELICACY!
GRAB
OKAY, THEN, SENSEI...
H-HOW ABOUT YOU JOIN THE FUN...?
W-WHY, YOU...

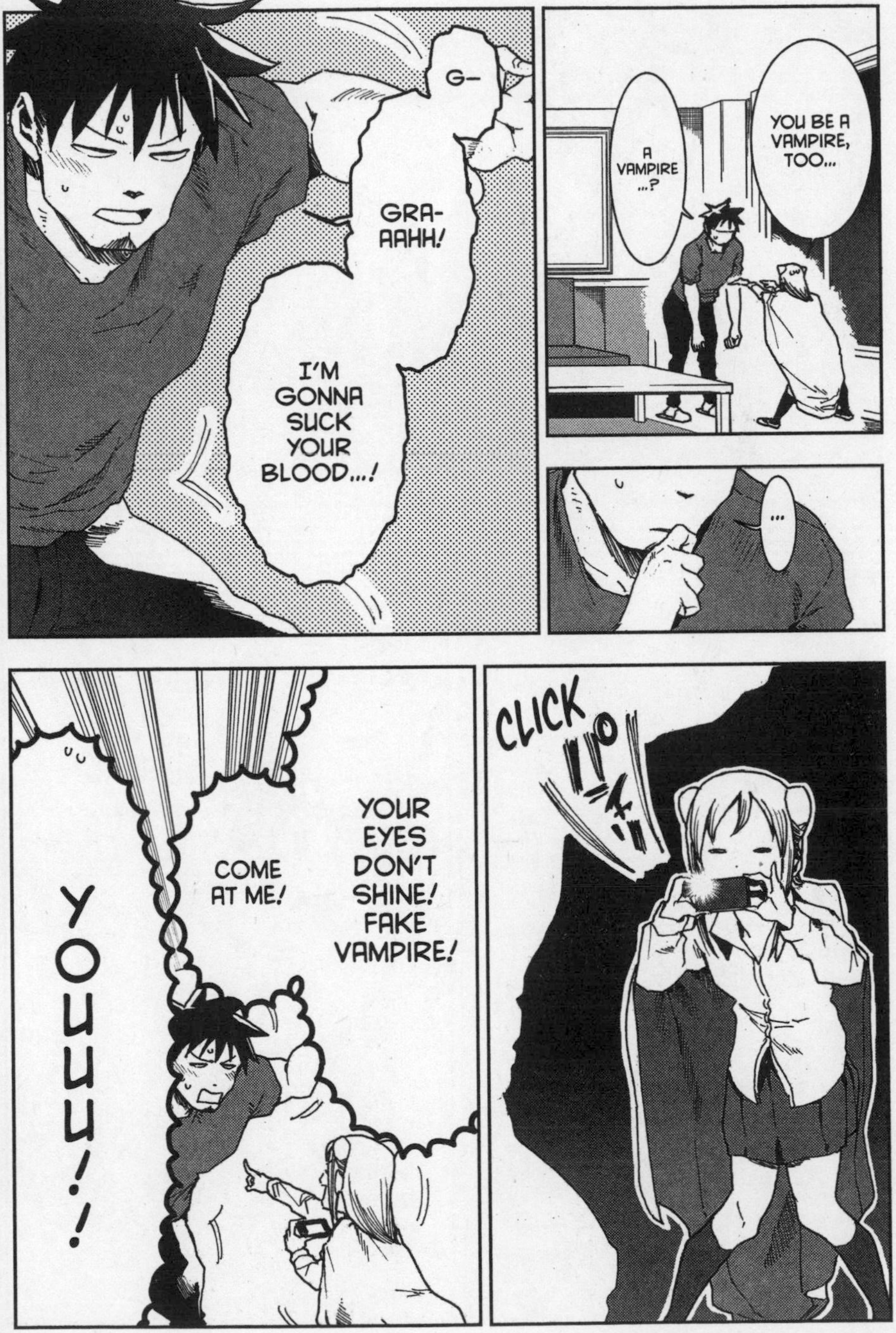
YOU BE A VAMPIRE, TOO...
A VAMPIRE ...?
...
G—
GRA-AAHH!
I'M GONNA SUCK YOUR BLOOD...!
CLICK
YOUR EYES DON'T SHINE! FAKE VAMPIRE!
COME AT ME!
YOUUU!!!

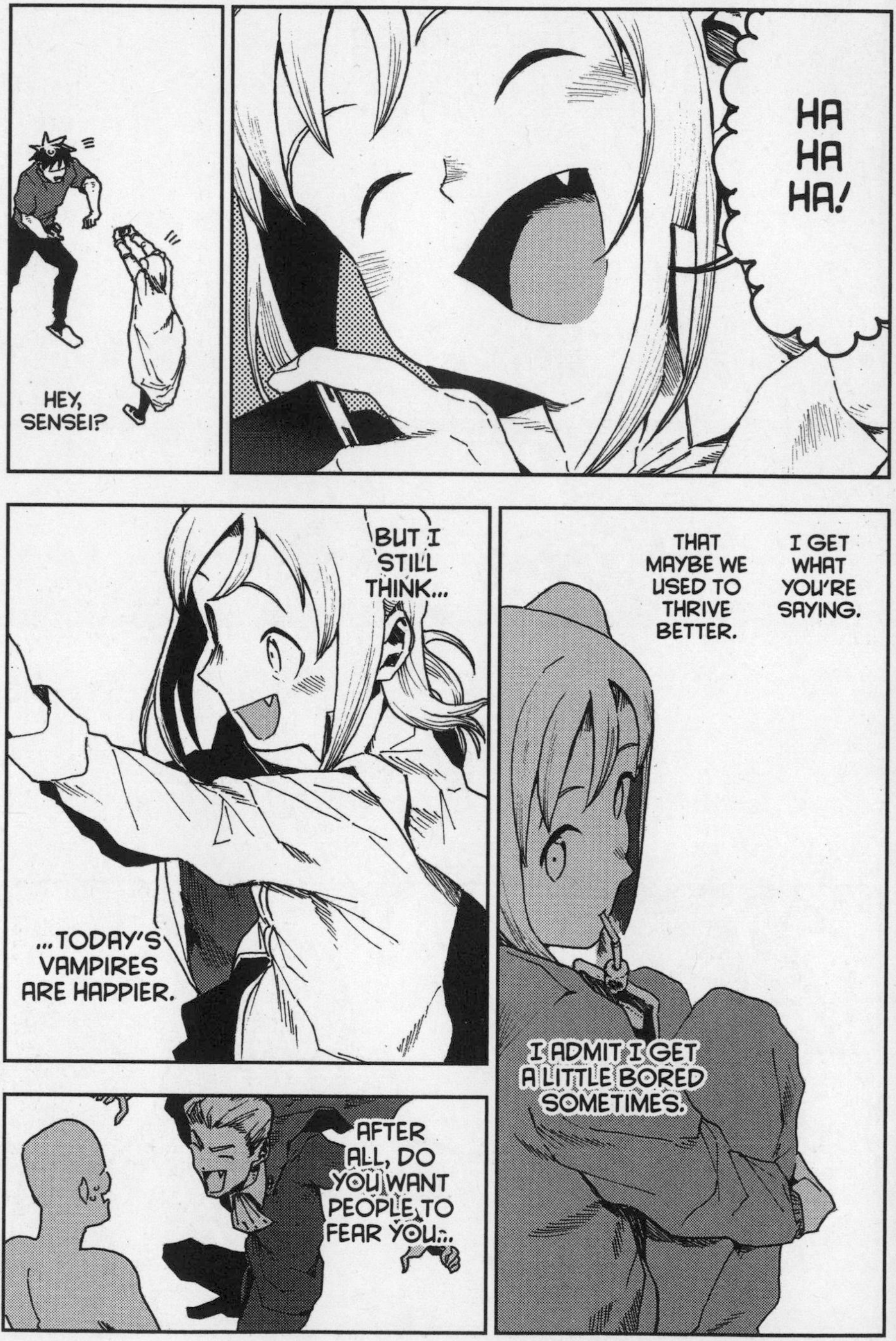
HA HA HA!
HEY, SENSEI?
I GET WHAT YOU'RE SAYING.
THAT MAYBE WE USED TO THRIVE BETTER.
I ADMIT I GET A LITTLE BORED SOMETIMES.
BUT I STILL THINK...
...TODAY'S VAMPIRES ARE HAPPIER.
AFTER ALL, DO YOU WANT PEOPLE TO FEAR YOU...

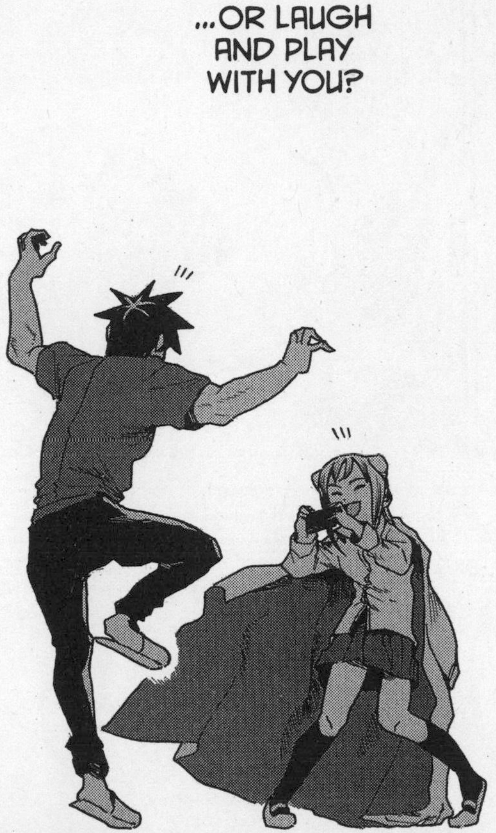
...OR LAUGH AND PLAY WITH YOU?

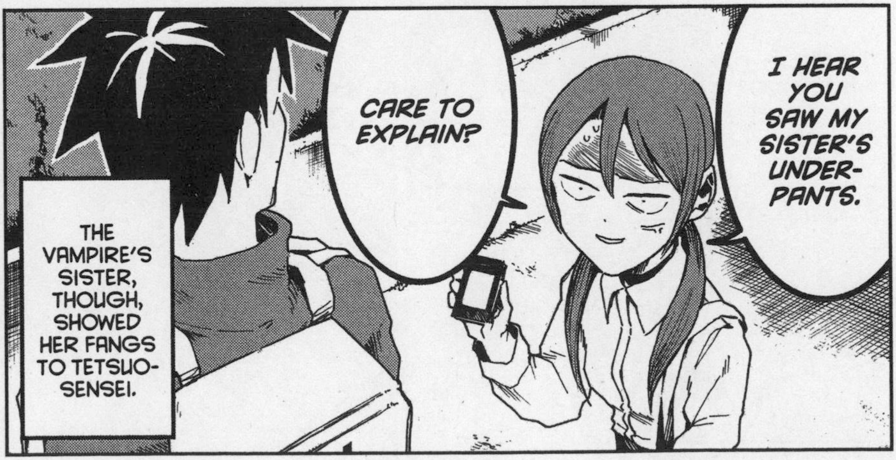
I HEAR YOU SAW MY SISTER'S UNDER-PANTS.
CARE TO EXPLAIN?
THE VAMPIRE'S SISTER, THOUGH, SHOWED HER FANGS TO TETSUO-SENSEI.

TALKING TO YOU, I'VE REALIZED...
*SUCKS BLOOD
*WEAK TO SUNLIGHT
*HATES GARLIC (ETC.)
...MOST VAMPIRE MYTHS EITHER HAVE A KERNEL OF TRUTH...
...OR WERE INVENTED BY FEARFUL HUMANS LARGELY ON A RELIGIOUS BASIS.
*VULNERABLE TO CROSSES
*DON'T APPEAR IN MIRRORS
I SEE!
AND? AND?
WHAT'S YOUR CONCLUSION?
HM?
THAT I ENJOYED FINDING OUT!
JUST IN IT FOR THE KNOWLEDGE.

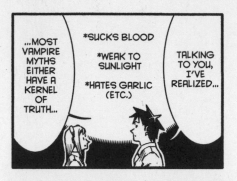

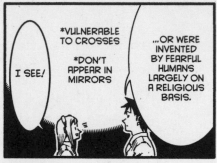

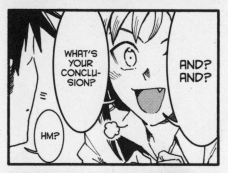

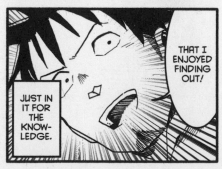

INTERVIEWS WITH
MONSTER GIRLS

Chapter 29: Tetsuo Takahashi Wants To Help

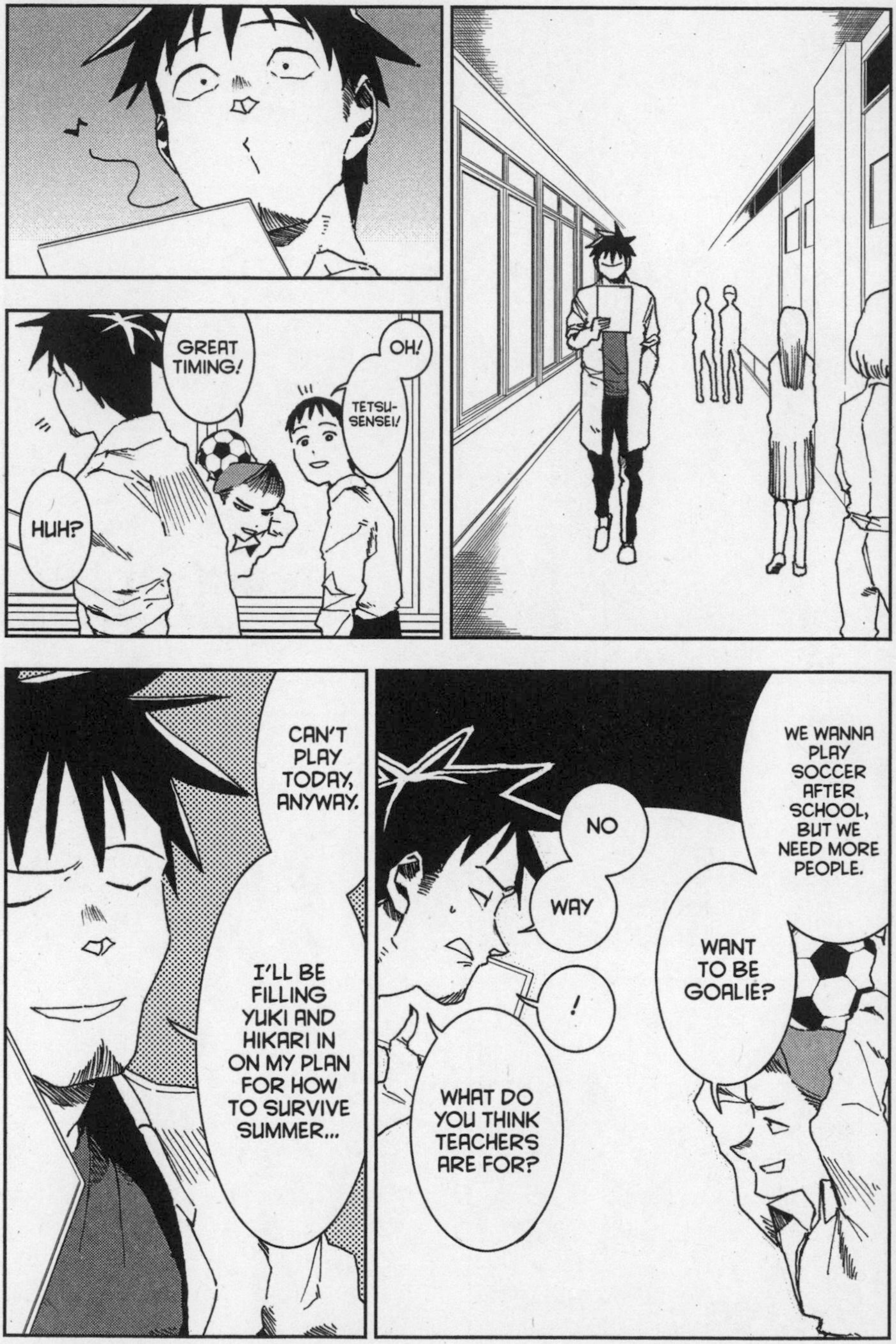
OH!
TETSU-SENSEI!
GREAT TIMING!
HUH?
WE WANNA PLAY SOCCER AFTER SCHOOL, BUT WE NEED MORE PEOPLE.
WANT TO BE GOALIE?
NO WAY
!
WHAT DO YOU THINK TEACHERS ARE FOR?
CAN'T PLAY TODAY, ANYWAY.
I'LL BE FILLING YUKI AND HIKARI IN ON MY PLAN FOR HOW TO SURVIVE SUMMER...

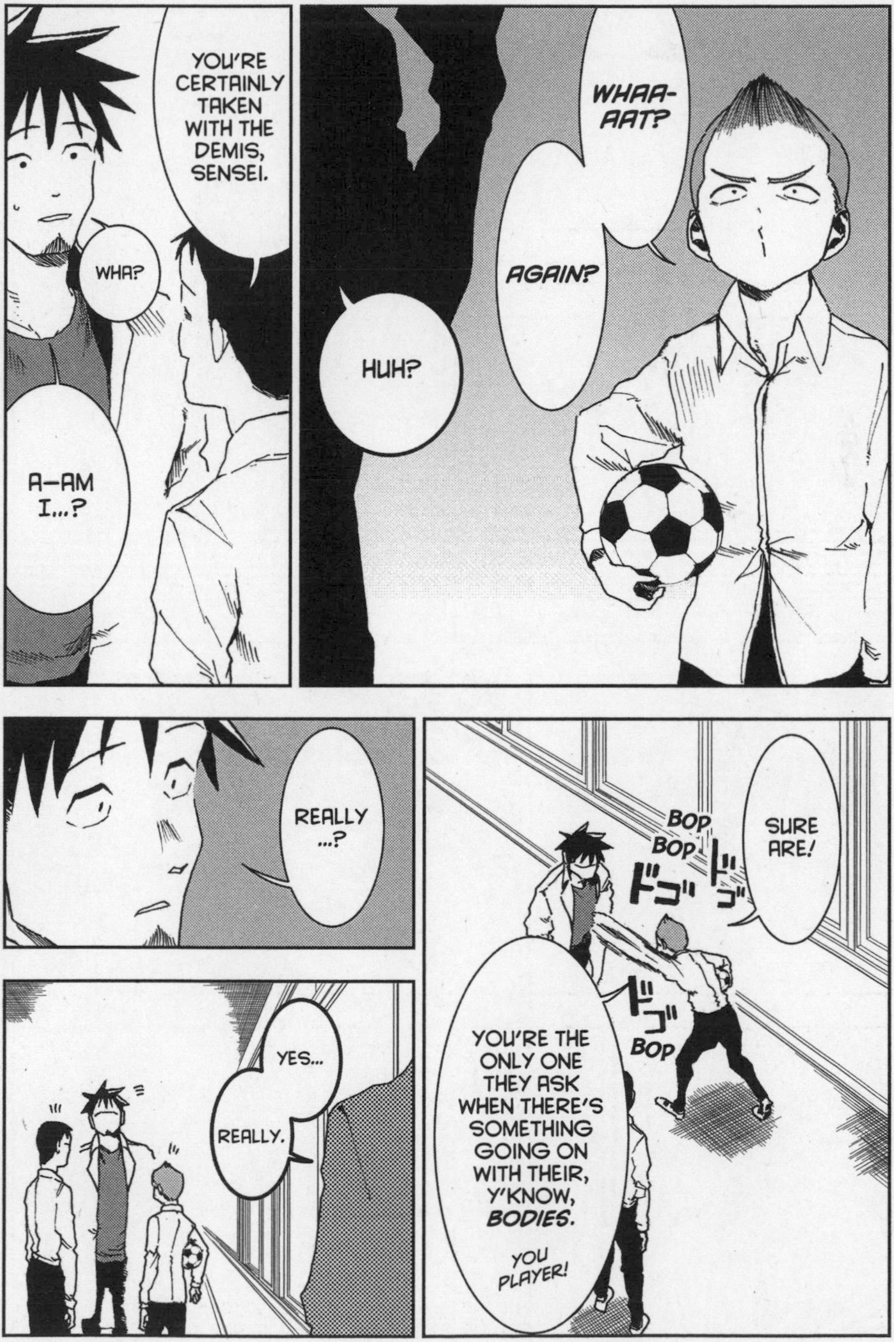
WHAA-AAT?
AGAIN?
HUH?
YOU'RE CERTAINLY TAKEN WITH THE DEMIS, SENSEI.
WHA?
A—AM I...?
SURE ARE!
BOP BOP ドゴ ドゴ
ドゴ BOP
YOU'RE THE ONLY ONE THEY ASK WHEN THERE'S SOMETHING GOING ON WITH THEIR, Y'KNOW, *BODIES*.
YOU PLAYER!
REALLY ...?
YES...
REALLY.

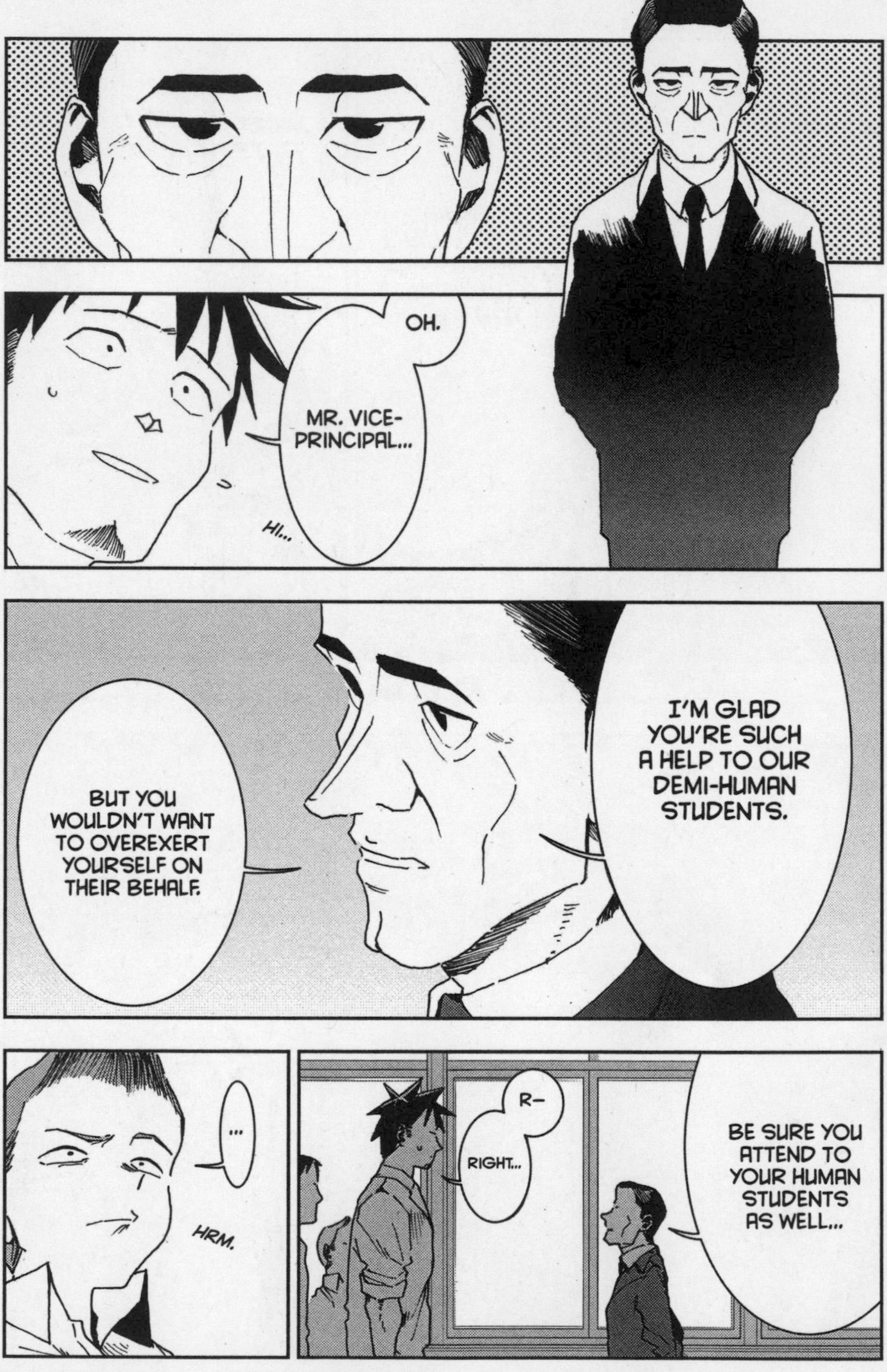
OH.
MR. VICE-PRINCIPAL...
HI...
I'M GLAD YOU'RE SUCH A HELP TO OUR DEMI-HUMAN STUDENTS.
BUT YOU WOULDN'T WANT TO OVEREXERT YOURSELF ON THEIR BEHALF.
BE SURE YOU ATTEND TO YOUR HUMAN STUDENTS AS WELL...
R-
RIGHT...
...
HRM.

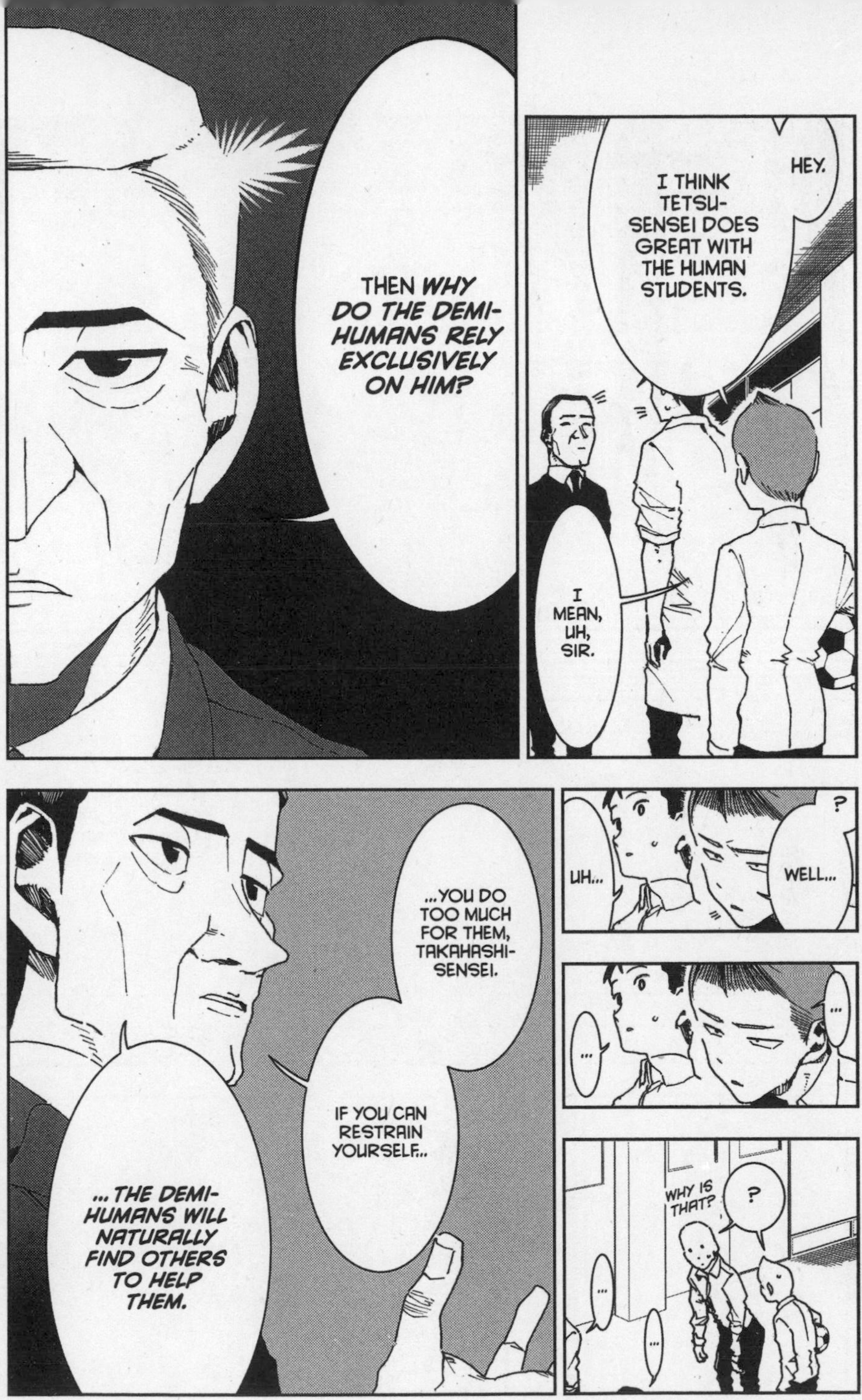
HEY.
I THINK TETSU-SENSEI DOES GREAT WITH THE HUMAN STUDENTS.
I MEAN, UH, SIR.
THEN *WHY DO THE DEMI-HUMANS RELY EXCLUSIVELY ON HIM?*
?
WELL...
UH...
...
...
?
WHY IS THAT?
...
...
...YOU DO TOO MUCH FOR THEM, TAKAHASHI-SENSEI.
IF YOU CAN RESTRAIN YOURSELF...
...THE DEMI-HUMANS WILL NATURALLY FIND OTHERS TO HELP THEM.

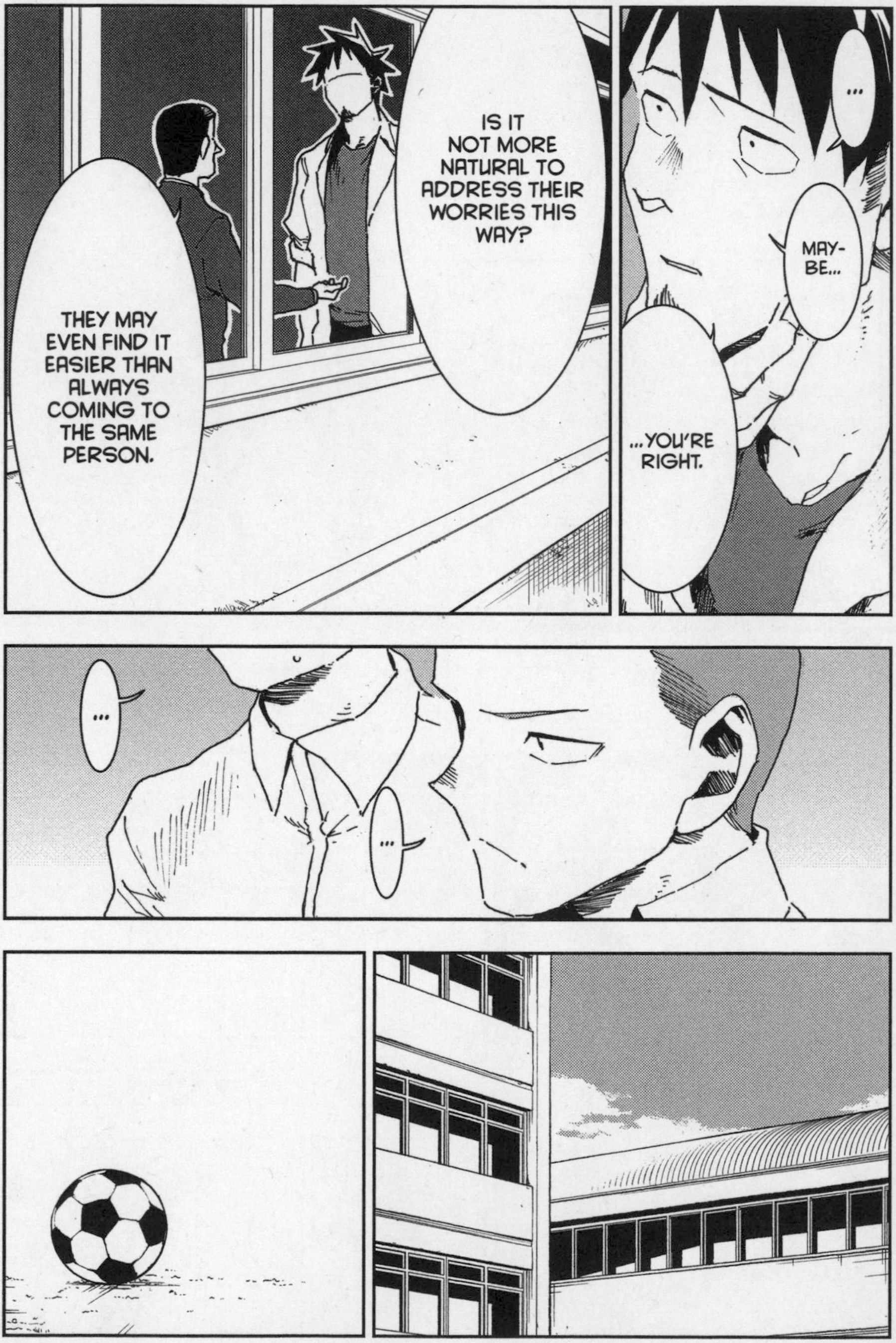
...
MAY-BE...
...YOU'RE RIGHT.
IS IT NOT MORE NATURAL TO ADDRESS THEIR WORRIES THIS WAY?
THEY MAY EVEN FIND IT EASIER THAN ALWAYS COMING TO THE SAME PERSON.
...
...

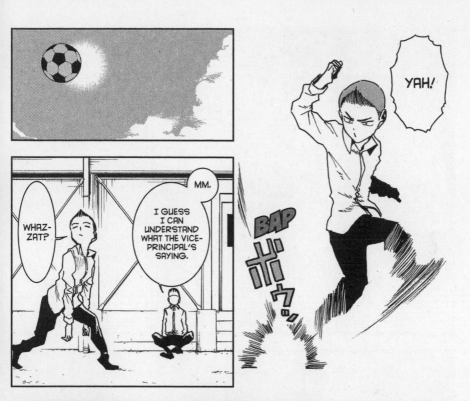

YAH!
BAP
ボウッ
MM.
I GUESS I CAN UNDERSTAND WHAT THE VICE-PRINCIPAL'S SAYING.
WHAZ-ZAT?
THERE ARE PLENTY OF OTHER TEACHERS. THE MORE YOU TALK TO, THE BETTER, RIGHT?
HA HA.
...
YOU THINK THAT'LL HAPPEN IF TETSU-SENSEI HOLDS BACK?
DON'T YOU?
THE VICE-PRINCIPAL SAID...

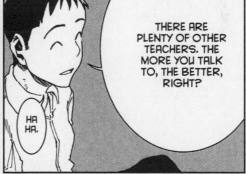

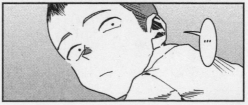

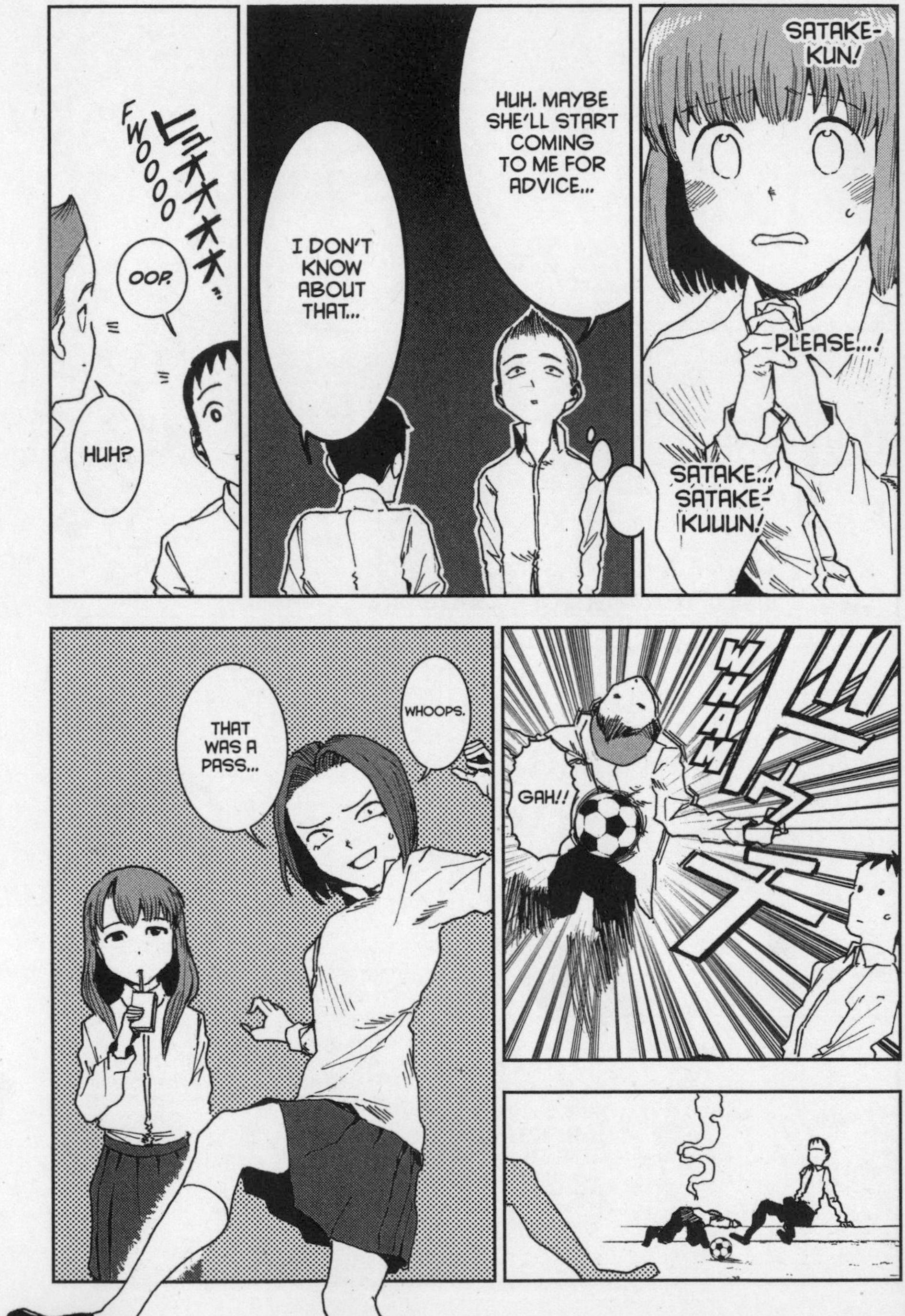
SATAKE-KUN!
PLEASE...!
SATAKE... SATAKE-KUUUN!
HUH. MAYBE SHE'LL START COMING TO ME FOR ADVICE...
I DON'T KNOW ABOUT THAT...
FWOOOOO
OOP.
HUH?
WHAM
GAH!!
WHOOPS.
THAT WAS A PASS...

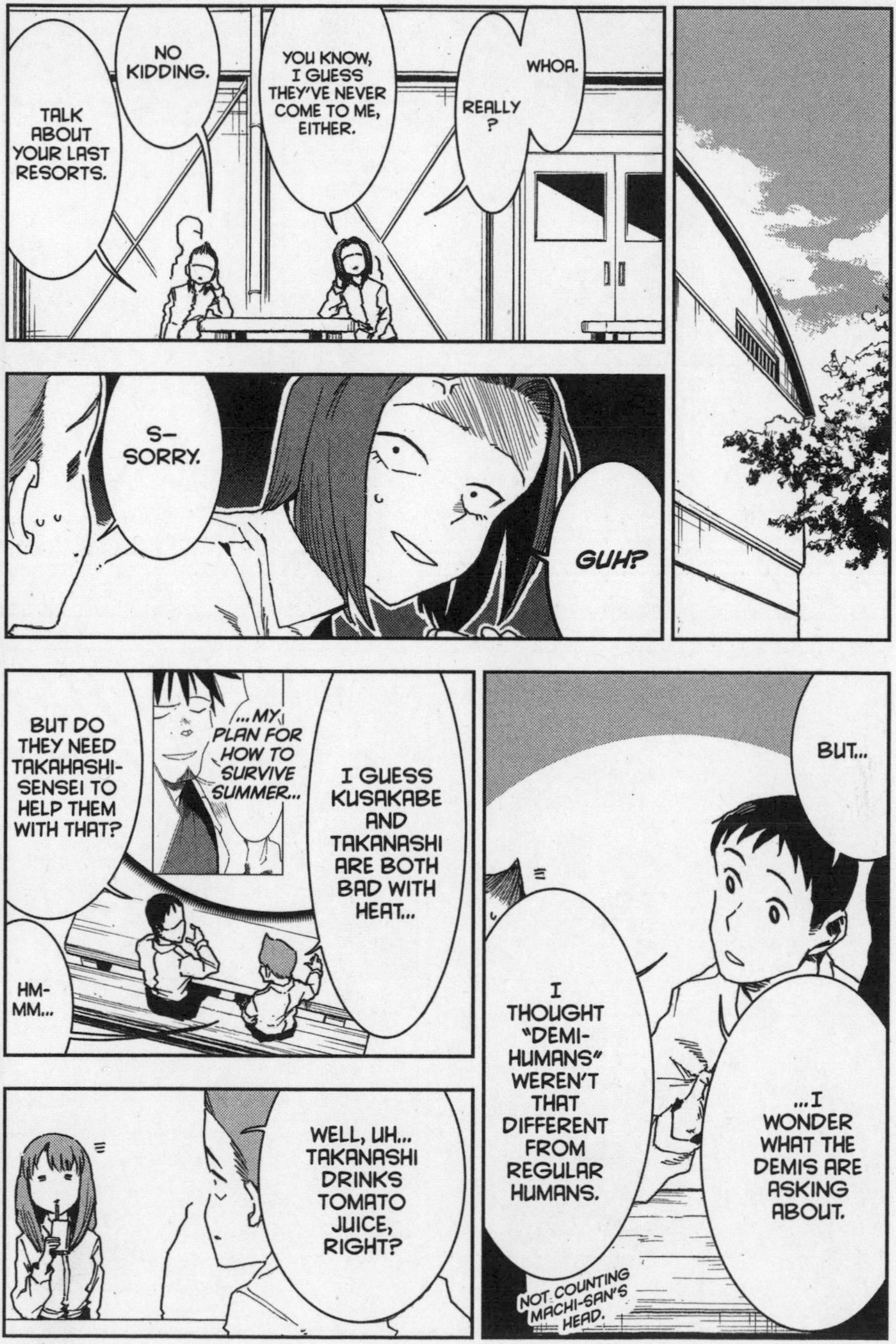
WHOA.
REALLY?
YOU KNOW, I GUESS THEY'VE NEVER COME TO ME, EITHER.
NO KIDDING.
TALK ABOUT YOUR LAST RESORTS.
GUH?
S— SORRY.
BUT...
...I WONDER WHAT THE DEMIS ARE ASKING ABOUT.
I THOUGHT "DEMI-HUMANS" WEREN'T THAT DIFFERENT FROM REGULAR HUMANS.
NOT COUNTING MACHI-SAN'S HEAD.
I GUESS KUSAKABE AND TAKANASHI ARE BOTH BAD WITH HEAT...
...MY PLAN FOR HOW TO SURVIVE SUMMER...
BUT DO THEY NEED TAKAHASHI-SENSEI TO HELP THEM WITH THAT?
HM-MM...
WELL, UH... TAKANASHI DRINKS TOMATO JUICE, RIGHT?

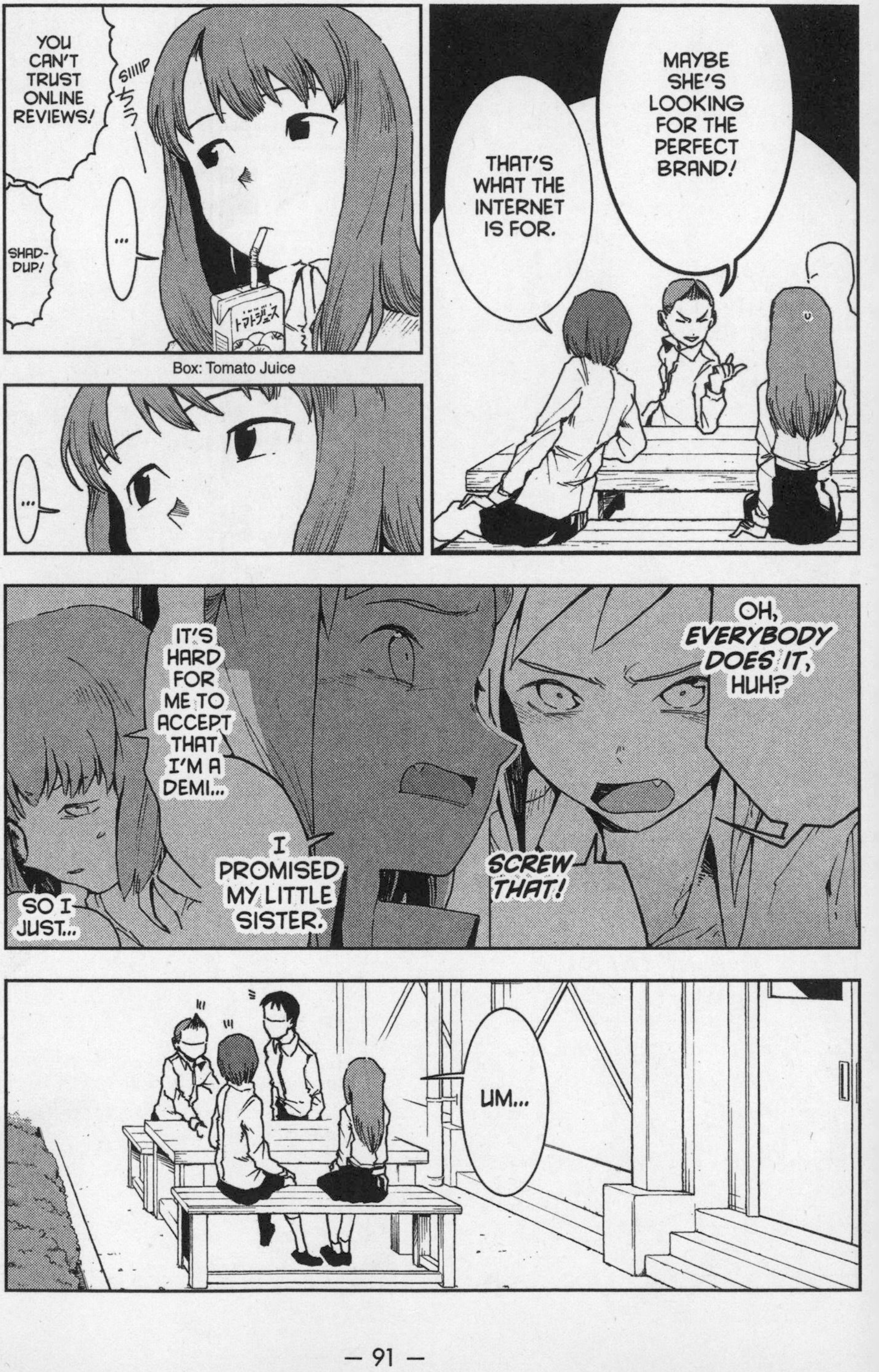
MAYBE SHE'S LOOKING FOR THE PERFECT BRAND!
THAT'S WHAT THE INTERNET IS FOR.
YOU CAN'T TRUST ONLINE REVIEWS!
SIIIIP
ちう
...
SHAD-DUP!
...
OH, EVERYBODY DOES IT, HUH?
SCREW THAT!
IT'S HARD FOR ME TO ACCEPT THAT I'M A DEMI...
I PROMISED MY LITTLE SISTER.
SO I JUST...
UM...
Box: Tomato Juice

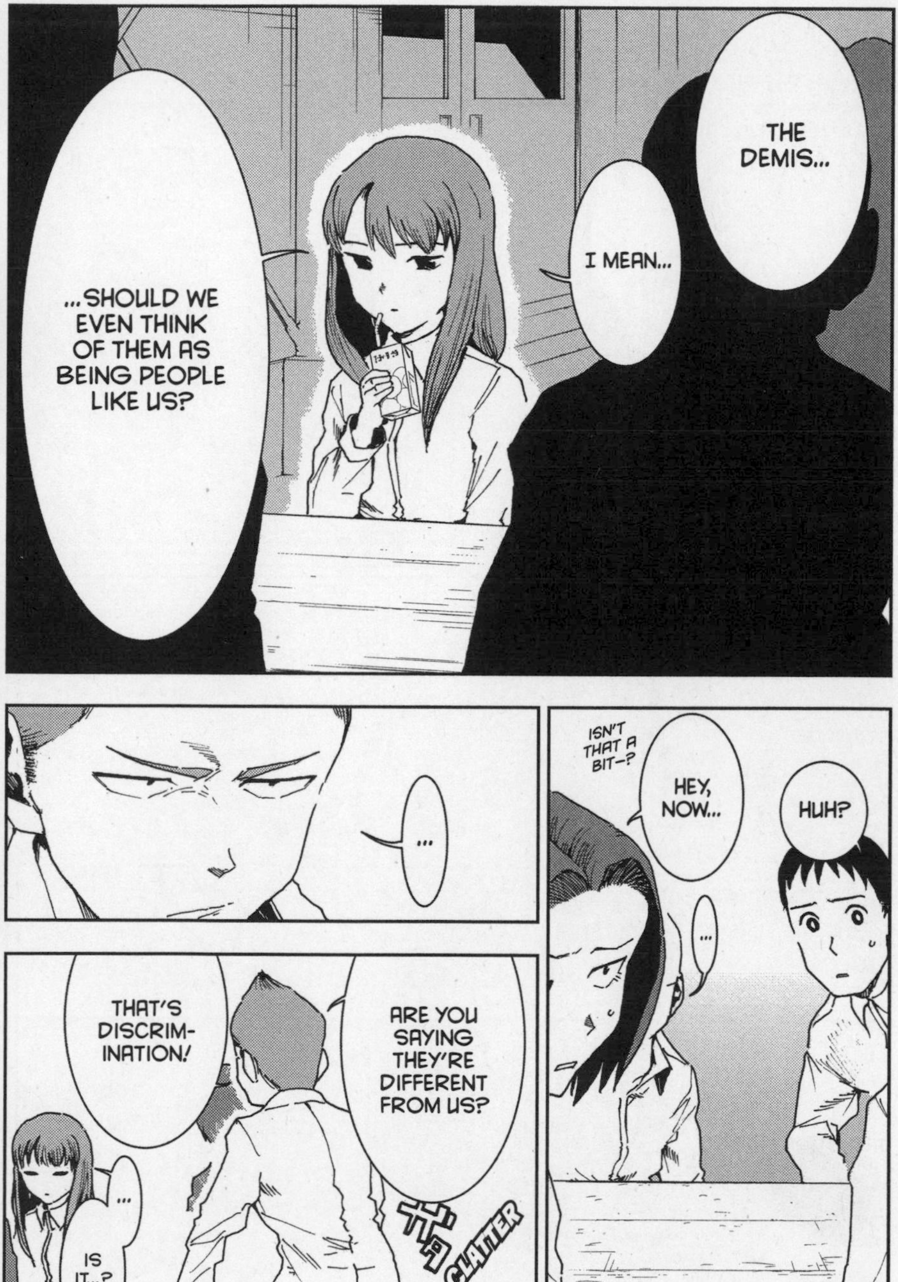
THE DEMIS...
I MEAN...
...SHOULD WE EVEN THINK OF THEM AS BEING PEOPLE LIKE US?
HUH?
HEY, NOW...
ISN'T THAT A BIT–?
...
...
ARE YOU SAYING THEY'RE DIFFERENT FROM US?
THAT'S DISCRIM- INATION!
CLATTER
...
IS IT...?

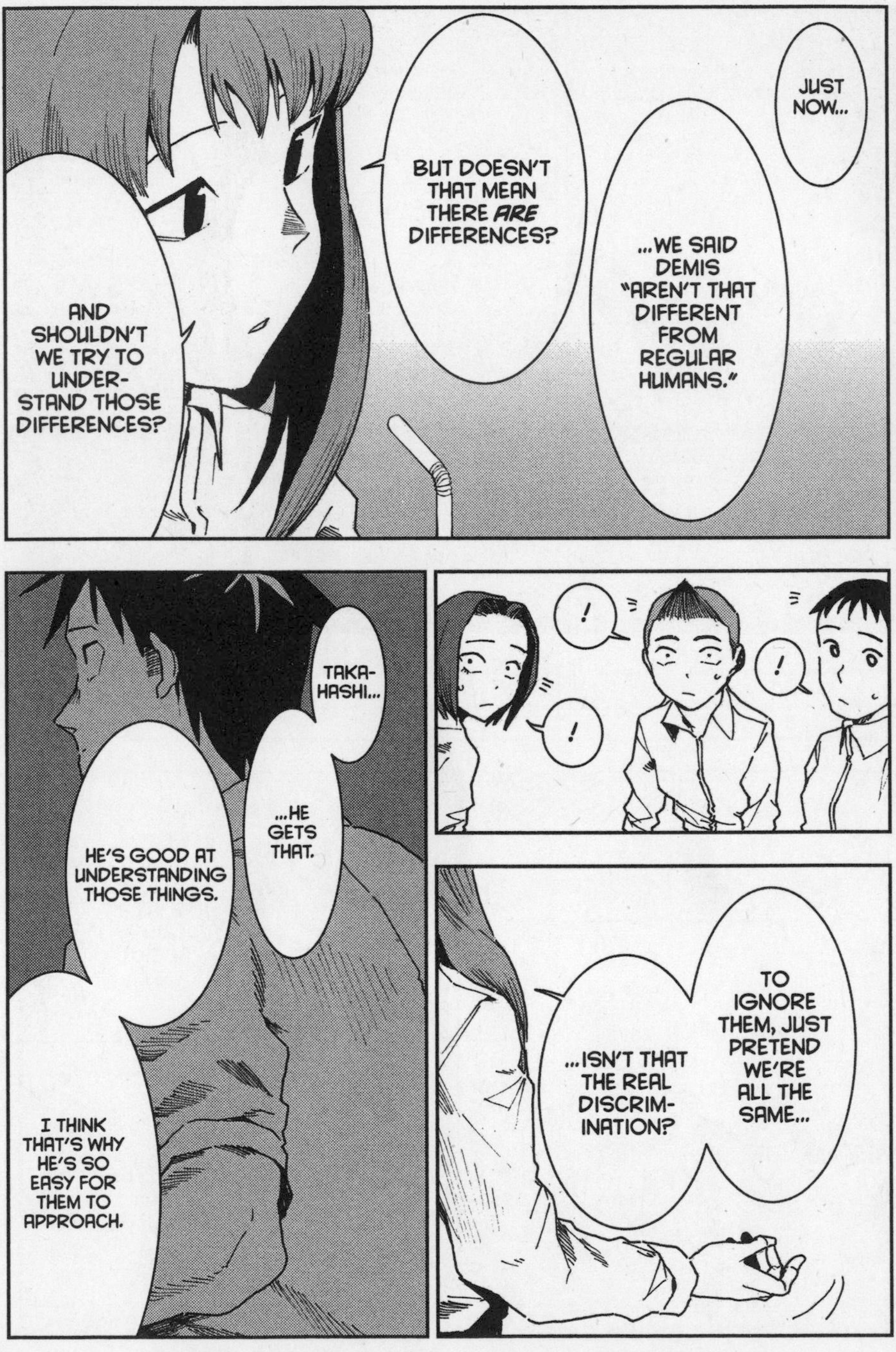
JUST NOW...
...WE SAID DEMIS "AREN'T THAT DIFFERENT FROM REGULAR HUMANS."
BUT DOESN'T THAT MEAN THERE *ARE* DIFFERENCES?
AND SHOULDN'T WE TRY TO UNDER-STAND THOSE DIFFERENCES?
!
!
!
TO IGNORE THEM, JUST PRETEND WE'RE ALL THE SAME...
...ISN'T THAT THE REAL DISCRIM-INATION?
TAKA-HASHI...
...HE GETS THAT.
HE'S GOOD AT UNDERSTANDING THOSE THINGS.
I THINK THAT'S WHY HE'S SO EASY FOR THEM TO APPROACH.

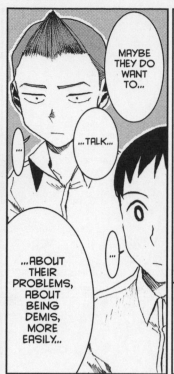

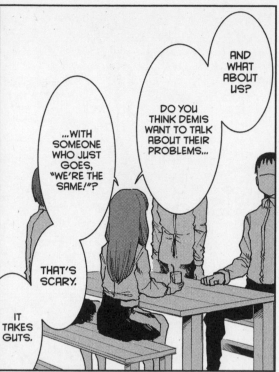

AND WHAT ABOUT US?
DO YOU THINK DEMIS WANT TO TALK ABOUT THEIR PROBLEMS...
...WITH SOMEONE WHO JUST GOES, "WE'RE THE SAME!"?
THAT'S SCARY.
IT TAKES GUTS.
MAYBE THEY DO WANT TO...
...TALK...
...
...
...ABOUT THEIR PROBLEMS, ABOUT BEING DEMIS, MORE EASILY...
AS FOR US...
...WE STILL DON'T KNOW THE FIRST THING ABOUT THEM.
...
...
I MEAN...
...JUST A THOUGHT.
...
MAY-BE...
SIIIP

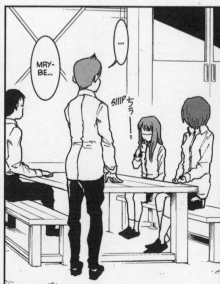

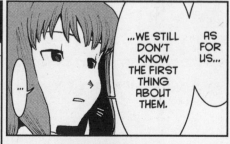

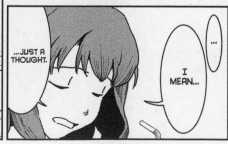

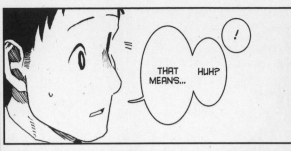

HEY...

...

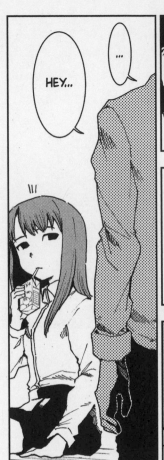

THAT MEANS...

HUH?

!

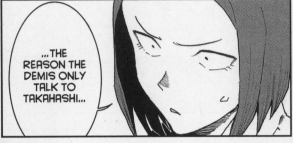

...THE REASON THE DEMIS ONLY TALK TO TAKAHASHI...

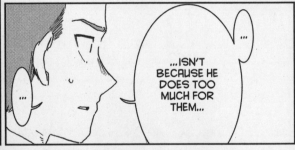

...ISN'T BECAUSE HE DOES TOO MUCH FOR THEM...

...

...

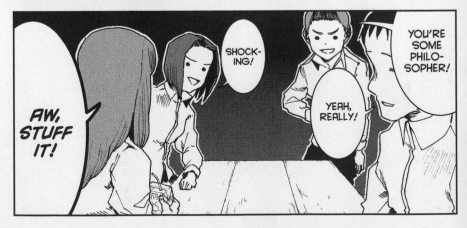

SHOCK-ING!

YOU'RE SOME PHILO-SOPHER!

YEAH, REALLY!

AW, STUFF IT!

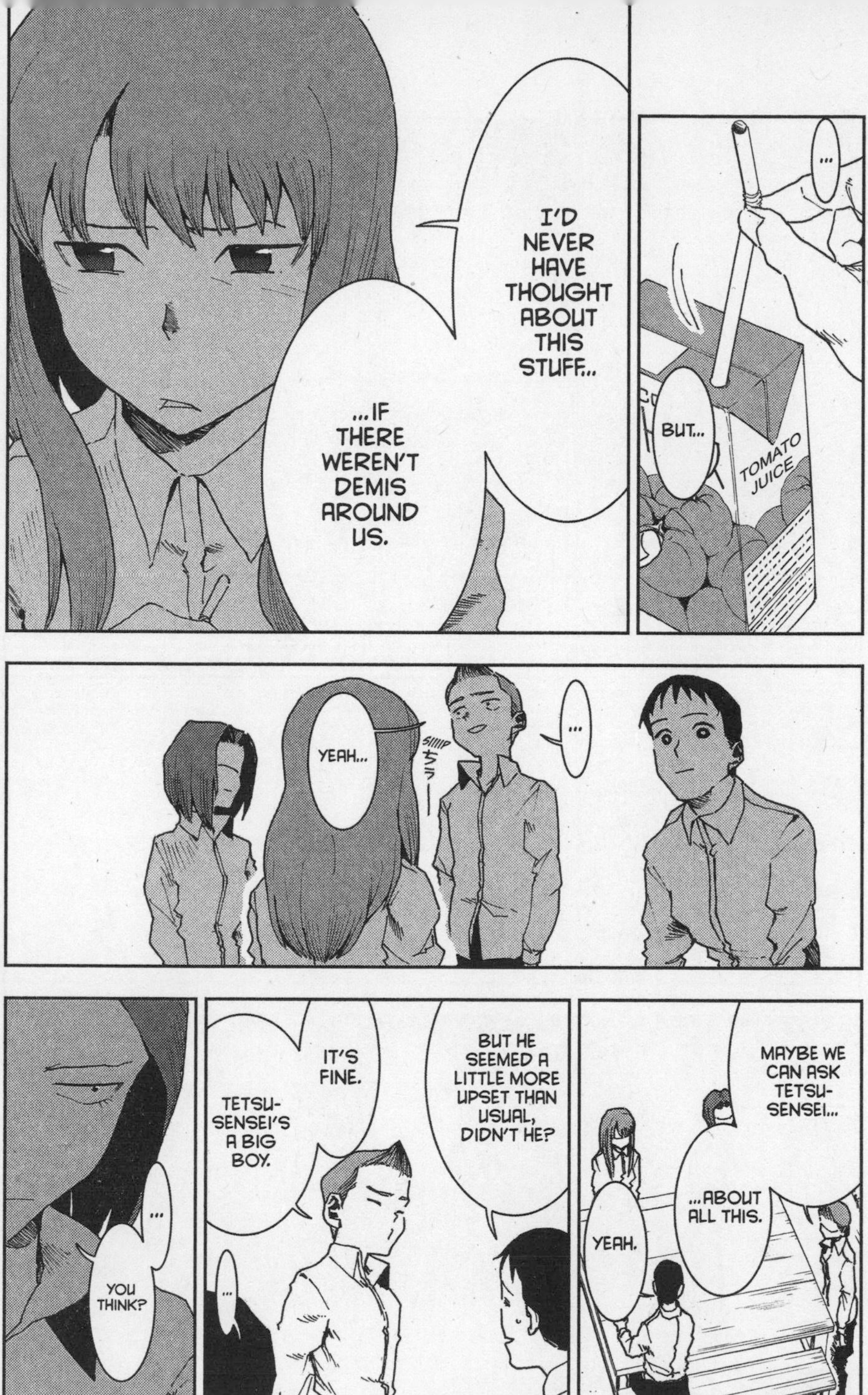
...
BUT...
TOMATO JUICE
I'D NEVER HAVE THOUGHT ABOUT THIS STUFF...
...IF THERE WEREN'T DEMIS AROUND US.
...
SIIIP
YEAH...
MAYBE WE CAN ASK TETSU-SENSEI...
...ABOUT ALL THIS.
YEAH.
BUT HE SEEMED A LITTLE MORE UPSET THAN USUAL, DIDN'T HE?
IT'S FINE.
TETSU-SENSEI'S A BIG BOY.
...
...
YOU THINK?

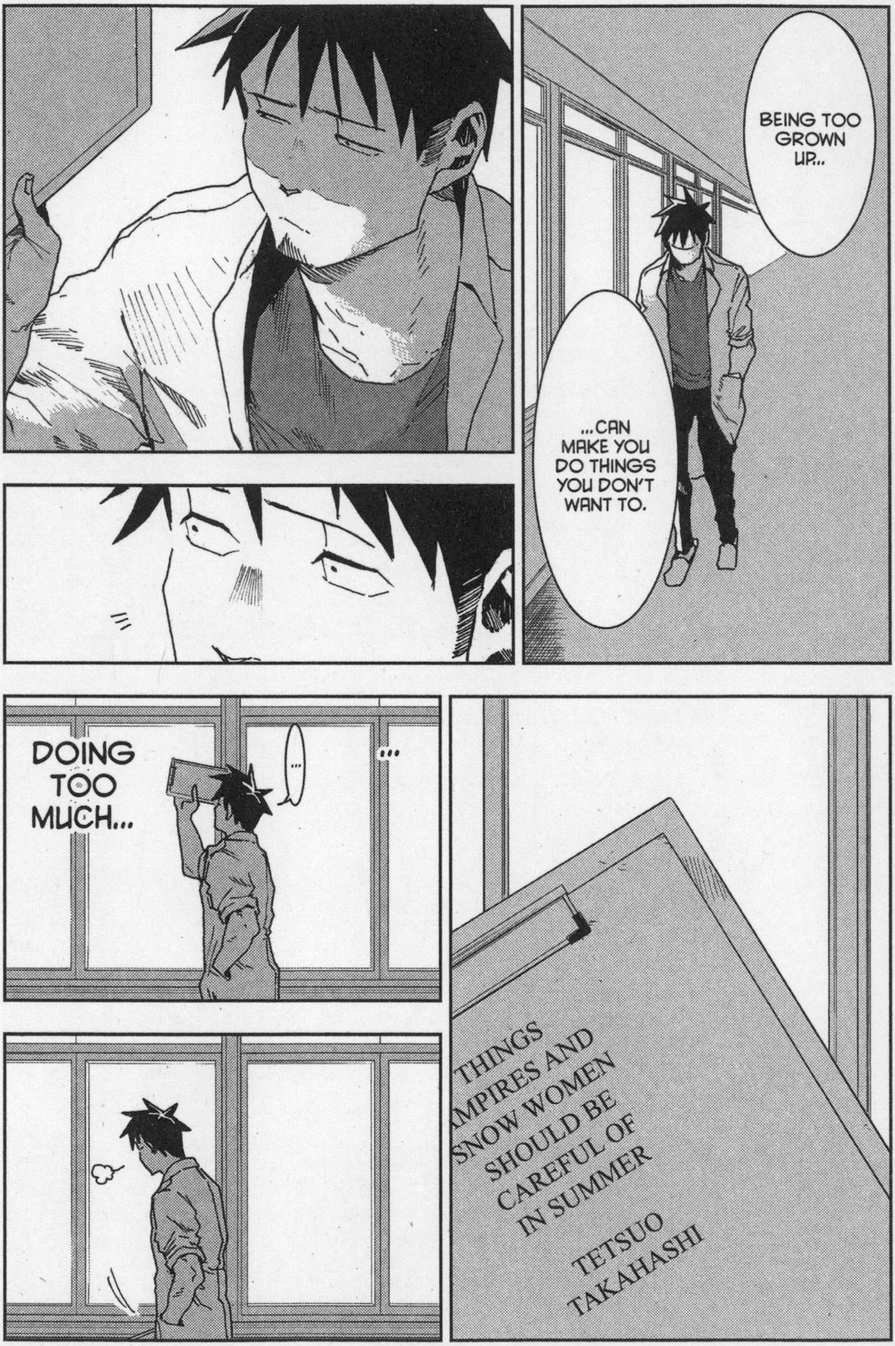
BEING TOO GROWN UP...
...CAN MAKE YOU DO THINGS YOU DON'T WANT TO.
THINGS
AMPIRES AND
SNOW WOMEN
SHOULD BE
CAREFUL OF
IN SUMMER
TETSUO
TAKAHASHI
...
DOING TOO MUCH...
...

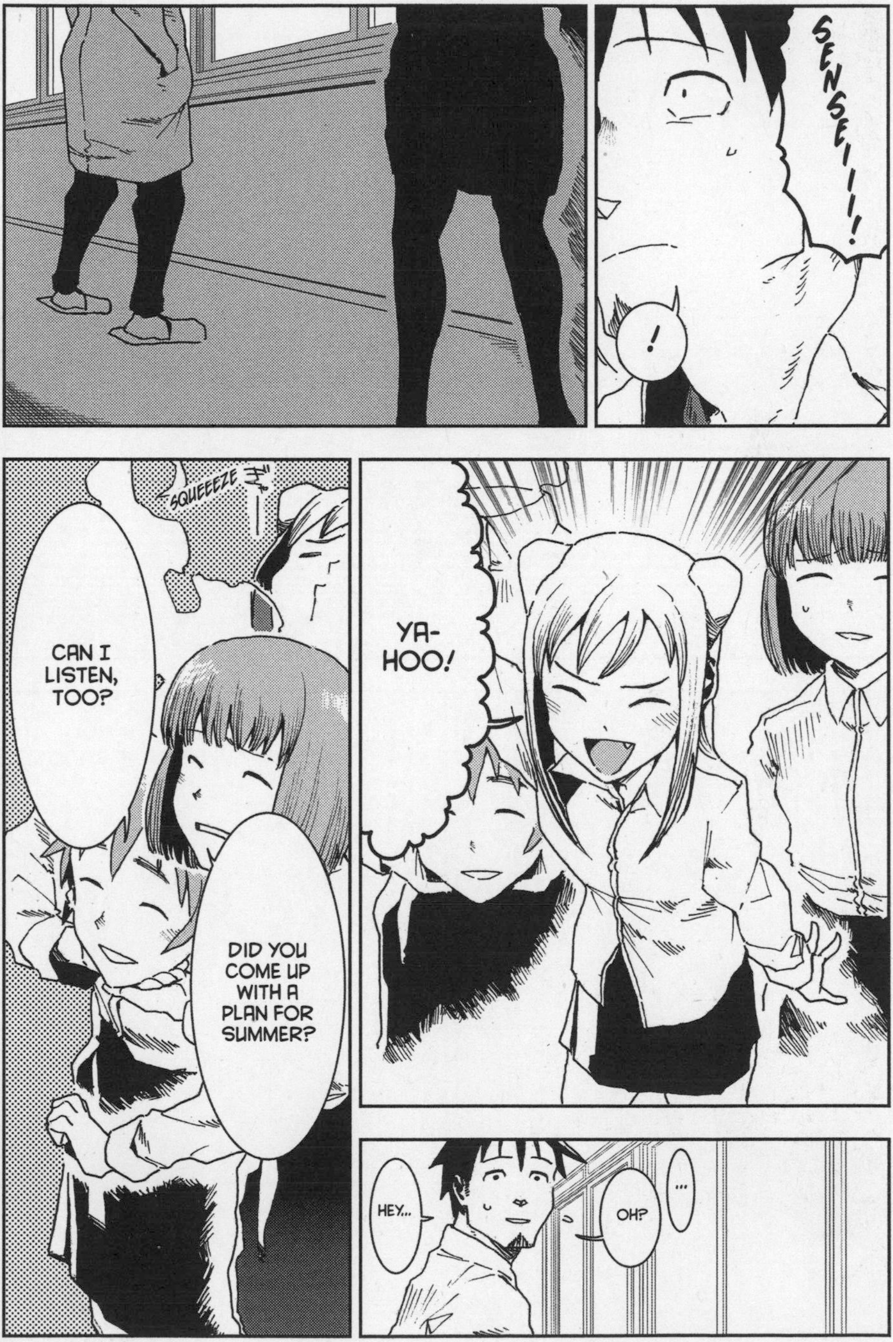
SENSEI!!!
!
YA-HOO!
...
OH?
HEY...
SQUEEEZE
CAN I LISTEN, TOO?
DID YOU COME UP WITH A PLAN FOR SUMMER?

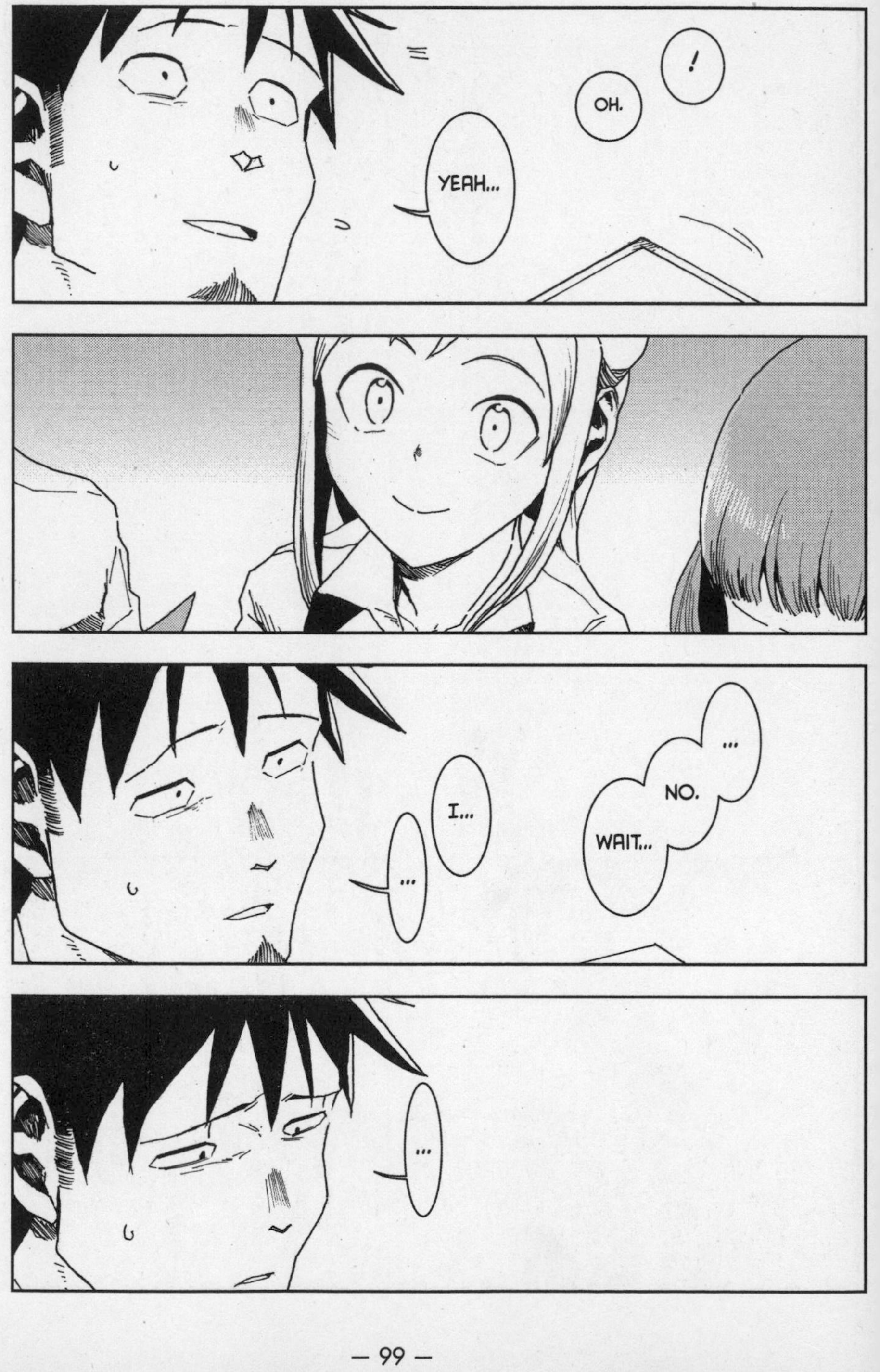
!
OH.
YEAH...
WAIT...
NO.
...
I...
...
...

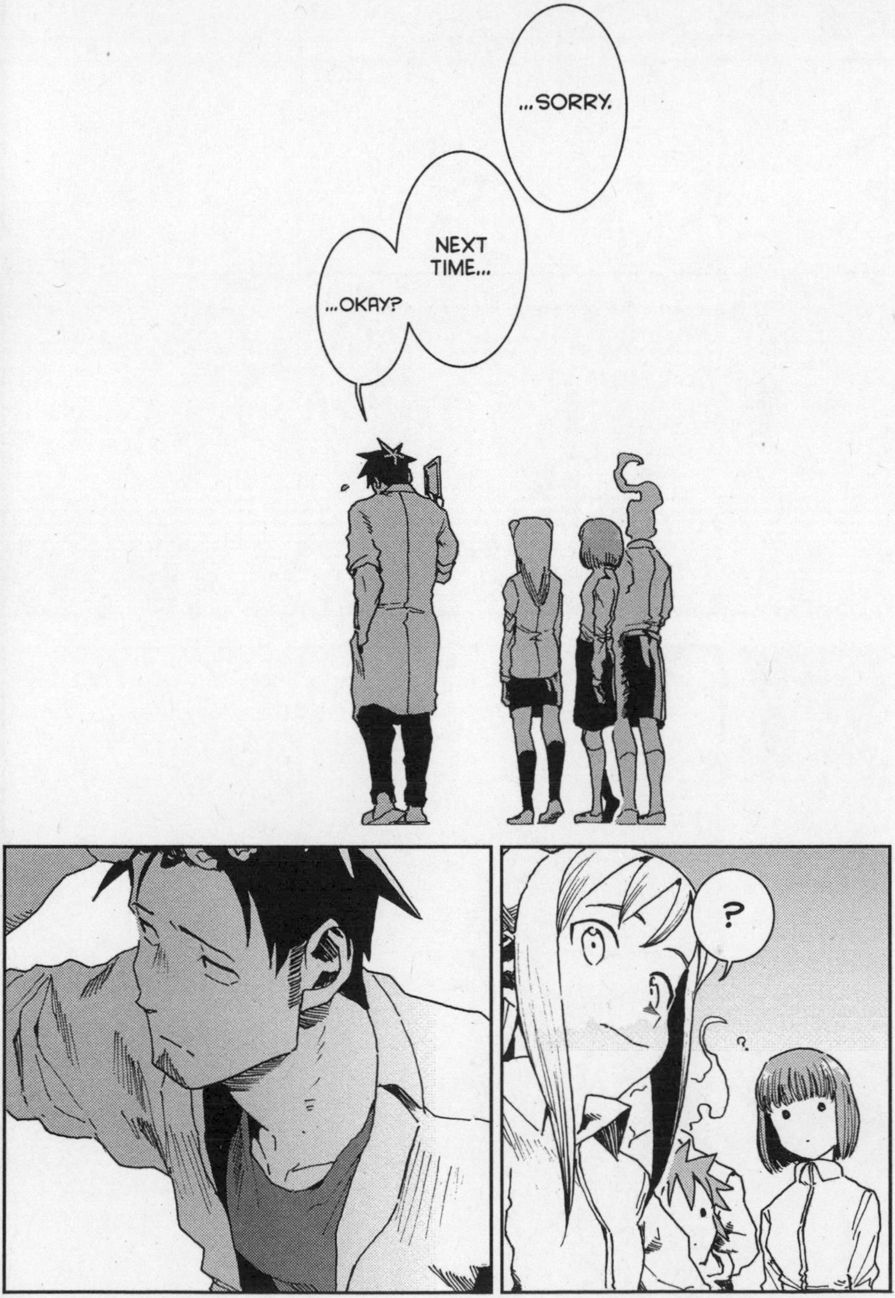
...SORRY.
NEXT TIME...
...OKAY?
?
?

...AND THAT'S THE STORY.
...
I SEE!
GOT IT!
I'LL SEE WHAT I CAN DO.
THANKS, SATA-KKEE!
...
"SATA-KKEE"...
IS THAT A *NICK-NAME*?!
SOUNDS LIKE SOME MONSTER!
HUH? HUH?
OH...
YEAH...
OTA
KIMURA
IMORI
LUCKY GUY...

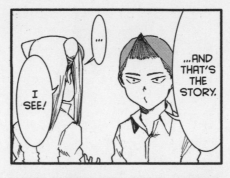

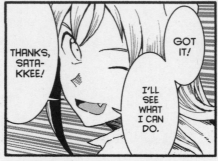

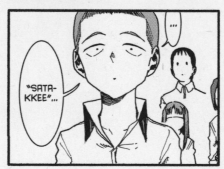

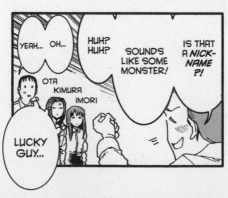

INTERVIEWS WITH MONSTER GIRLS

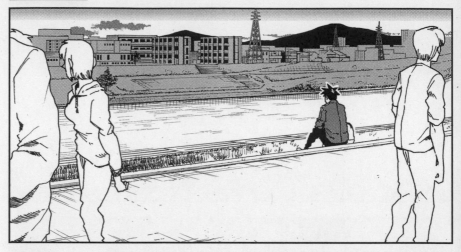

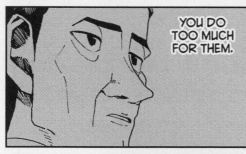

Chapter 30: Demis Want to Help

SIIIGH
ボケー…
YOU DO TOO MUCH FOR THEM.
DO I REALLY...?
MAYBE I DO...

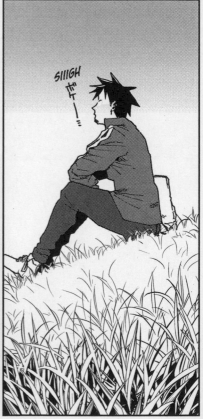

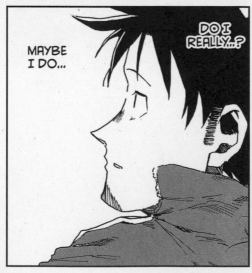

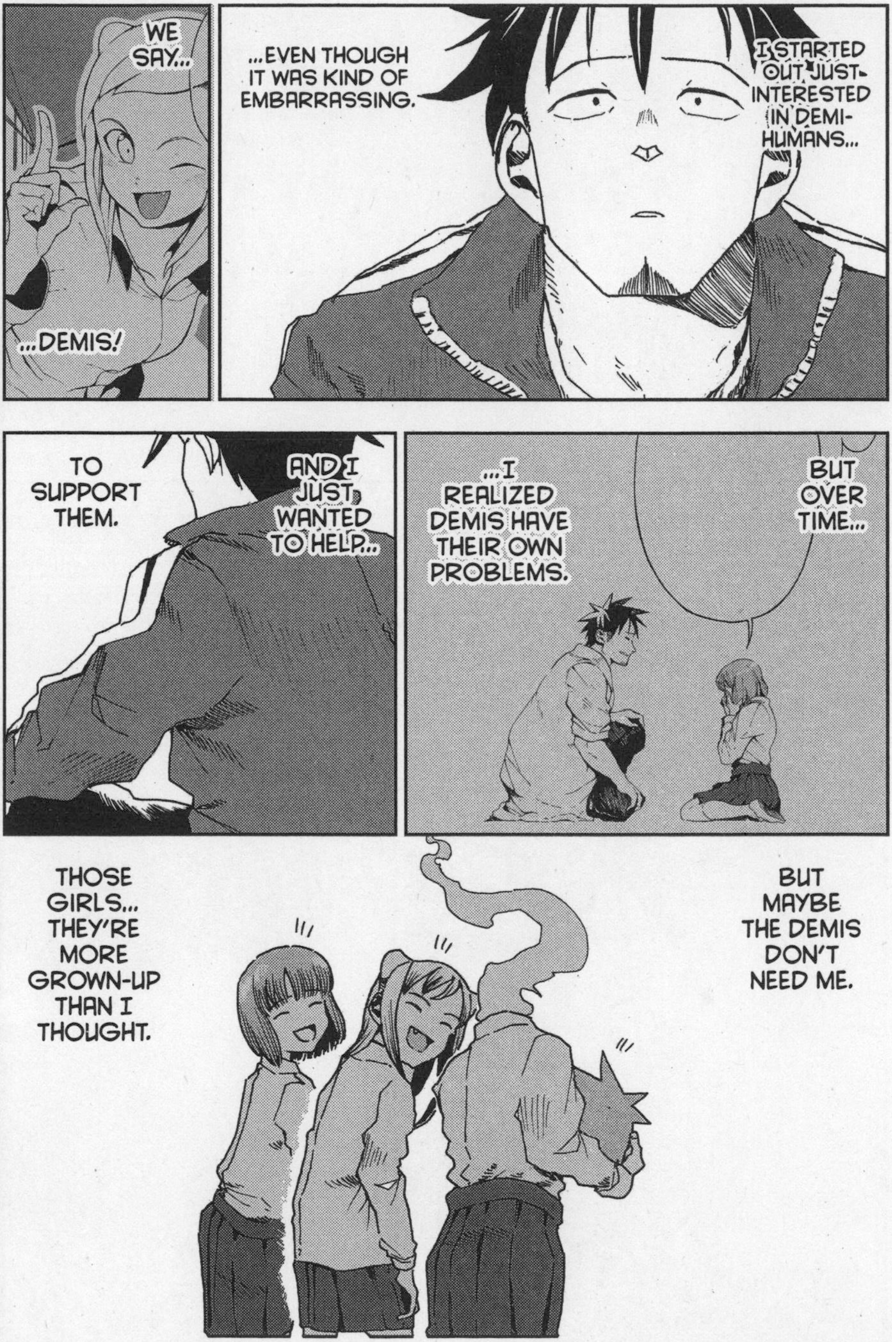
I STARTED OUT JUST INTERESTED IN DEMI-HUMANS...
...EVEN THOUGH IT WAS KIND OF EMBARRASSING.
WE SAY...
...DEMIS!
BUT OVER TIME...
...I REALIZED DEMIS HAVE THEIR OWN PROBLEMS.
AND I JUST WANTED TO HELP...
TO SUPPORT THEM.
BUT MAYBE THE DEMIS DON'T NEED ME.
THOSE GIRLS... THEY'RE MORE GROWN-UP THAN I THOUGHT.

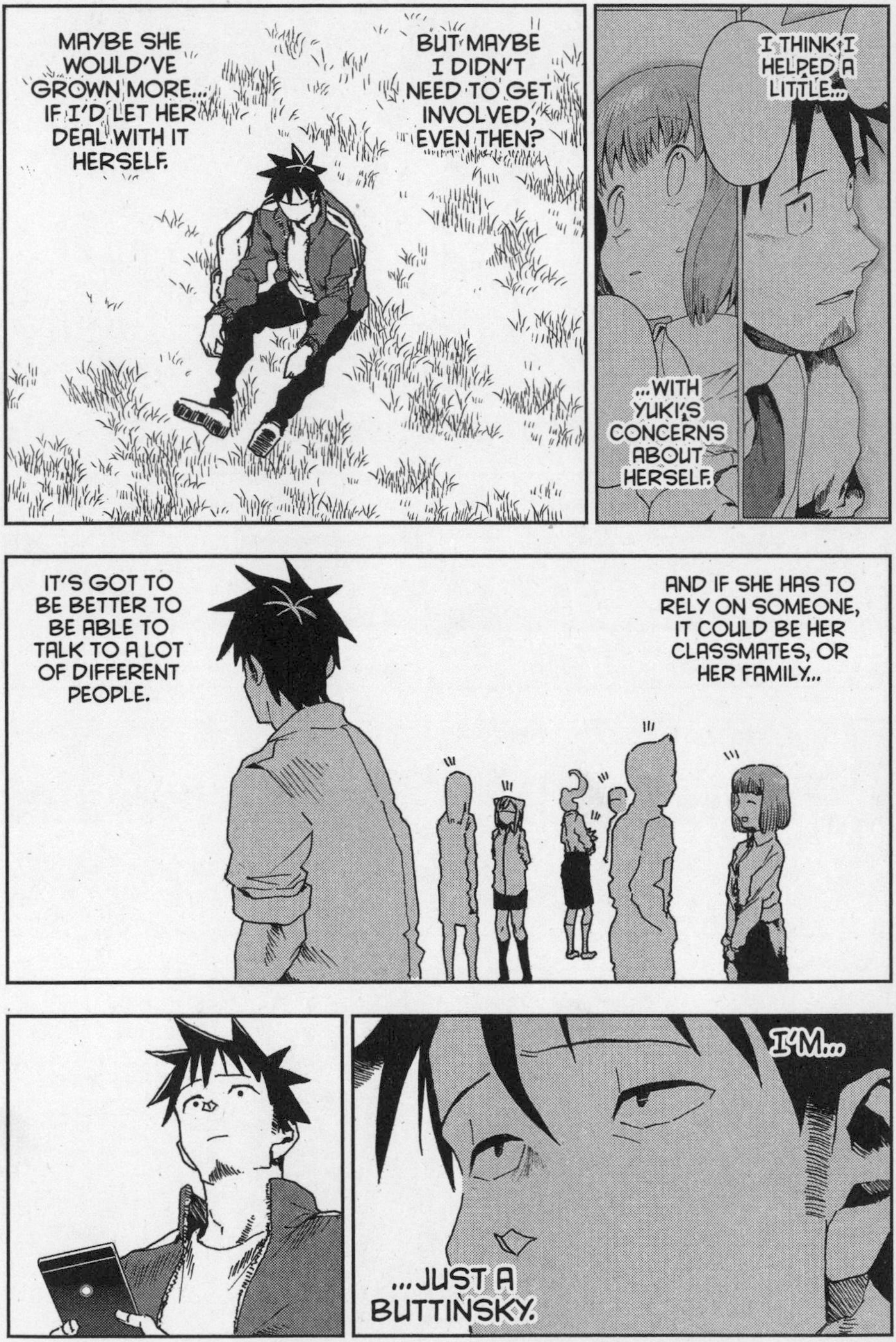
I THINK I HELPED A LITTLE...
...WITH YUKI'S CONCERNS ABOUT HERSELF.
BUT MAYBE I DIDN'T NEED TO GET INVOLVED, EVEN THEN?
MAYBE SHE WOULD'VE GROWN MORE... IF I'D LET HER DEAL WITH IT HERSELF.
AND IF SHE HAS TO RELY ON SOMEONE, IT COULD BE HER CLASSMATES, OR HER FAMILY...
IT'S GOT TO BE BETTER TO BE ABLE TO TALK TO A LOT OF DIFFERENT PEOPLE.
I'M...
...JUST A BUTTINSKY.

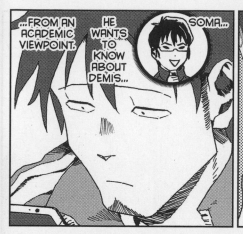

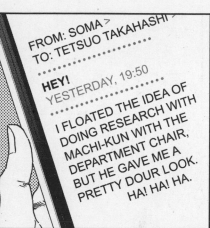

FROM: SOMA
TO: TETSUO TAKAHASHI
HEY!
YESTERDAY, 19:50
I FLOATED THE IDEA OF DOING RESEARCH WITH MACHI-KUN WITH THE DEPARTMENT CHAIR, BUT HE GAVE ME A PRETTY DOUR LOOK. HA! HA! HA.
SOMA...
HE WANTS TO KNOW ABOUT DEMIS...
...FROM AN ACADEMIC VIEWPOINT.
I'M SURE THAT WOULD HELP THEM IN THE LONG RUN.
IT MIGHT EVEN...
...HELP CHANGE THE WORLD ONE DAY.
THERE'S MORE THAN ONE WAY...
...TO HELP THE DEMIS.
MAYBE I'VE GOTTEN TOO CLOSE TO THEM AS A TEACHER.
I COULD...
...BE A SCHOLAR INSTEAD, GET SOME DISTANCE...

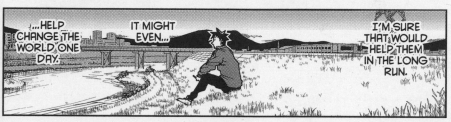

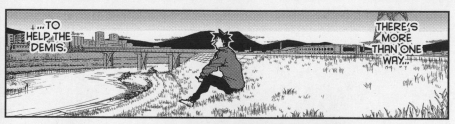

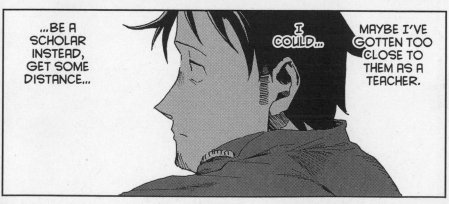

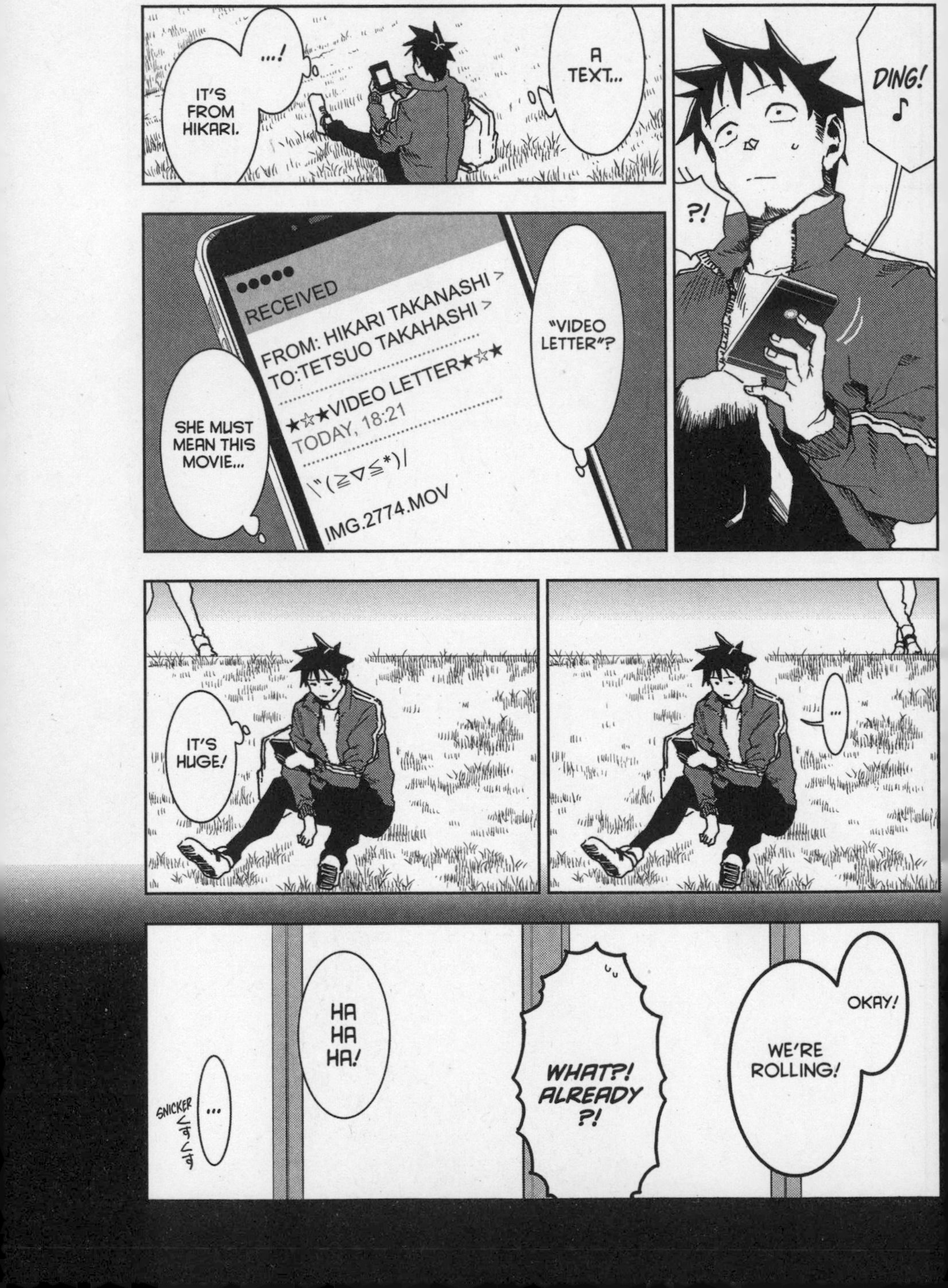
DING! ♪
?!
A TEXT...
...!
IT'S FROM HIKARI.
"VIDEO LETTER"?
RECEIVED
FROM: HIKARI TAKANASHI >
TO:TETSUO TAKAHASHI >
★☆★VIDEO LETTER★☆★
TODAY, 18:21
\"(≧▽≦*)/
IMG.2774.MOV
SHE MUST MEAN THIS MOVIE...
...
IT'S HUGE!
OKAY! WE'RE ROLLING!
WHAT?! ALREADY?!
HA HA HA!
...
SNICKER くすくす

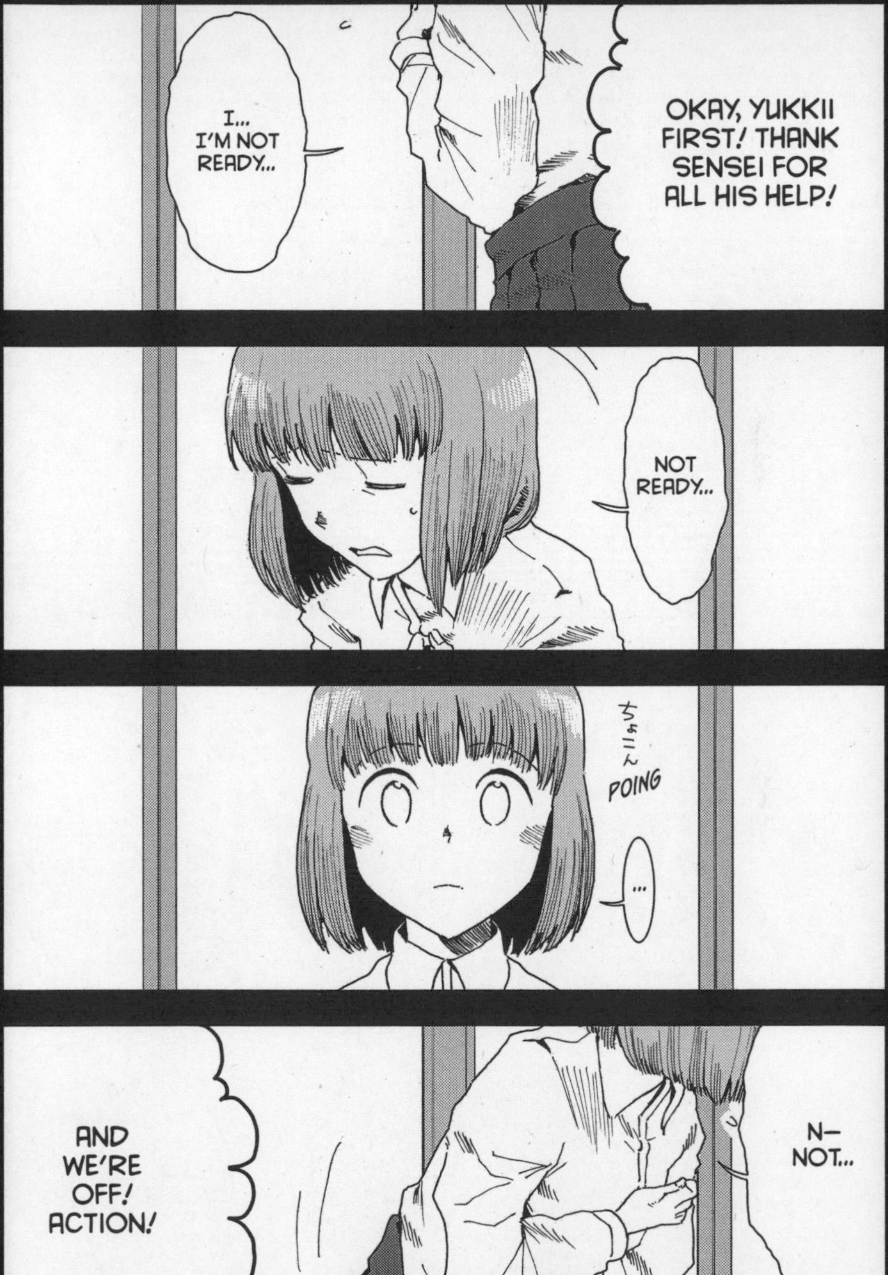
OKAY, YUKKII FIRST! THANK SENSEI FOR ALL HIS HELP!
I... I'M NOT READY...
NOT READY...
ちょこん
POING
...
N— NOT...
AND WE'RE OFF! ACTION!

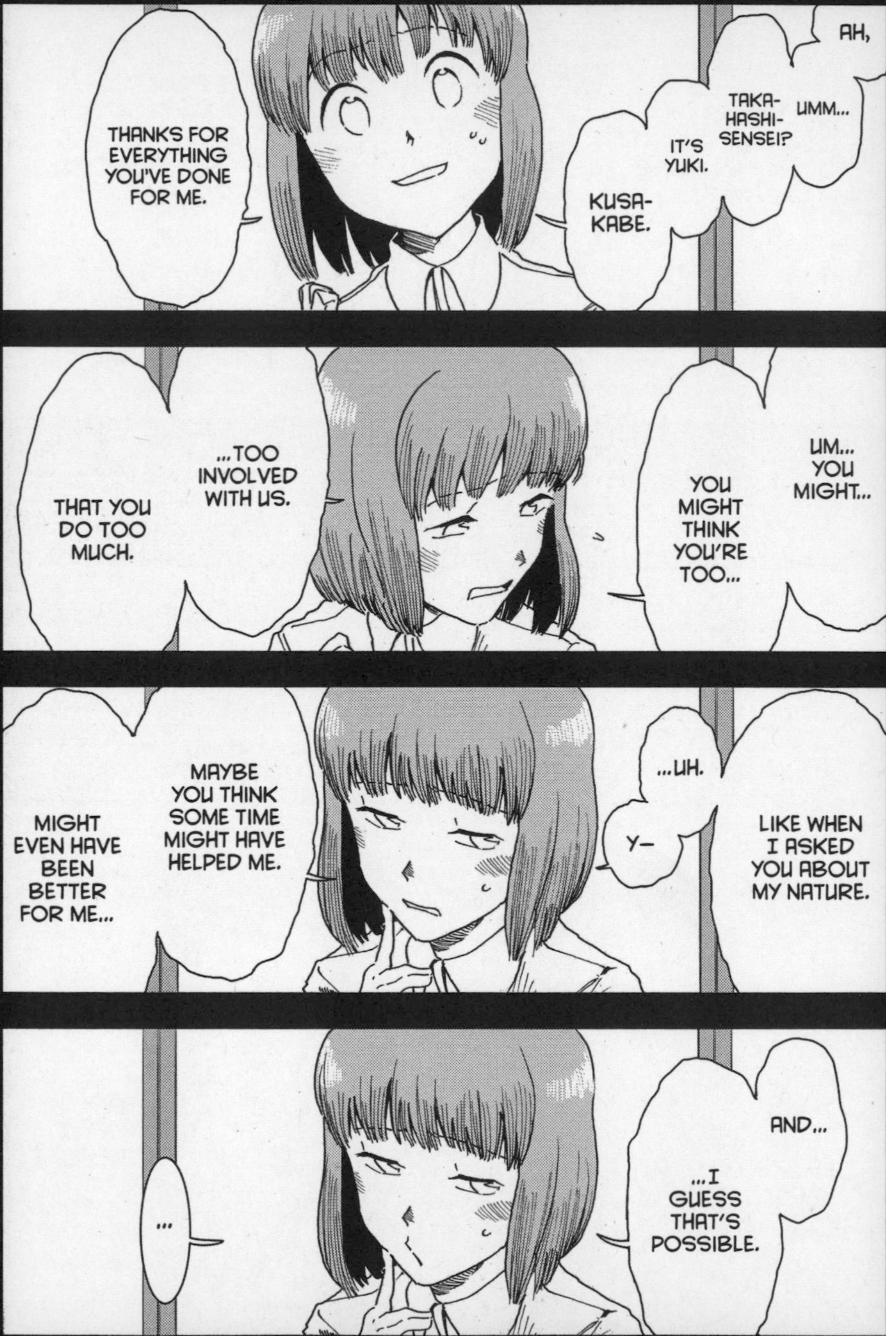
AH,
UMM...
TAKA-HASHI-SENSEI?
IT'S YUKI.
KUSA-KABE.
THANKS FOR EVERYTHING YOU'VE DONE FOR ME.
UM... YOU MIGHT...
YOU MIGHT THINK YOU'RE TOO...
...TOO INVOLVED WITH US.
THAT YOU DO TOO MUCH.
LIKE WHEN I ASKED YOU ABOUT MY NATURE.
...UH.
Y–
MAYBE YOU THINK SOME TIME MIGHT HAVE HELPED ME.
MIGHT EVEN HAVE BEEN BETTER FOR ME...
AND...
...I GUESS THAT'S POSSIBLE.
...

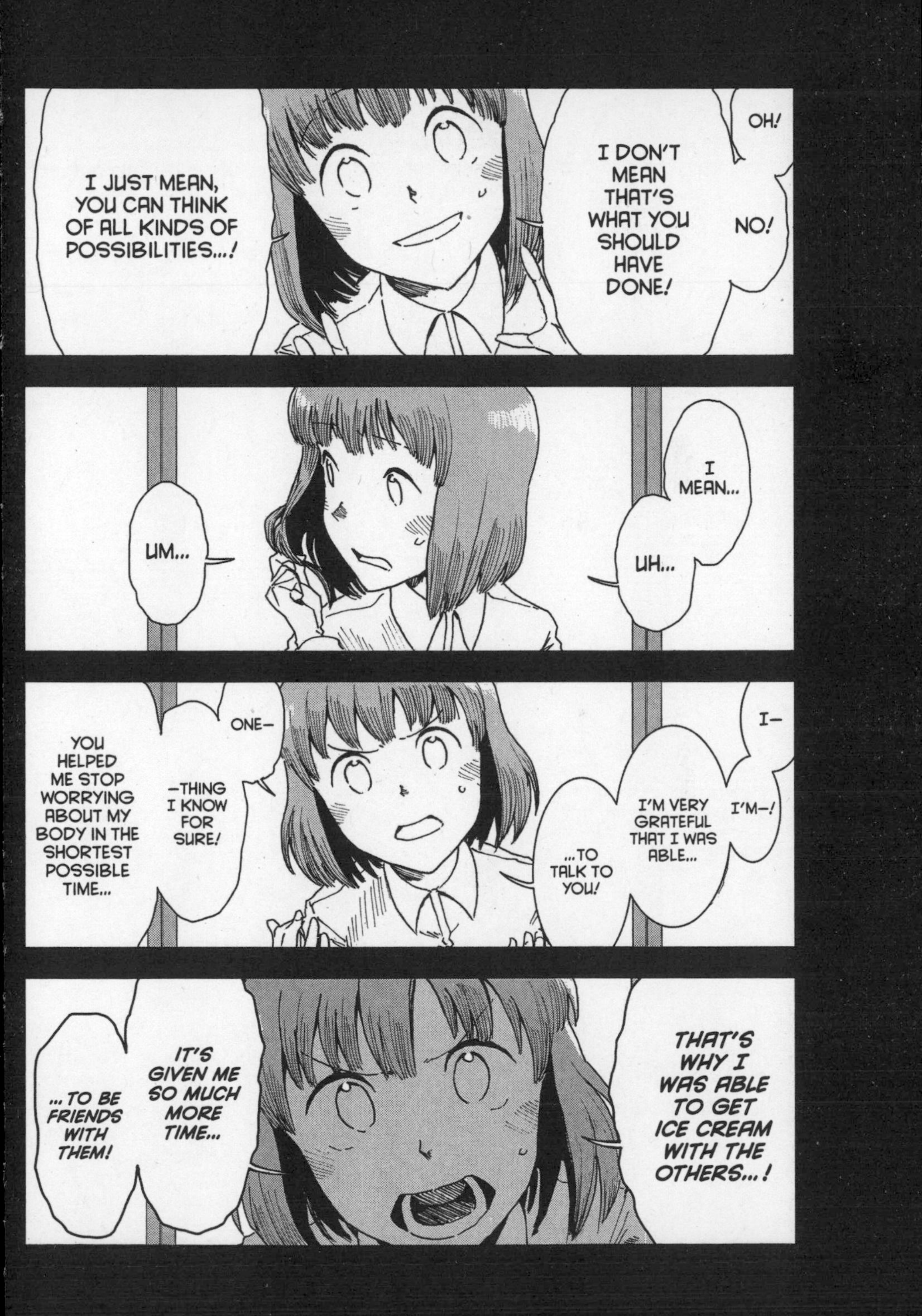
OH! NO!
I DON'T MEAN THAT'S WHAT YOU SHOULD HAVE DONE!
I JUST MEAN, YOU CAN THINK OF ALL KINDS OF POSSIBILITIES...!
I MEAN... UH...
UM...
I— I'M—!
I'M VERY GRATEFUL THAT I WAS ABLE... ...TO TALK TO YOU!
ONE— —THING I KNOW FOR SURE!
YOU HELPED ME STOP WORRYING ABOUT MY BODY IN THE SHORTEST POSSIBLE TIME...
THAT'S WHY I WAS ABLE TO GET ICE CREAM WITH THE OTHERS...!
IT'S GIVEN ME SO MUCH MORE TIME...
...TO BE FRIENDS WITH THEM!

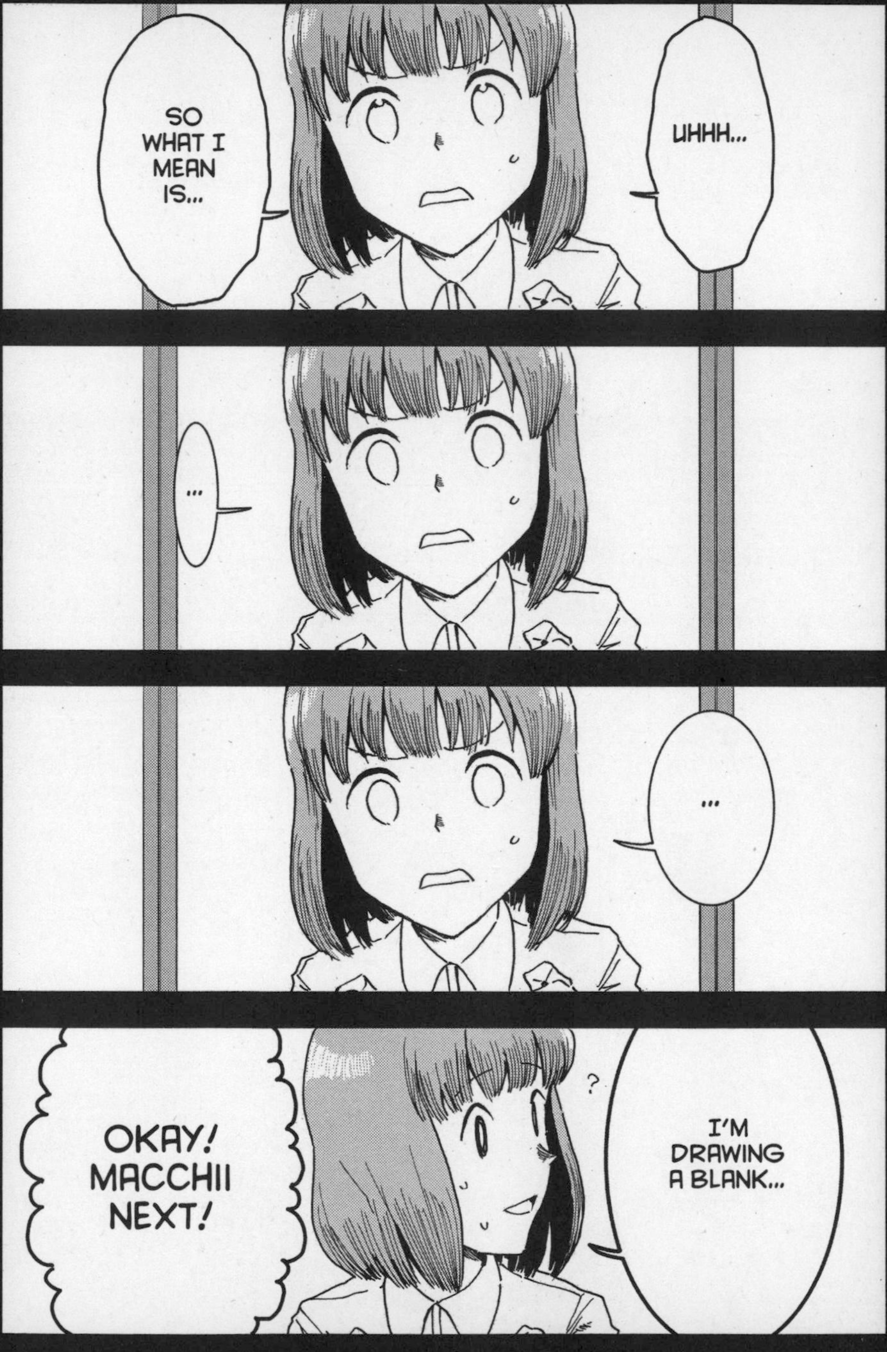
UHHH...
SO WHAT I MEAN IS...
...
...
I'M DRAWING A BLANK...
OKAY! MACCHII NEXT!

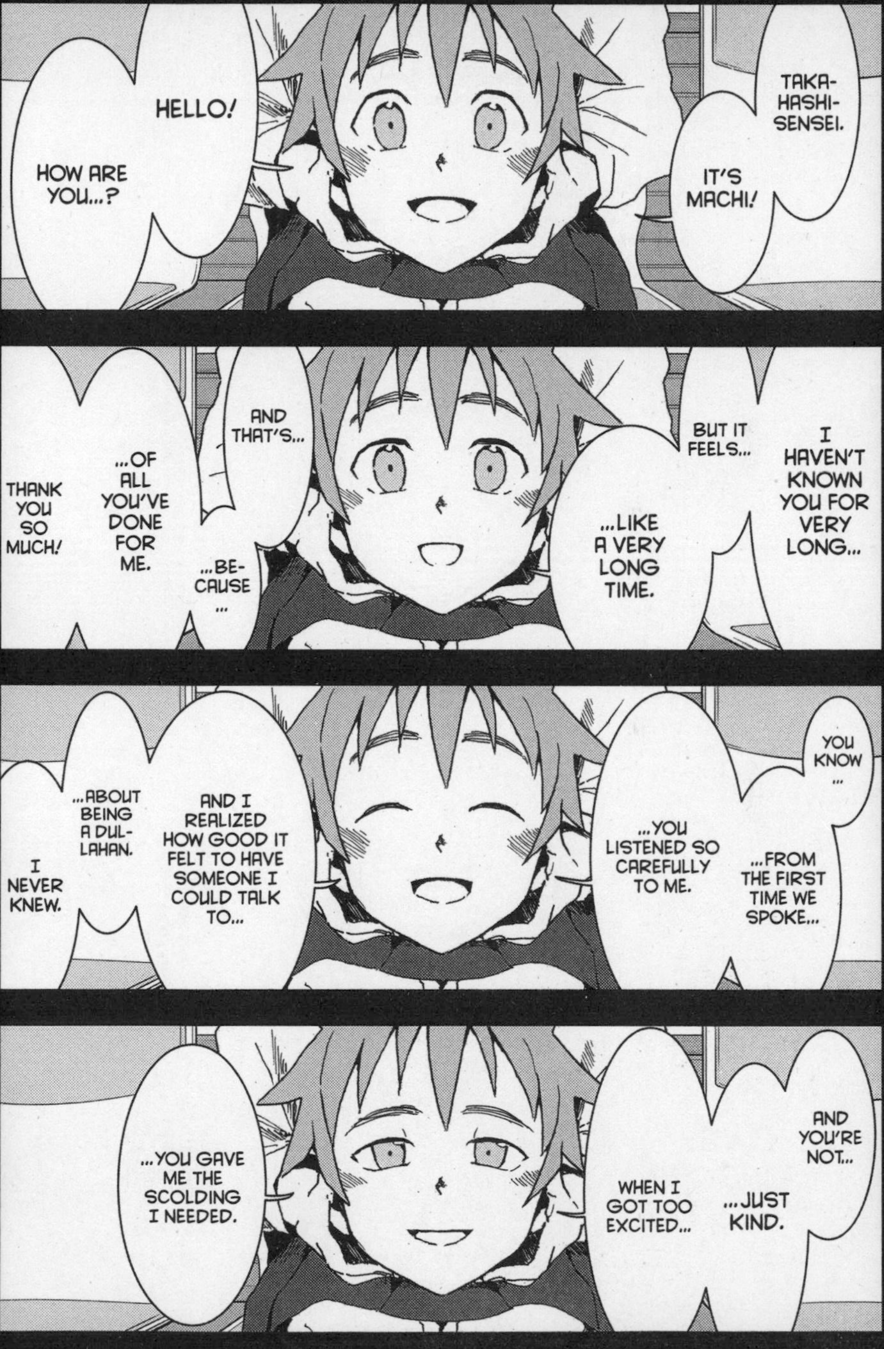
TAKAHASHI-SENSEI.
IT'S MACHI!
HELLO!
HOW ARE YOU...?
I HAVEN'T KNOWN YOU FOR VERY LONG...
BUT IT FEELS...
...LIKE A VERY LONG TIME.
AND THAT'S...
...BECAUSE...
...OF ALL YOU'VE DONE FOR ME.
THANK YOU SO MUCH!
YOU KNOW...
...FROM THE FIRST TIME WE SPOKE...
...YOU LISTENED SO CAREFULLY TO ME.
AND I REALIZED HOW GOOD IT FELT TO HAVE SOMEONE I COULD TALK TO...
...ABOUT BEING A DULLAHAN.
I NEVER KNEW.
AND YOU'RE NOT...
...JUST KIND.
WHEN I GOT TOO EXCITED...
...YOU GAVE ME THE SCOLDING I NEEDED.

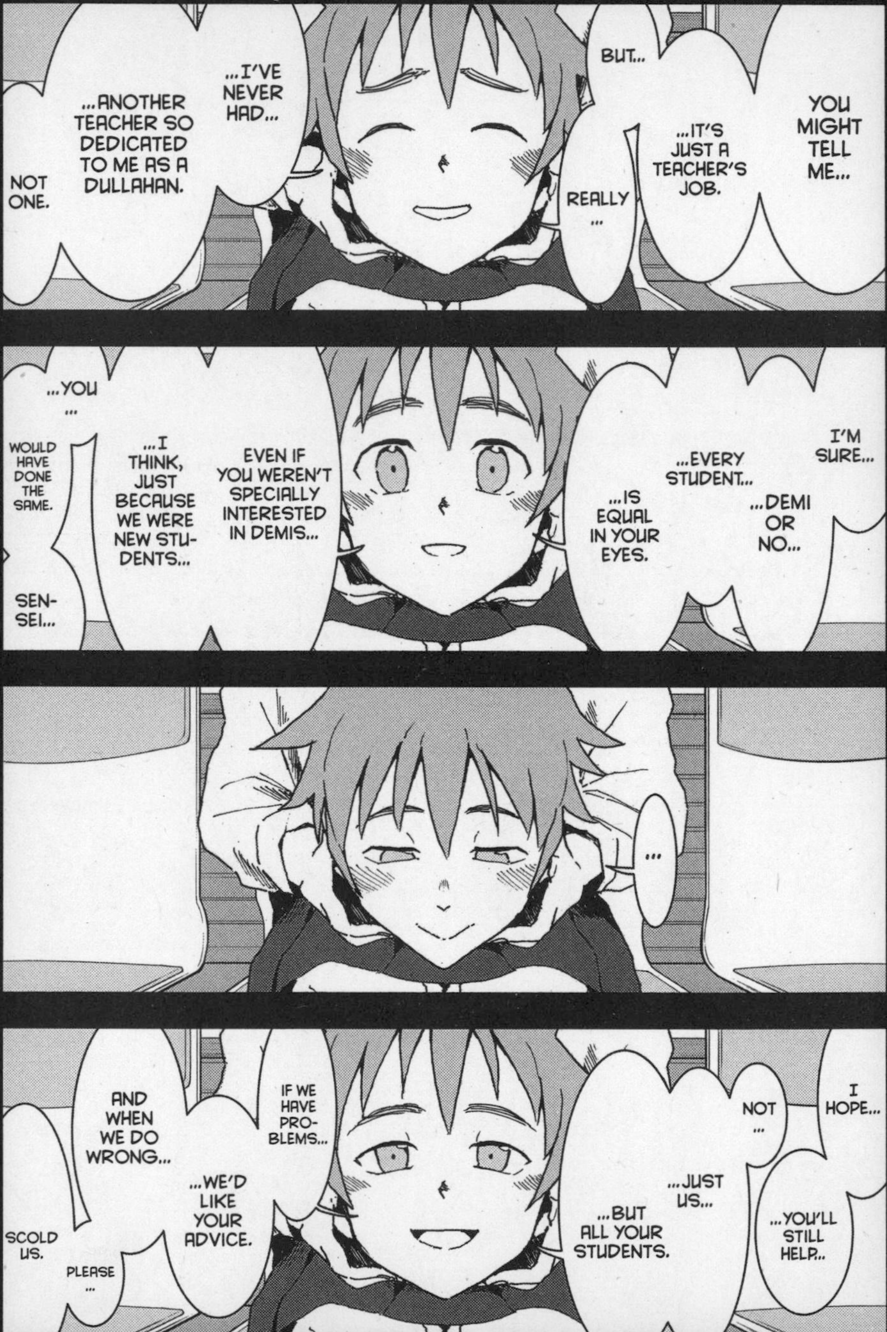
YOU MIGHT TELL ME...
...IT'S JUST A TEACHER'S JOB.
BUT...
REALLY ...
...I'VE NEVER HAD...
...ANOTHER TEACHER SO DEDICATED TO ME AS A DULLAHAN.
NOT ONE.
I'M SURE...
...DEMI OR NO...
...EVERY STUDENT...
...IS EQUAL IN YOUR EYES.
EVEN IF YOU WEREN'T SPECIALLY INTERESTED IN DEMIS...
...I THINK, JUST BECAUSE WE WERE NEW STU-DENTS...
...YOU ...
WOULD HAVE DONE THE SAME.
SEN-SEI...
...
I HOPE...
...YOU'LL STILL HELP...
NOT ...
...JUST US...
...BUT ALL YOUR STUDENTS.
IF WE HAVE PRO-BLEMS...
...WE'D LIKE YOUR ADVICE.
AND WHEN WE DO WRONG...
SCOLD US.
PLEASE ...

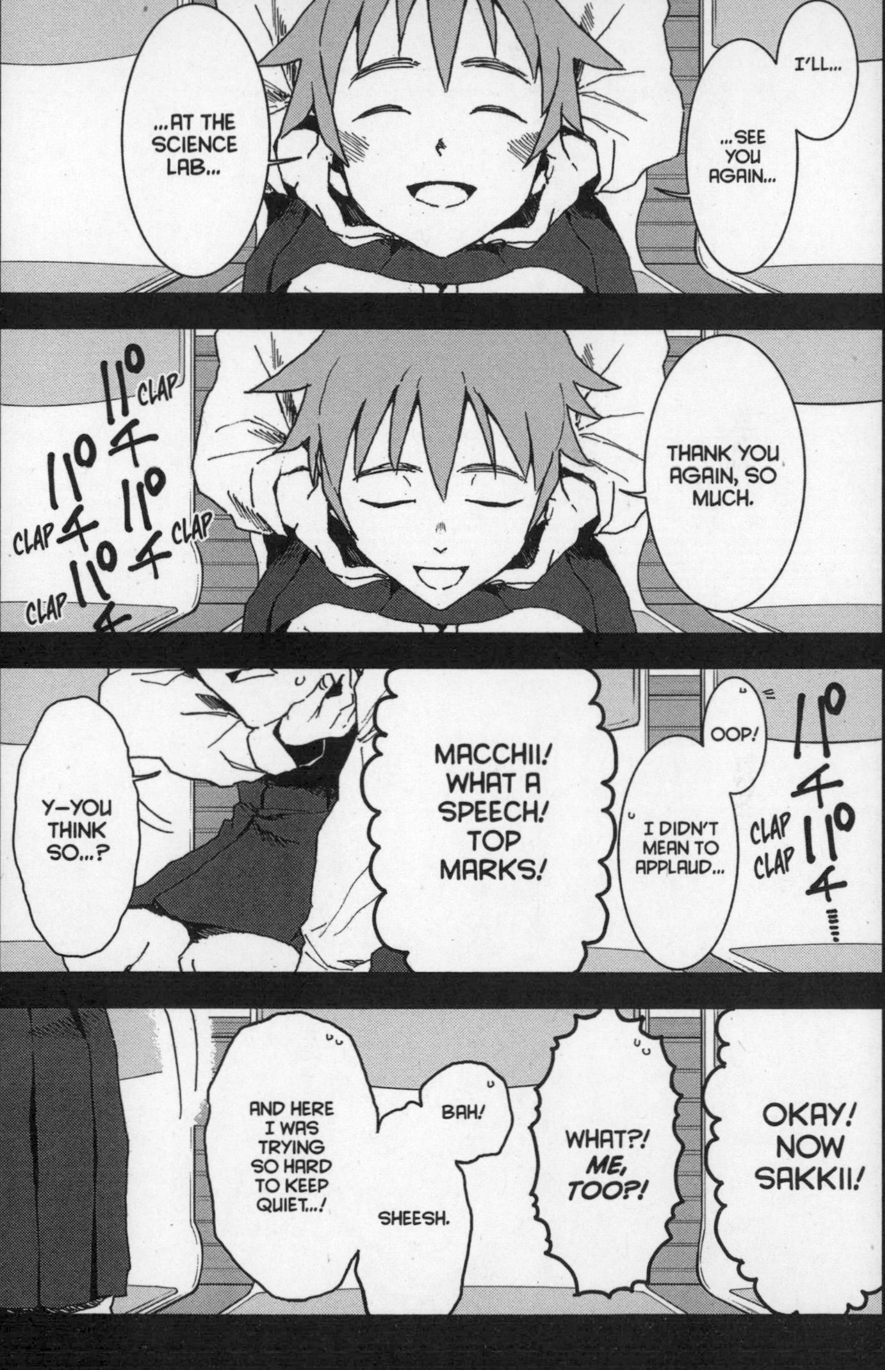
I'LL...
...SEE YOU AGAIN...
...AT THE SCIENCE LAB...
THANK YOU AGAIN, SO MUCH.
CLAP
CLAP
CLAP
CLAP
OOP!
CLAP
CLAP
I DIDN'T MEAN TO APPLAUD...
MACCHII! WHAT A SPEECH! TOP MARKS!
Y-YOU THINK SO...?
OKAY! NOW SAKKII!
WHAT?! *ME, TOO?!*
BAH!
AND HERE I WAS TRYING SO HARD TO KEEP QUIET...!
SHEESH.

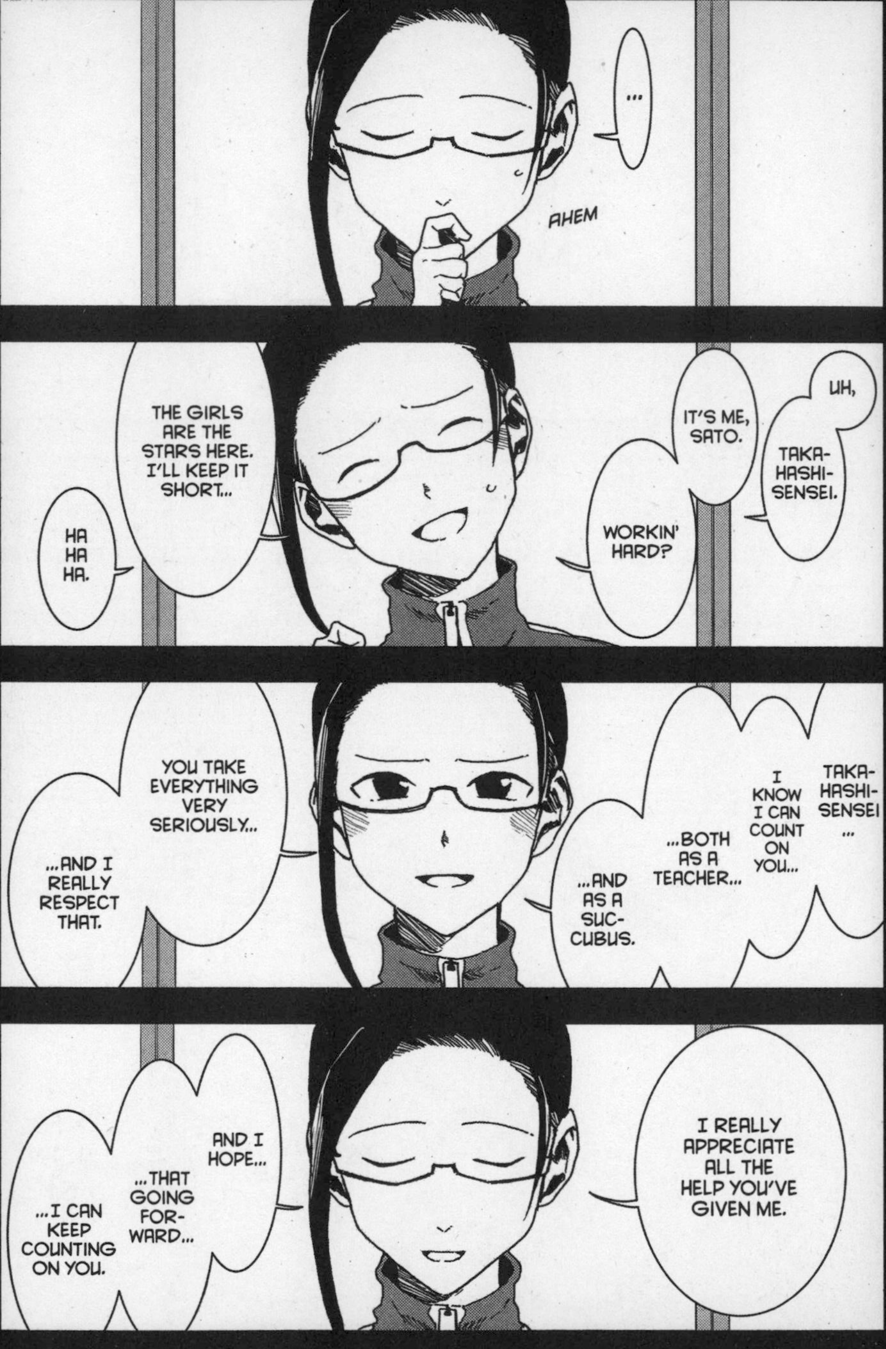
...
AHEM
UH, TAKA-HASHI-SENSEI.
IT'S ME, SATO.
WORKIN' HARD?
THE GIRLS ARE THE STARS HERE. I'LL KEEP IT SHORT...
HA HA HA.
TAKA-HASHI-SENSEI...
I KNOW I CAN COUNT ON YOU...
...BOTH AS A TEACHER...
...AND AS A SUC-CUBUS.
YOU TAKE EVERYTHING VERY SERIOUSLY...
...AND I REALLY RESPECT THAT.
I REALLY APPRECIATE ALL THE HELP YOU'VE GIVEN ME.
AND I HOPE...
...THAT GOING FOR-WARD...
...I CAN KEEP COUNTING ON YOU.

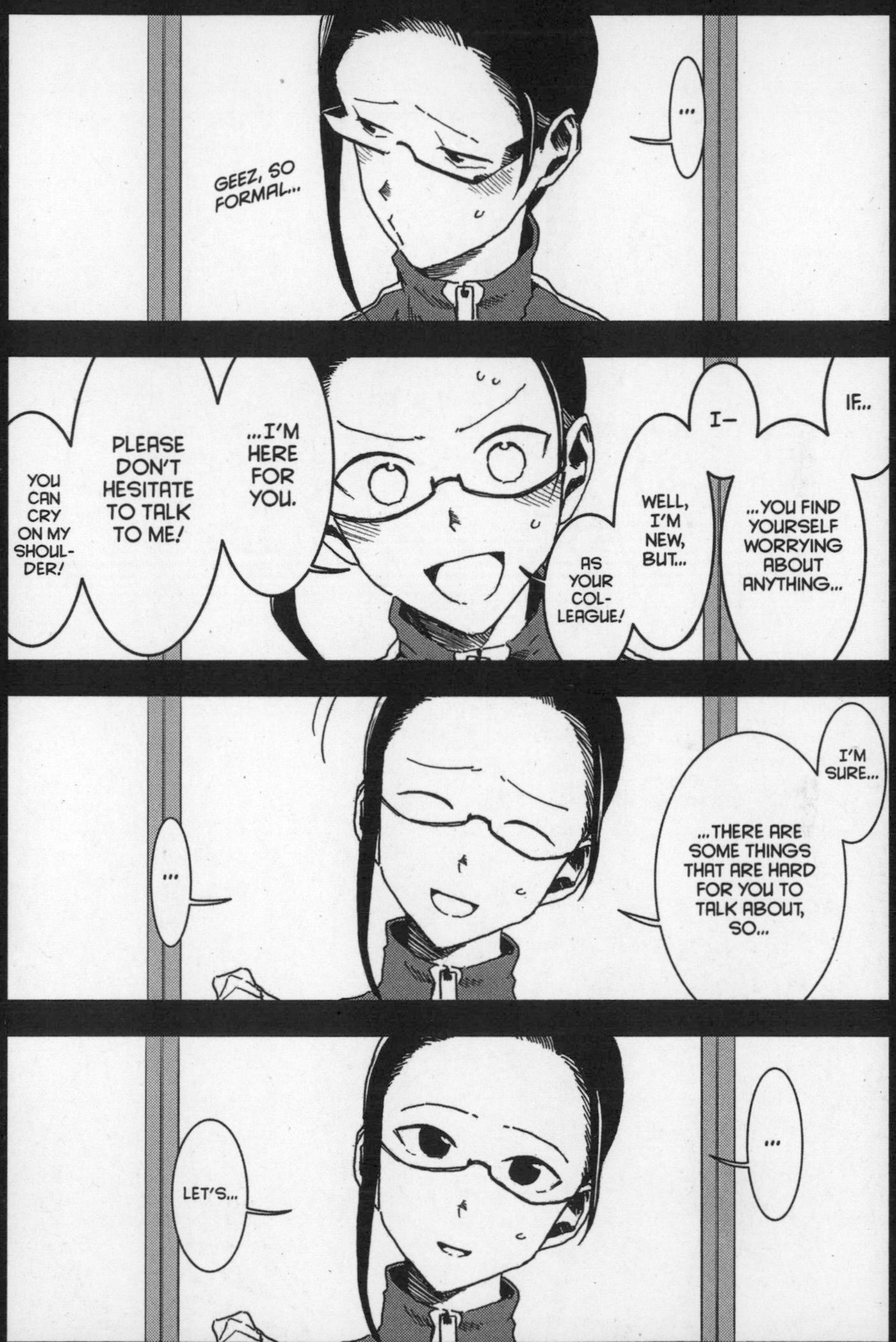
...
GEEZ, SO FORMAL...
IF...
...YOU FIND YOURSELF WORRYING ABOUT ANYTHING...
I—
WELL, I'M NEW, BUT...
AS YOUR COL-LEAGUE!
...I'M HERE FOR YOU.
PLEASE DON'T HESITATE TO TALK TO ME!
YOU CAN CRY ON MY SHOUL-DER!
I'M SURE...
...THERE ARE SOME THINGS THAT ARE HARD FOR YOU TO TALK ABOUT, SO...
...
...
LET'S...

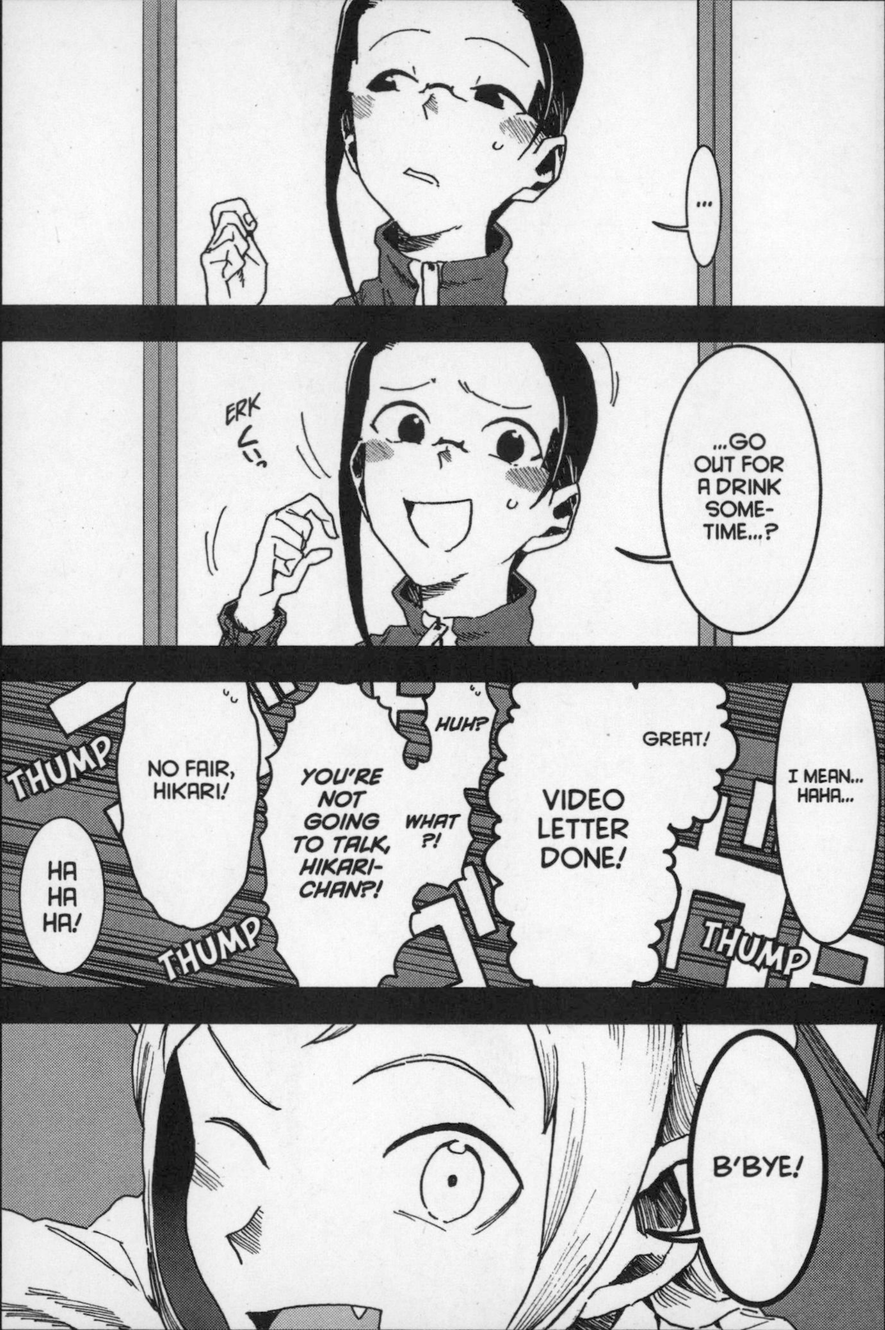
...
...GO OUT FOR A DRINK SOMETIME...?
ERK
I MEAN... HAHA...
GREAT!
VIDEO LETTER DONE!
THUMP
HUH?
WHAT?!
YOU'RE NOT GOING TO TALK, HIKARI-CHAN?!
NO FAIR, HIKARI!
THUMP
HA HA HA!
THUMP
B'BYE!

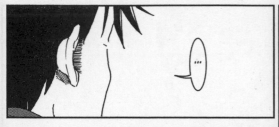

...

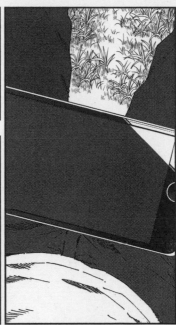

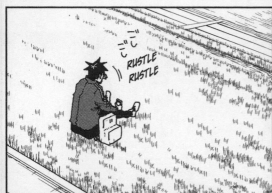

RUSTLE
RUSTLE

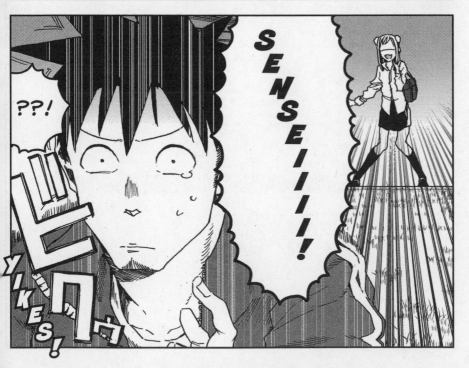

??!

YIKES!

SENSEIIII!

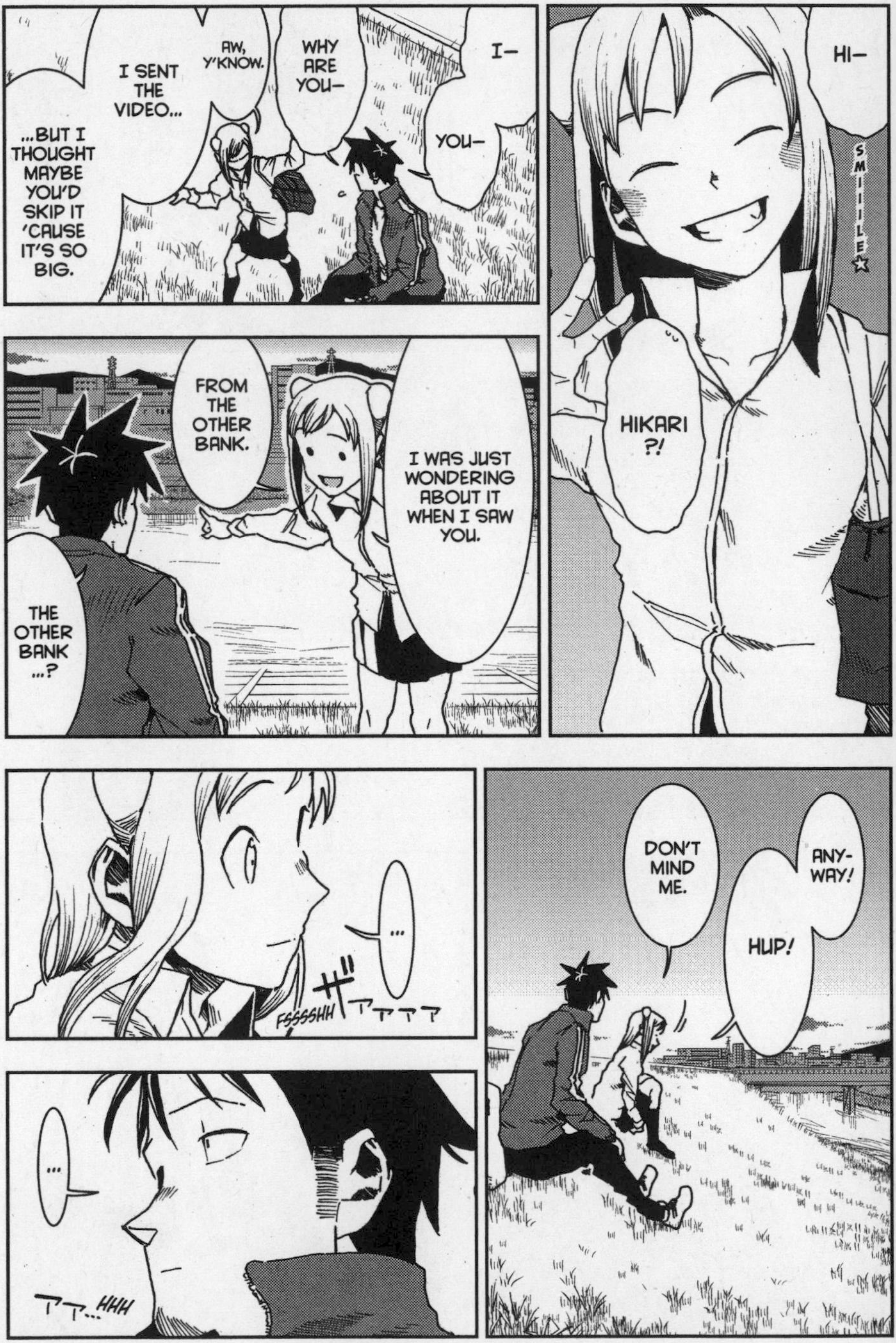
HI—
SMIIILE☆
HIKARI ?!
I—
YOU—
WHY ARE YOU—
AW, Y'KNOW.
I SENT THE VIDEO...
...BUT I THOUGHT MAYBE YOU'D SKIP IT 'CAUSE IT'S SO BIG.
I WAS JUST WONDERING ABOUT IT WHEN I SAW YOU.
FROM THE OTHER BANK.
THE OTHER BANK ...?
ANY-WAY!
DON'T MIND ME.
HUP!
...
ザァァァァ
FSSSSHH
...
ァァ...HHH

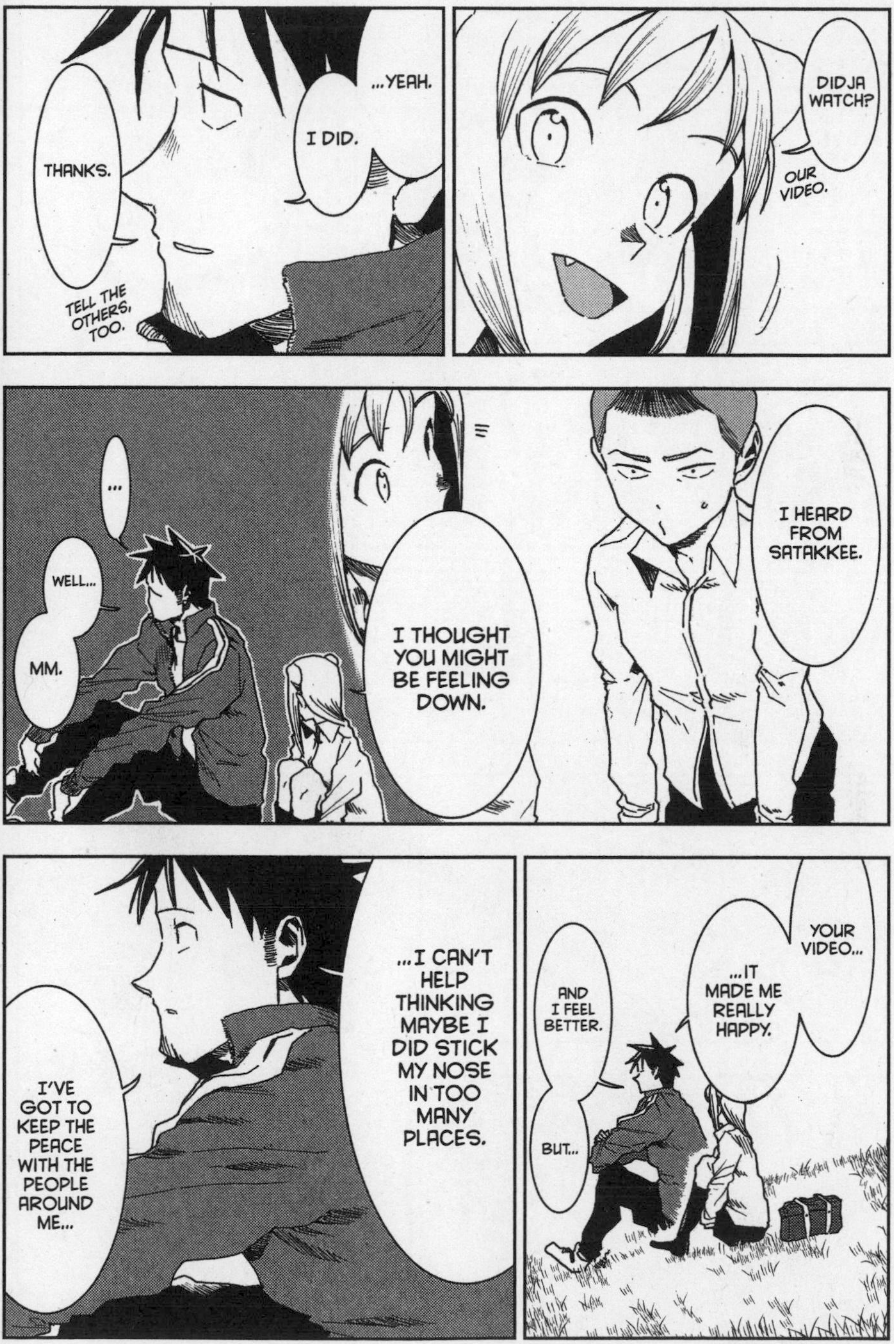
DIDJA WATCH?
OUR VIDEO.
...YEAH.
I DID.
THANKS.
TELL THE OTHERS, TOO.
I HEARD FROM SATAKKEE.
I THOUGHT YOU MIGHT BE FEELING DOWN.
...
WELL...
MM.
YOUR VIDEO...
...IT MADE ME REALLY HAPPY.
AND I FEEL BETTER.
BUT...
...I CAN'T HELP THINKING MAYBE I DID STICK MY NOSE IN TOO MANY PLACES.
I'VE GOT TO KEEP THE PEACE WITH THE PEOPLE AROUND ME...

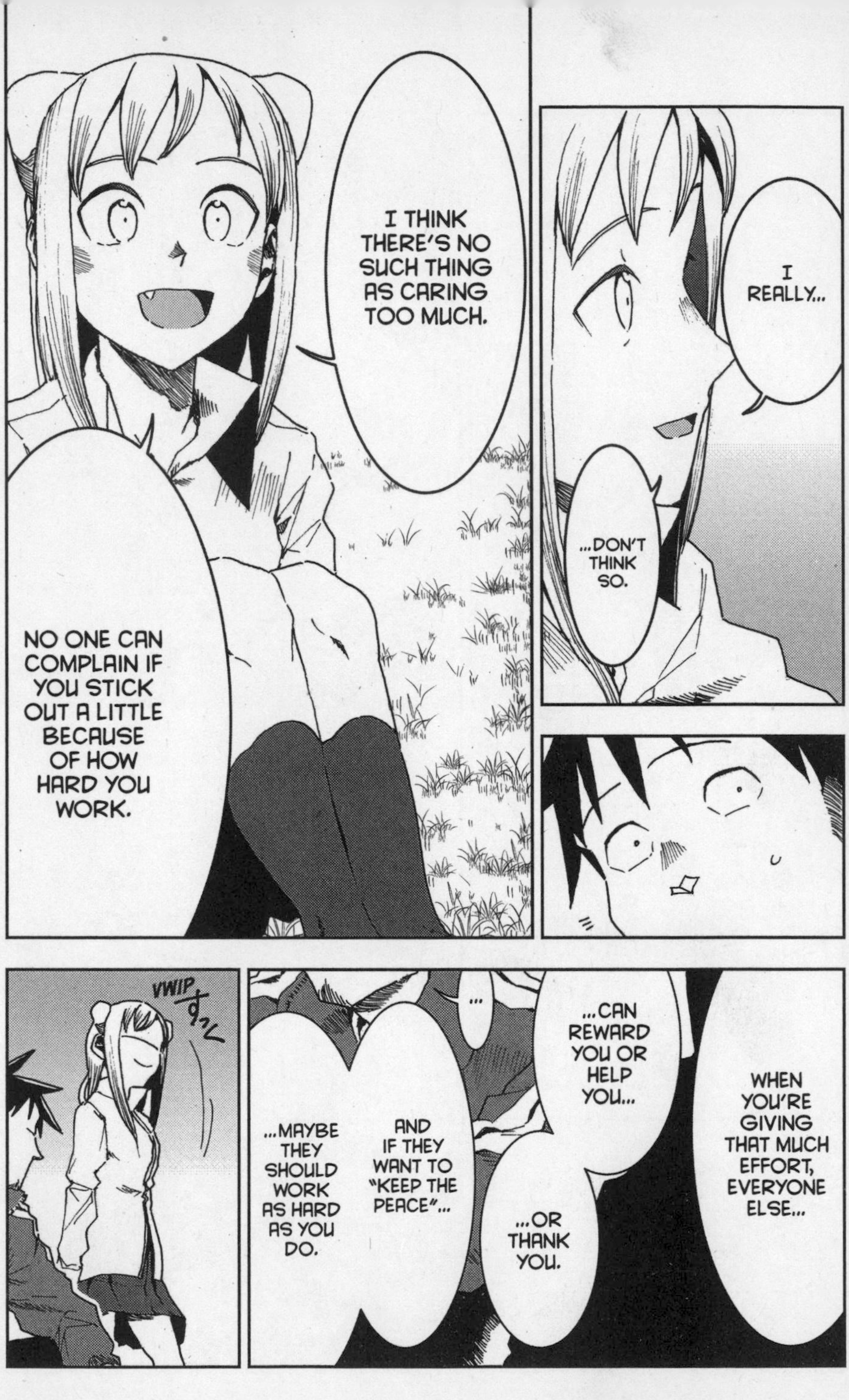
I REALLY...
...DON'T THINK SO.
I THINK THERE'S NO SUCH THING AS CARING TOO MUCH.
NO ONE CAN COMPLAIN IF YOU STICK OUT A LITTLE BECAUSE OF HOW HARD YOU WORK.
WHEN YOU'RE GIVING THAT MUCH EFFORT, EVERYONE ELSE...
...CAN REWARD YOU OR HELP YOU...
...OR THANK YOU.
...
AND IF THEY WANT TO "KEEP THE PEACE"...
...MAYBE THEY SHOULD WORK AS HARD AS YOU DO.
VWIP
すっ

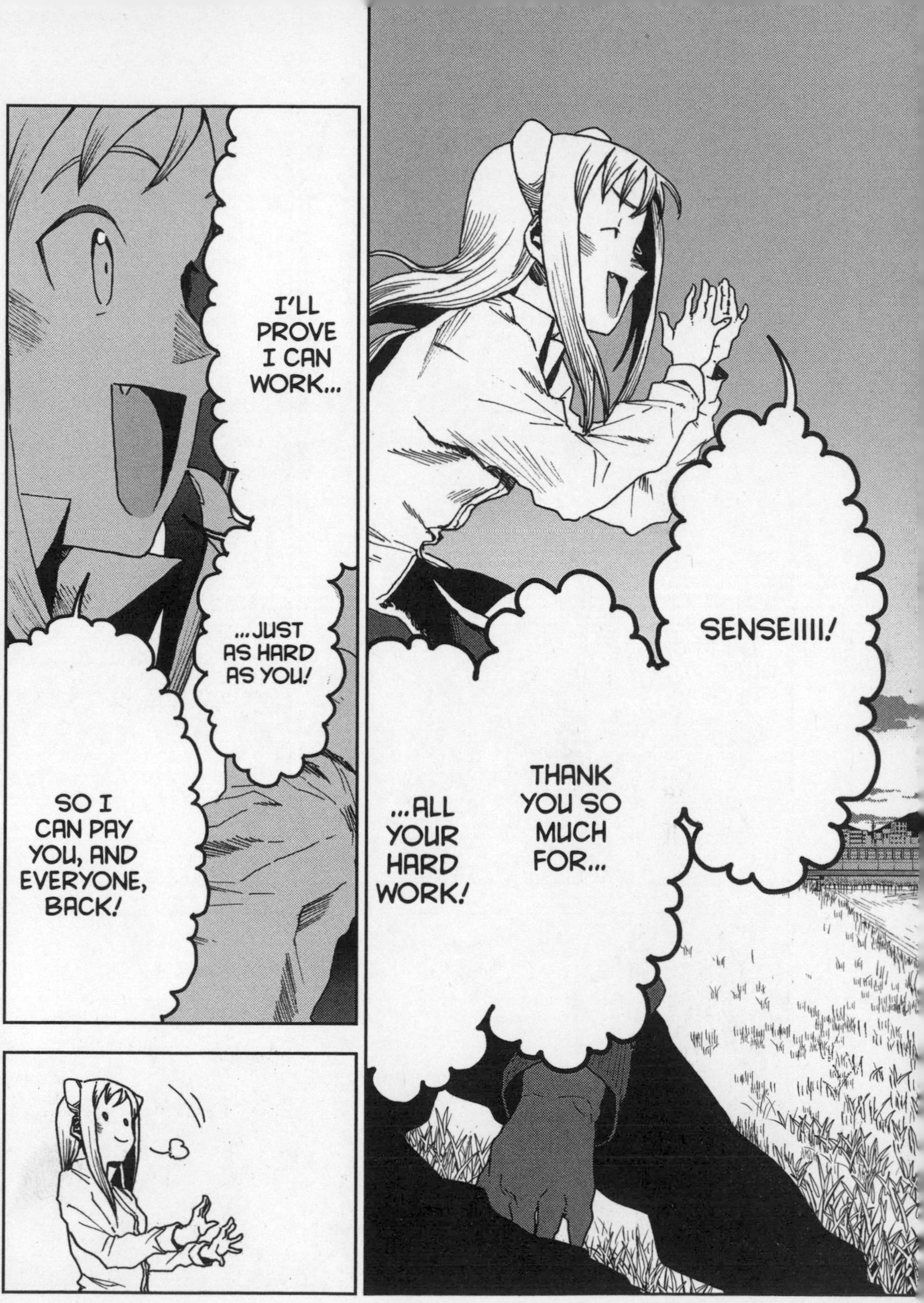
SENSEIIII!
THANK YOU SO MUCH FOR...
...ALL YOUR HARD WORK!
I'LL PROVE I CAN WORK...
...JUST AS HARD AS YOU!
SO I CAN PAY YOU, AND EVERYONE, BACK!

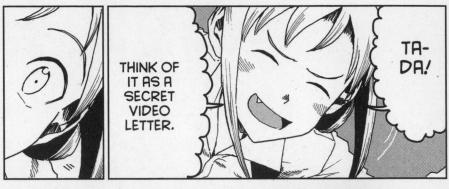

THINK OF IT AS A SECRET VIDEO LETTER.

TA-DA!

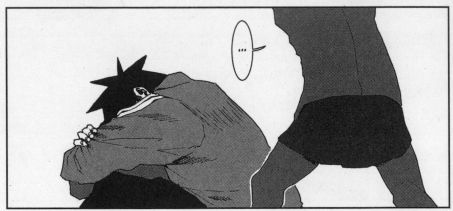

...

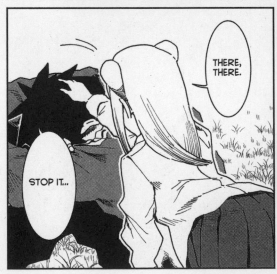

THERE, THERE.

STOP IT...

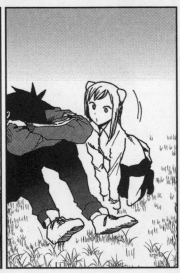

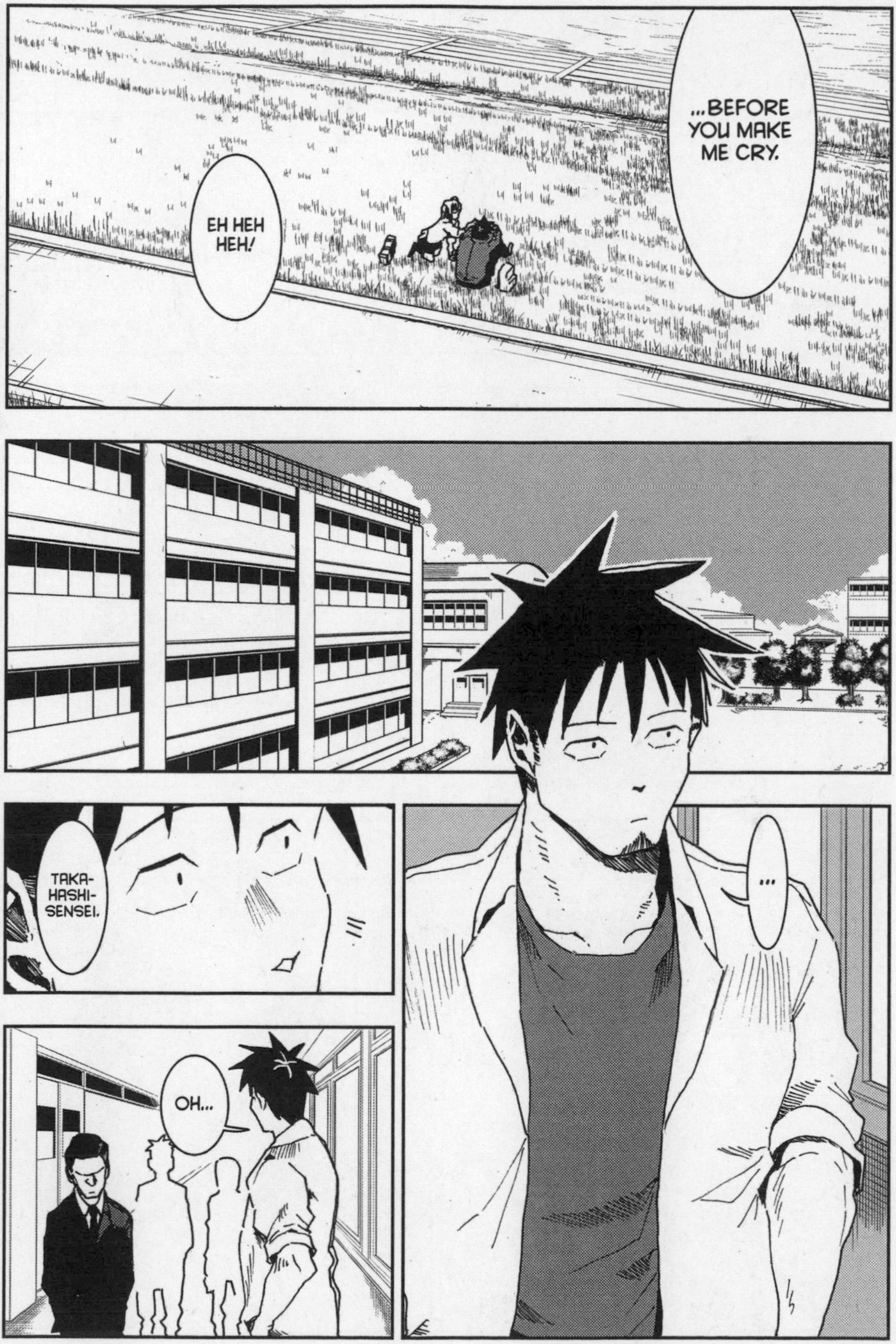
...BEFORE YOU MAKE ME CRY.
EH HEH HEH!
...
TAKA-HASHI-SENSEI.
OH...

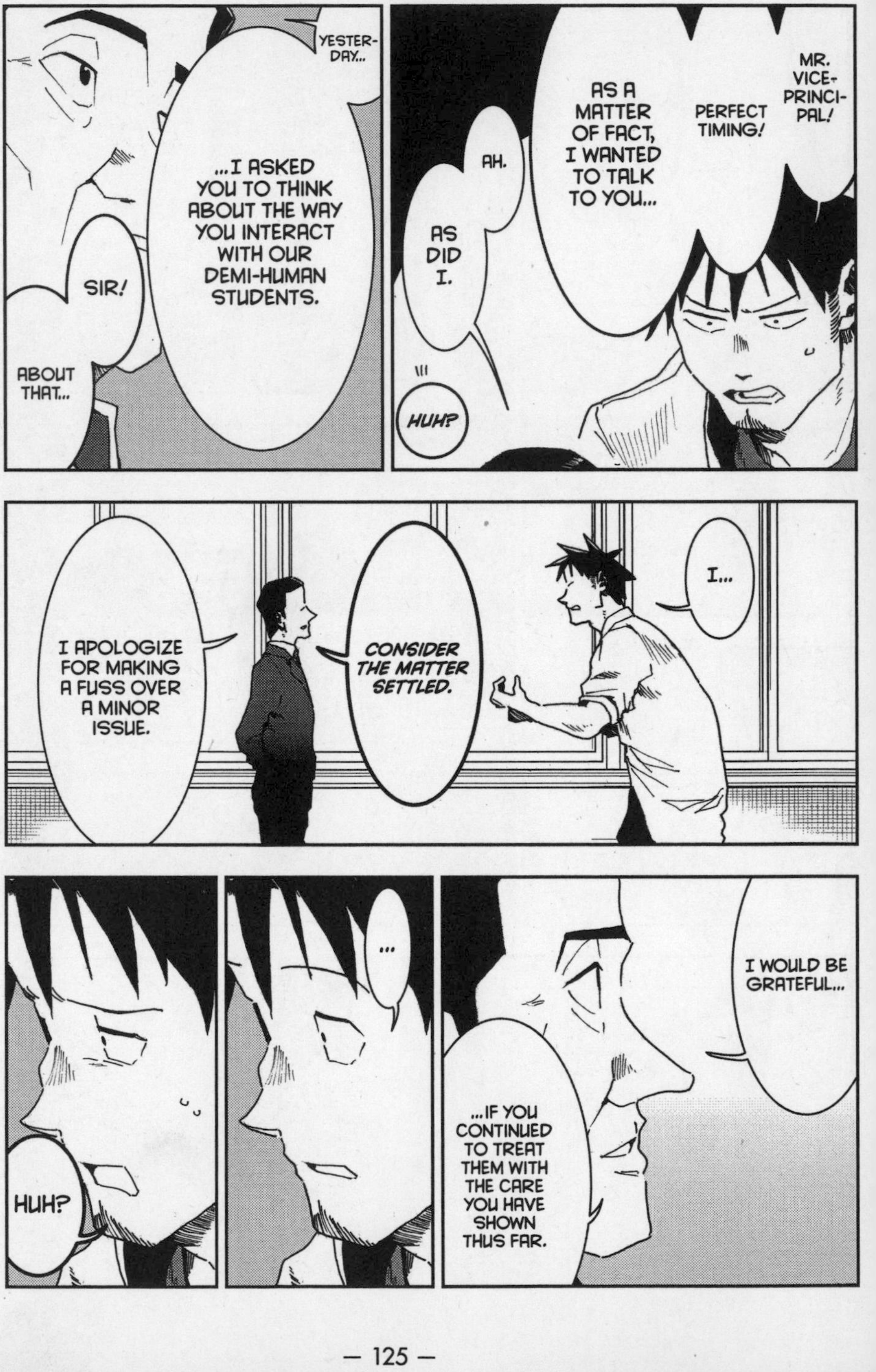
MR. VICE-PRINCIPAL!
PERFECT TIMING!
AS A MATTER OF FACT, I WANTED TO TALK TO YOU...
AH.
AS DID I.
HUH?
YESTER-DAY...
...I ASKED YOU TO THINK ABOUT THE WAY YOU INTERACT WITH OUR DEMI-HUMAN STUDENTS.
SIR!
ABOUT THAT...
I...
CONSIDER THE MATTER SETTLED.
I APOLOGIZE FOR MAKING A FUSS OVER A MINOR ISSUE.
I WOULD BE GRATEFUL...
...IF YOU CONTINUED TO TREAT THEM WITH THE CARE YOU HAVE SHOWN THUS FAR.
...
HUH?

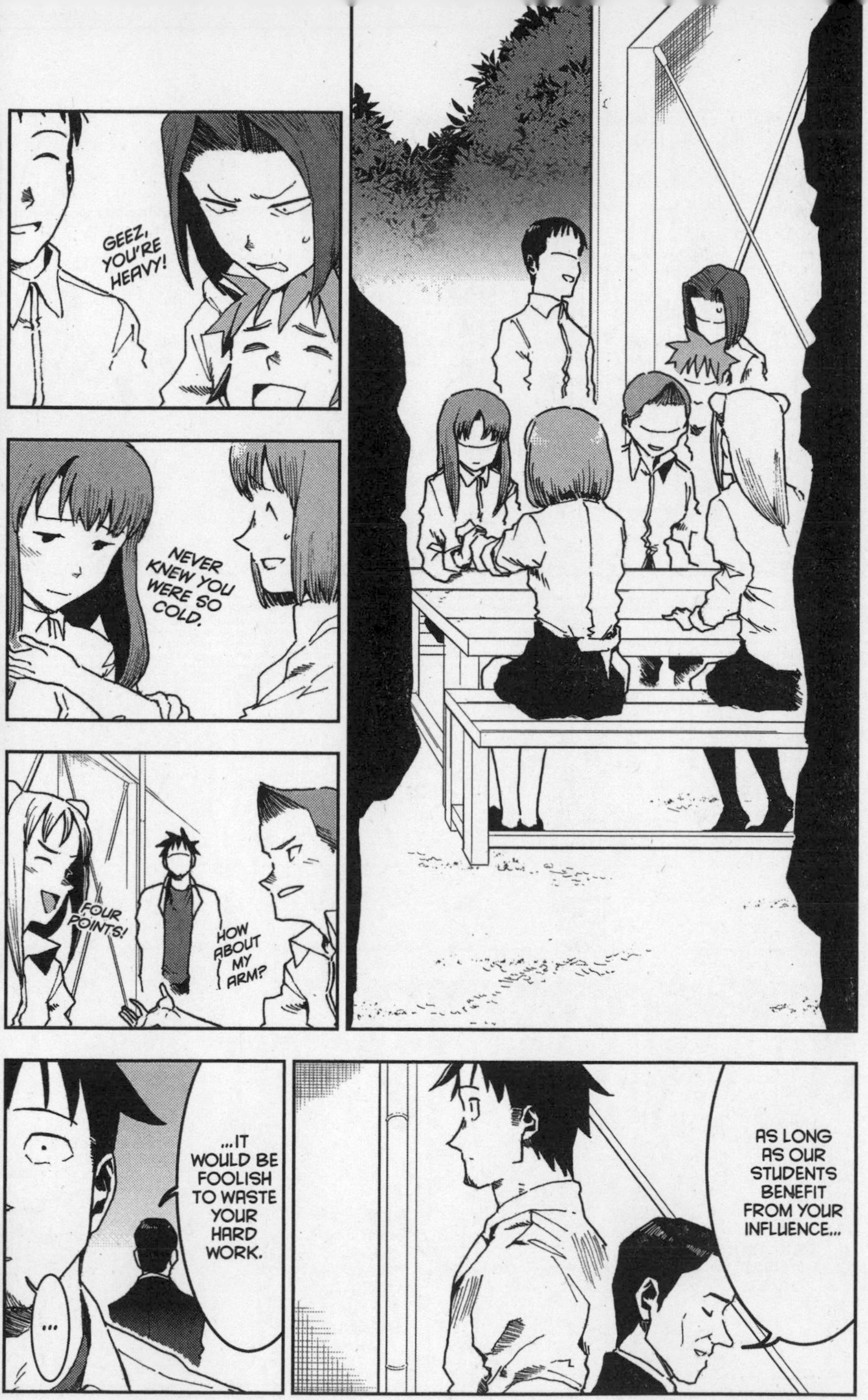
GEEZ, YOU'RE HEAVY!
NEVER KNEW YOU WERE SO COLD.
HOW ABOUT MY ARM?
FOUR POINTS!
AS LONG AS OUR STUDENTS BENEFIT FROM YOUR INFLUENCE...
...IT WOULD BE FOOLISH TO WASTE YOUR HARD WORK.
...

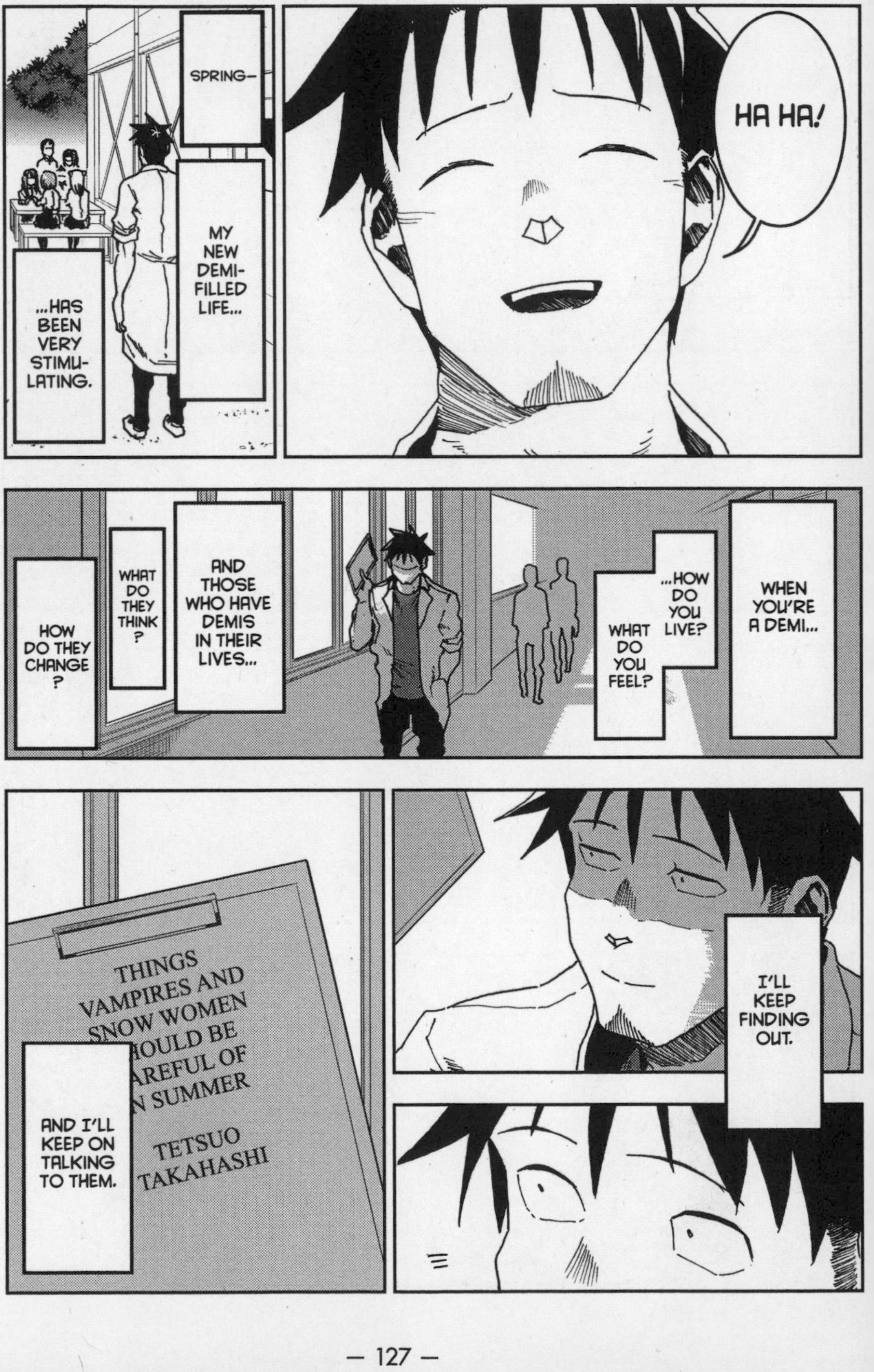
HA HA!
SPRING—
MY NEW DEMI-FILLED LIFE...
...HAS BEEN VERY STIMULATING.
WHEN YOU'RE A DEMI...
...HOW DO YOU LIVE?
WHAT DO YOU FEEL?
AND THOSE WHO HAVE DEMIS IN THEIR LIVES...
WHAT DO THEY THINK?
HOW DO THEY CHANGE?
I'LL KEEP FINDING OUT.
THINGS VAMPIRES AND SNOW WOMEN
TETSUO TAKAHASHI
AND I'LL KEEP ON TALKING TO THEM.

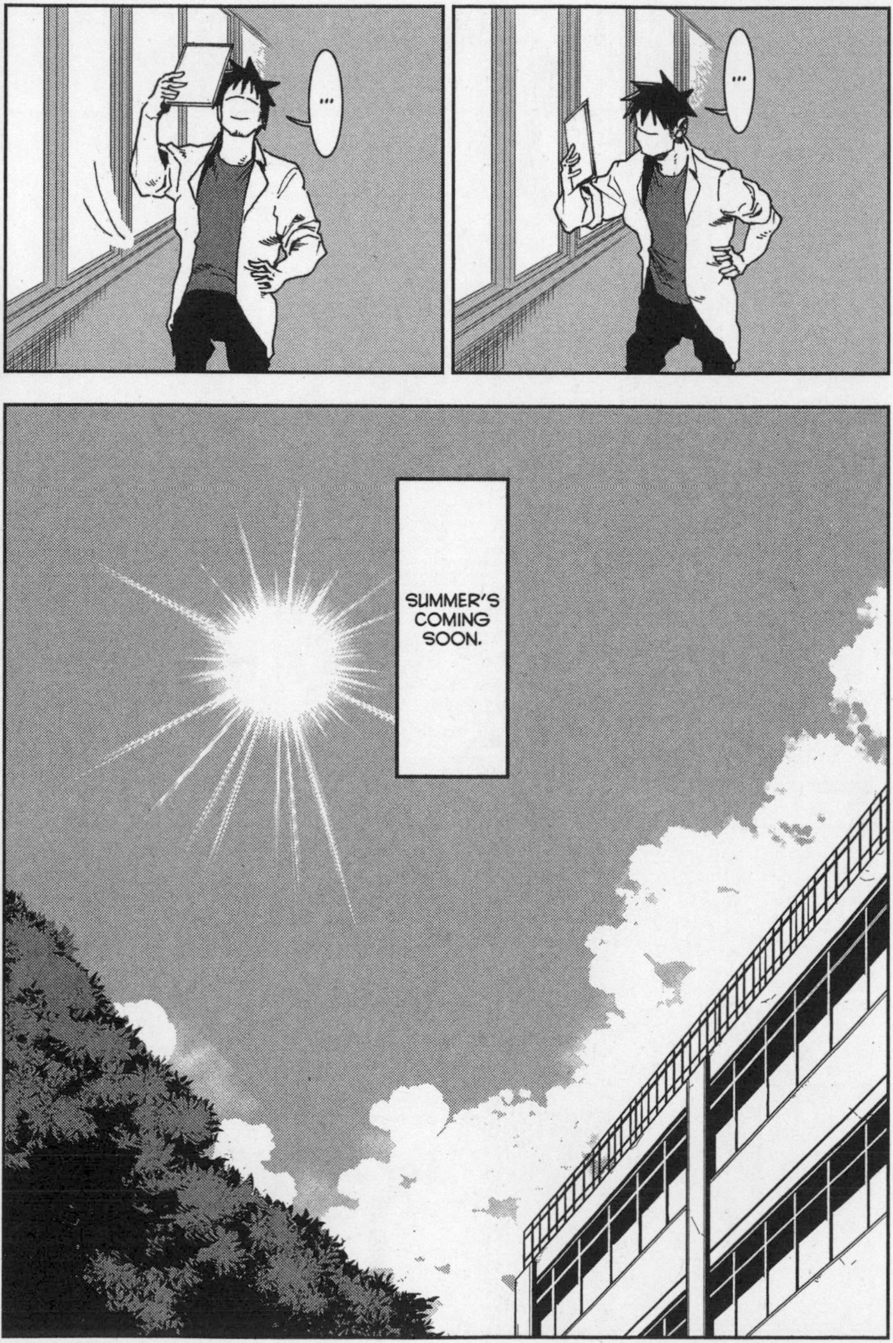
...
...
SUMMER'S COMING SOON.

VOLUME 4/END

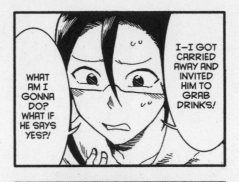

I—I GOT CARRIED AWAY AND INVITED HIM TO GRAB DRINKS!
WHAT AM I GONNA DO? WHAT IF HE SAYS YES?!
WH— WHAT SHOULD I ORDER ...?
I LIKE BEER, BUT IS THAT JUST WHAT OLD GUYS DRINK?
M-MAYBE A COCKTAIL? OR A *CHUHAI*...?
BUT A... A LEMON *CHUHAI* IS KIND OF AN OLD GUY DRINK, TOO...
AND WHAT IF—
OH!!
WHAT IF I GET DRUNK AND *DO* SOMETHING?!
3:00 AM
WHAT SHOULD I DO, UGAKI-SAN?!
CAN WE TALK TOMORROW ...?

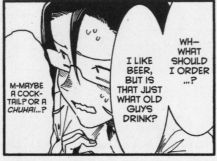

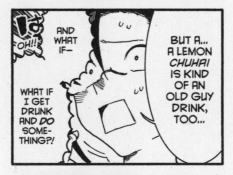

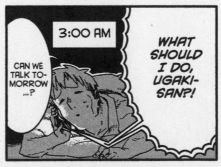

INTERVIEWS WITH MONSTER GIRLS

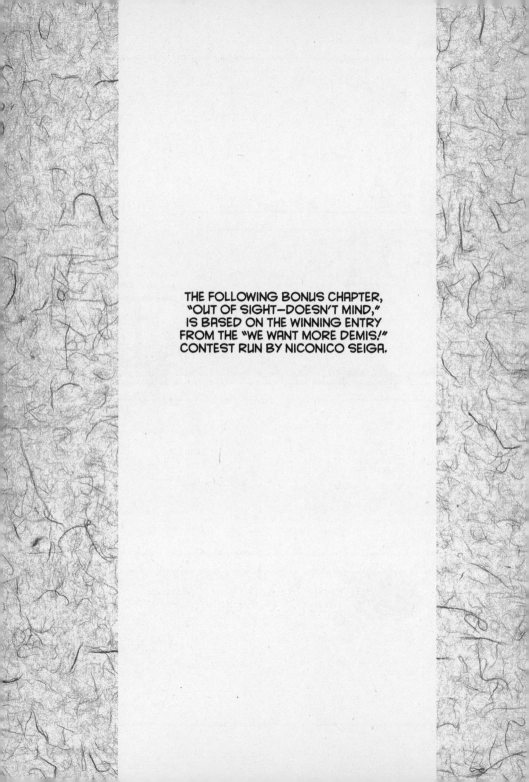

THE FOLLOWING BONUS CHAPTER,
"OUT OF SIGHT—DOESN'T MIND,"
IS BASED ON THE WINNING ENTRY
FROM THE "WE WANT MORE DEMIS!"
CONTEST RUN BY NICONICO SEIGA.

Bonus Chapter: Out of Sight—Doesn't Mind

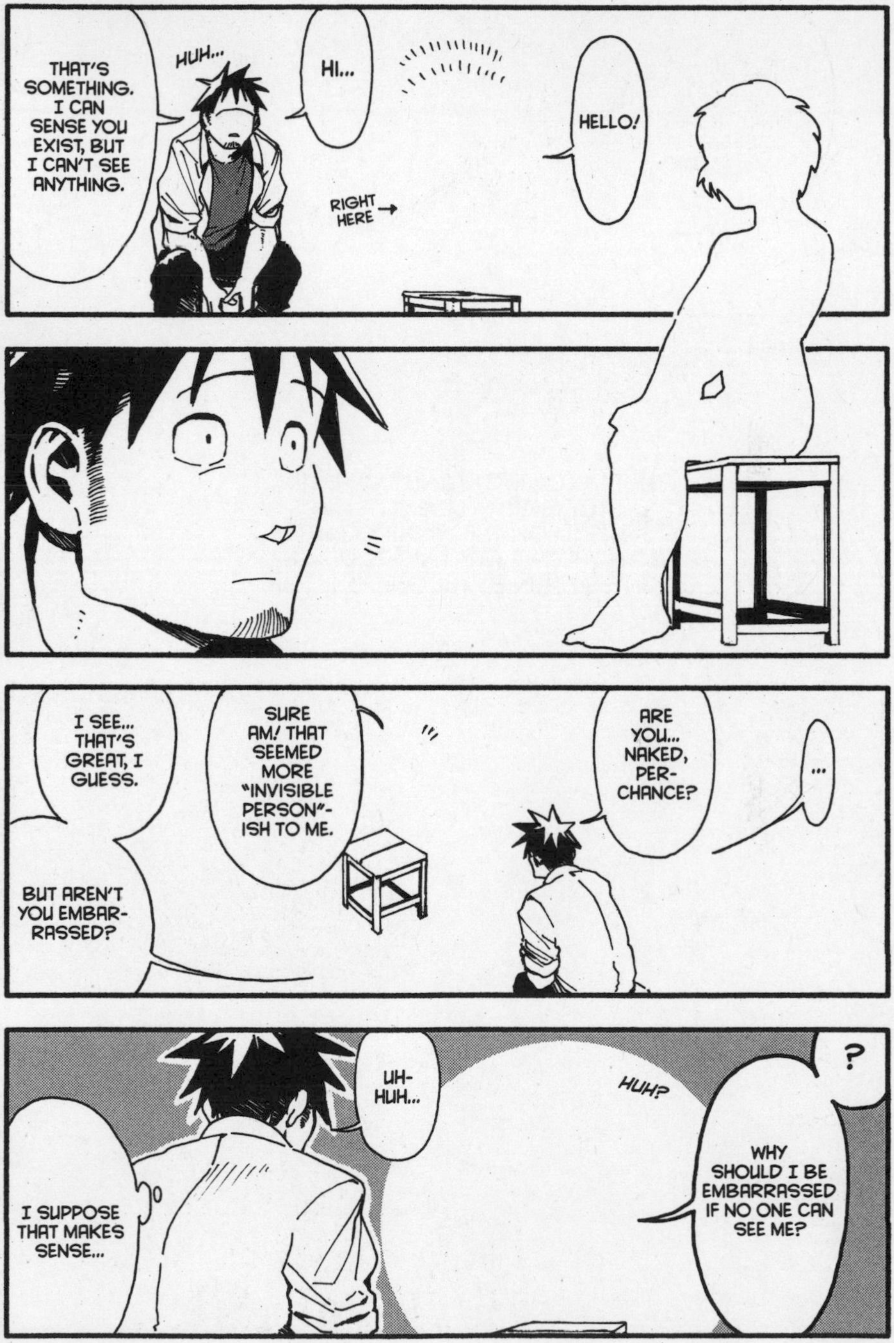
HELLO!
HI...
HUH...
RIGHT HERE →
THAT'S SOMETHING. I CAN SENSE YOU EXIST, BUT I CAN'T SEE ANYTHING.
...
ARE YOU... NAKED, PER-CHANCE?
SURE AM! THAT SEEMED MORE "INVISIBLE PERSON"-ISH TO ME.
I SEE... THAT'S GREAT, I GUESS.
BUT AREN'T YOU EMBARRASSED?
?
HUH?
WHY SHOULD I BE EMBARRASSED IF NO ONE CAN SEE ME?
UH-HUH...
I SUPPOSE THAT MAKES SENSE...

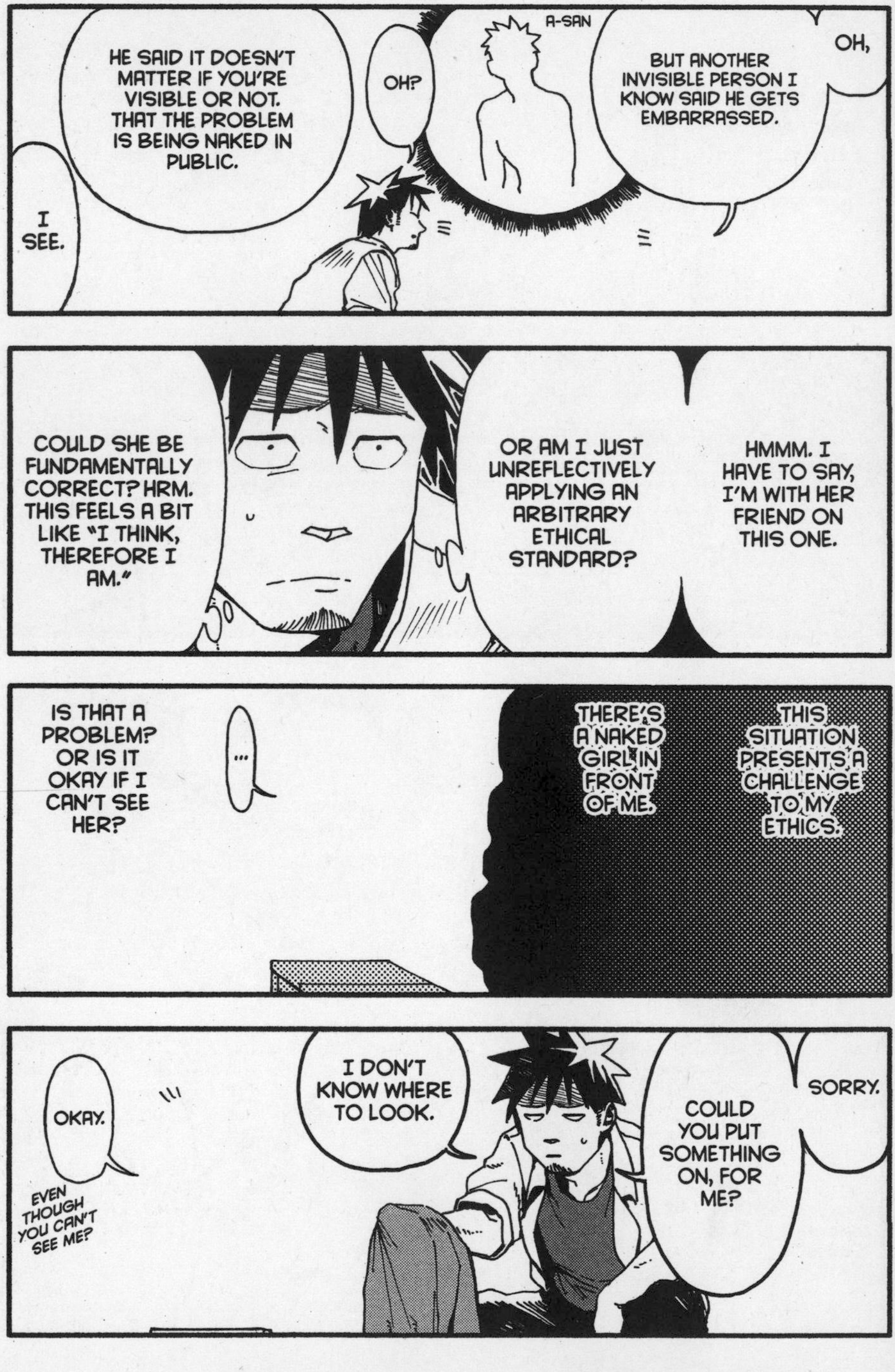
OH,
BUT ANOTHER INVISIBLE PERSON I KNOW SAID HE GETS EMBARRASSED.
A-SAN
OH?
HE SAID IT DOESN'T MATTER IF YOU'RE VISIBLE OR NOT. THAT THE PROBLEM IS BEING NAKED IN PUBLIC.
I SEE.
HMMM. I HAVE TO SAY, I'M WITH HER FRIEND ON THIS ONE.
OR AM I JUST UNREFLECTIVELY APPLYING AN ARBITRARY ETHICAL STANDARD?
COULD SHE BE FUNDAMENTALLY CORRECT? HRM. THIS FEELS A BIT LIKE "I THINK, THEREFORE I AM."
THIS SITUATION PRESENTS A CHALLENGE TO MY ETHICS.
THERE'S A NAKED GIRL IN FRONT OF ME.
...
IS THAT A PROBLEM? OR IS IT OKAY IF I CAN'T SEE HER?
SORRY.
COULD YOU PUT SOMETHING ON, FOR ME?
I DON'T KNOW WHERE TO LOOK.
OKAY.
EVEN THOUGH YOU CAN'T SEE ME?

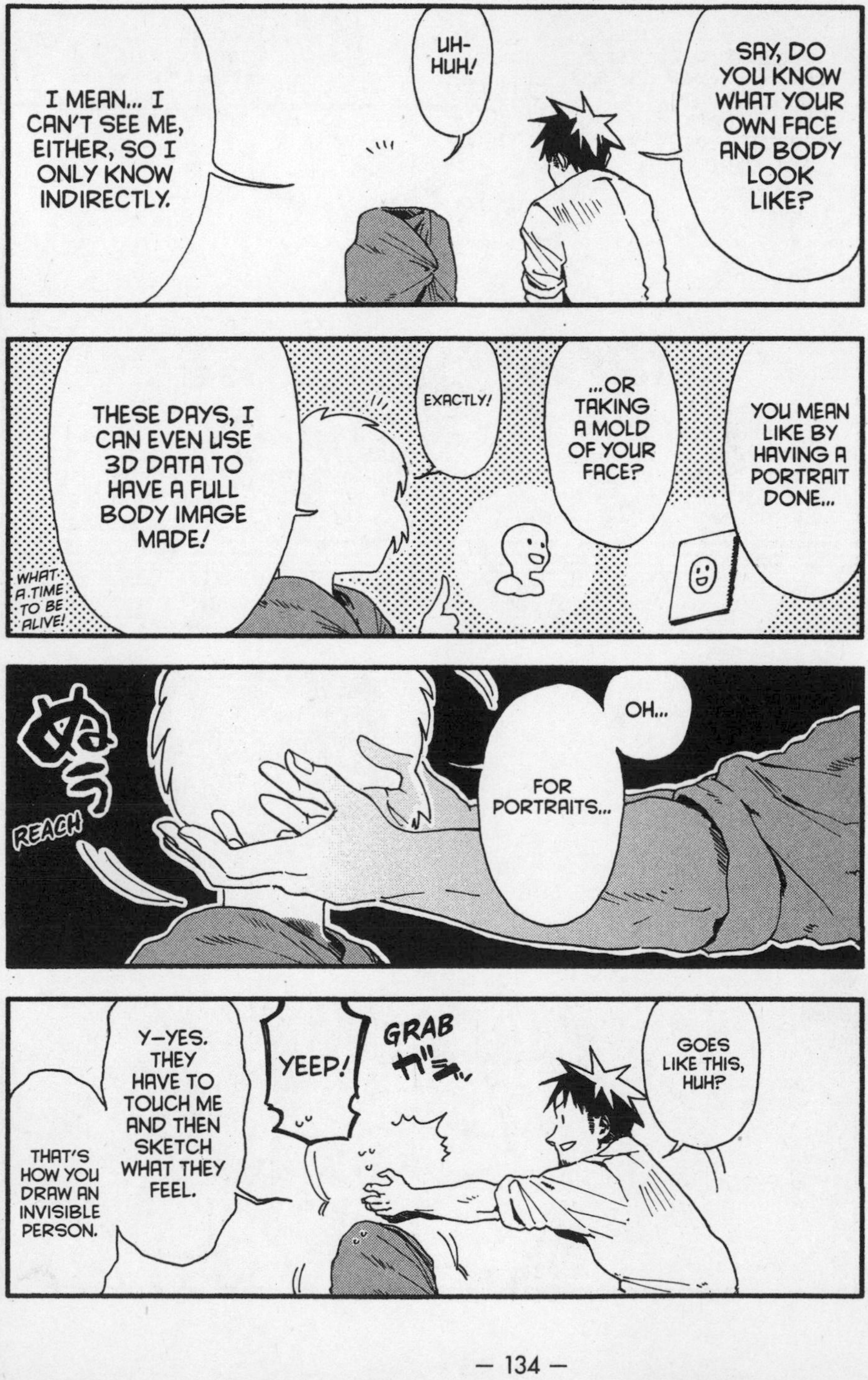
SAY, DO YOU KNOW WHAT YOUR OWN FACE AND BODY LOOK LIKE?
UH-HUH!
I MEAN... I CAN'T SEE ME, EITHER, SO I ONLY KNOW INDIRECTLY.
YOU MEAN LIKE BY HAVING A PORTRAIT DONE...
...OR TAKING A MOLD OF YOUR FACE?
EXACTLY!
THESE DAYS, I CAN EVEN USE 3D DATA TO HAVE A FULL BODY IMAGE MADE!
WHAT A TIME TO BE ALIVE!
OH...
FOR PORTRAITS...
ぬぅ
REACH
GOES LIKE THIS, HUH?
GRAB
ガシッ
YEEP!
Y-YES. THEY HAVE TO TOUCH ME AND THEN SKETCH WHAT THEY FEEL.
THAT'S HOW YOU DRAW AN INVISIBLE PERSON.

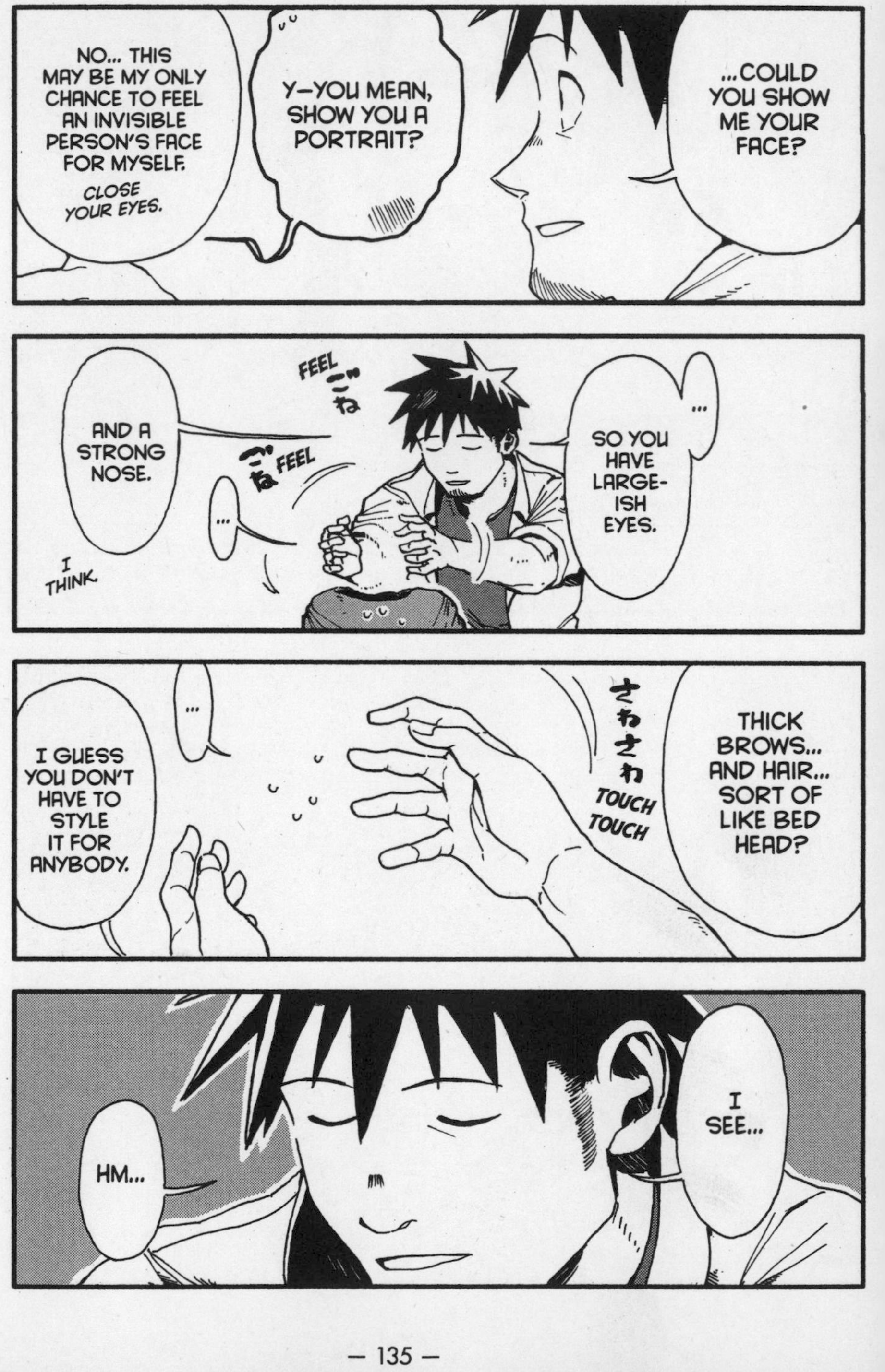
...COULD YOU SHOW ME YOUR FACE?
Y-YOU MEAN, SHOW YOU A PORTRAIT?
NO... THIS MAY BE MY ONLY CHANCE TO FEEL AN INVISIBLE PERSON'S FACE FOR MYSELF.
CLOSE YOUR EYES.
...
SO YOU HAVE LARGE-ISH EYES.
...
FEEL ごね
ごね FEEL
...
AND A STRONG NOSE.
I THINK.
THICK BROWS... AND HAIR... SORT OF LIKE BED HEAD?
さわさわ
TOUCH TOUCH
...
I GUESS YOU DON'T HAVE TO STYLE IT FOR ANYBODY.
I SEE...
HM...

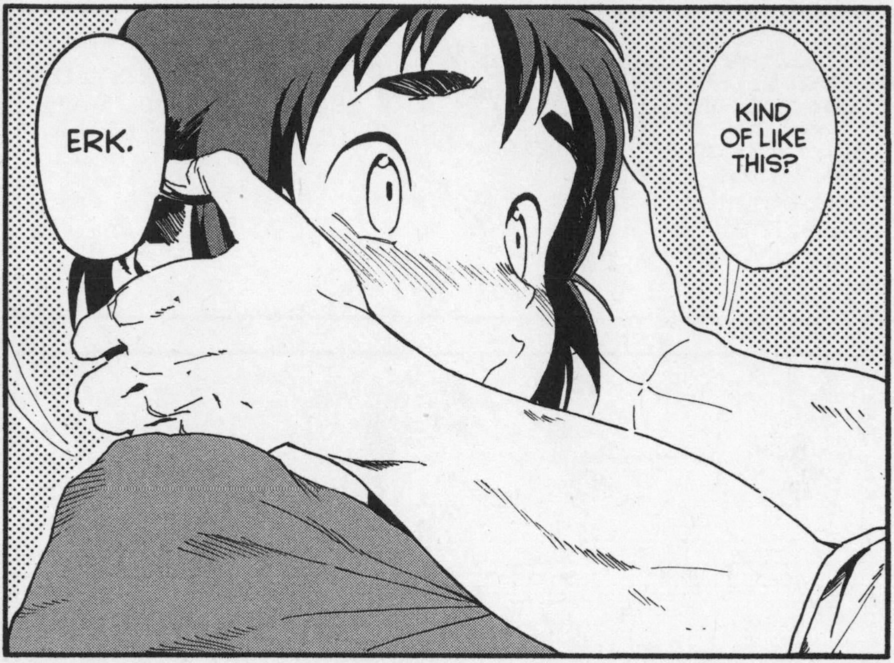
KIND OF LIKE THIS?
ERK.

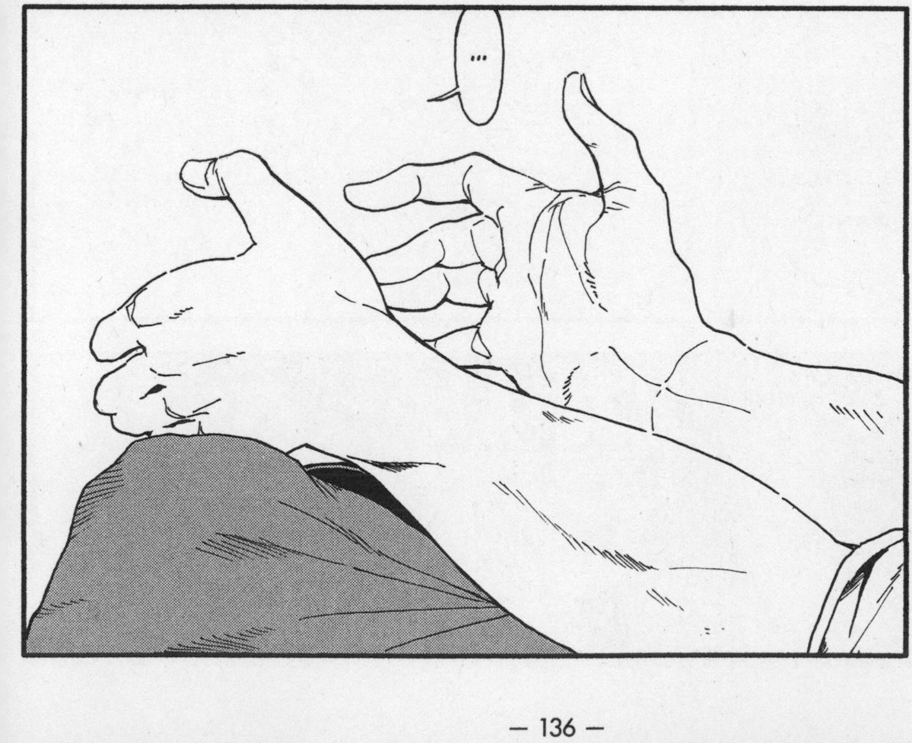
...

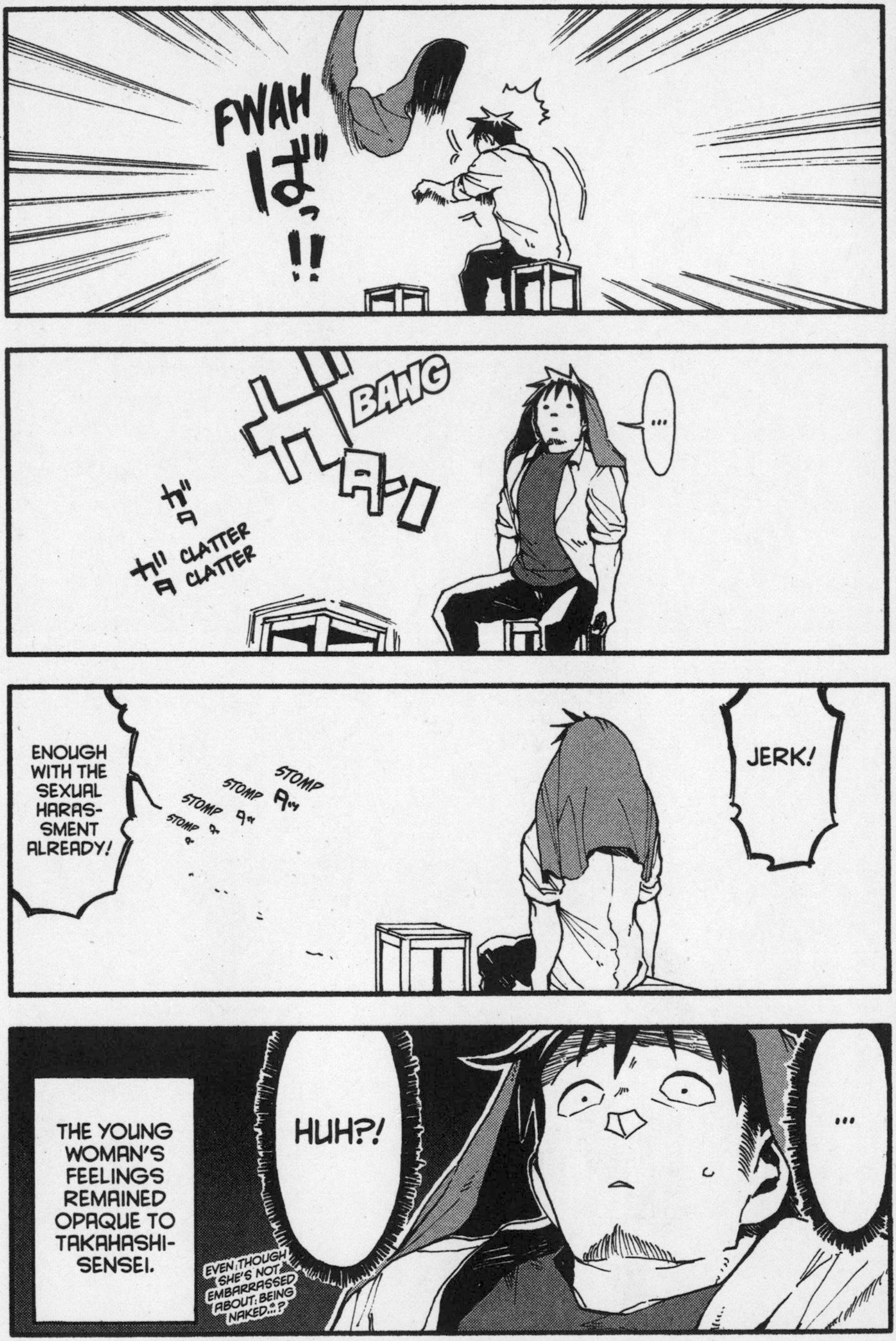

FWAH
ばっ!!
...
BANG
ガターン
ガタ
ガタ
CLATTER CLATTER
JERK!
STOMP
STOMP
STOMP
ENOUGH WITH THE SEXUAL HARASSMENT ALREADY!
...
HUH?!
EVEN THOUGH SHE'S NOT EMBARRASSED ABOUT BEING NAKED...?
THE YOUNG WOMAN'S FEELINGS REMAINED OPAQUE TO TAKAHASHI-SENSEI.

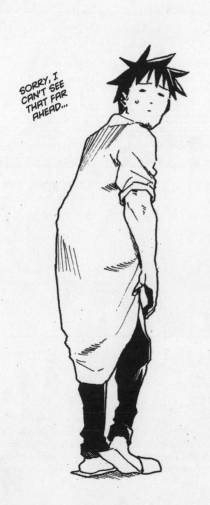

WILL INVISIBLE PEOPLE APPEAR IN THE MAIN STORY?
SORRY, I CAN'T SEE THAT FAR AHEAD...

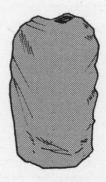

TRANSLATION NOTES

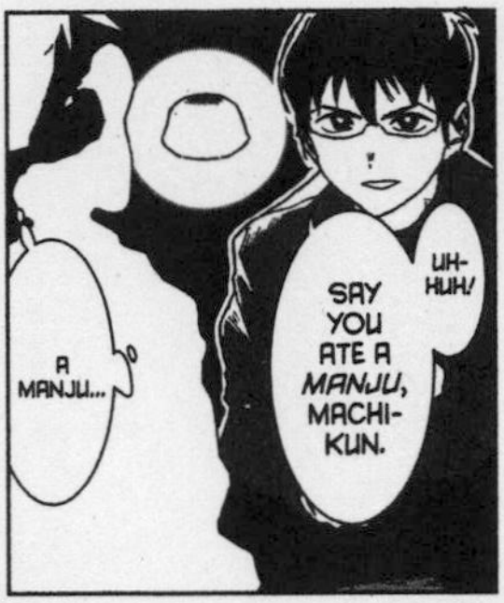
UH-HUH!
SAY YOU ATE A *MANJU*, MACHI-KUN.
A MANJU...

Manju, page 26
A *manju* is a small cake with a skin made of rice flour, usually stuffed with a filling like *anko* (red bean paste).

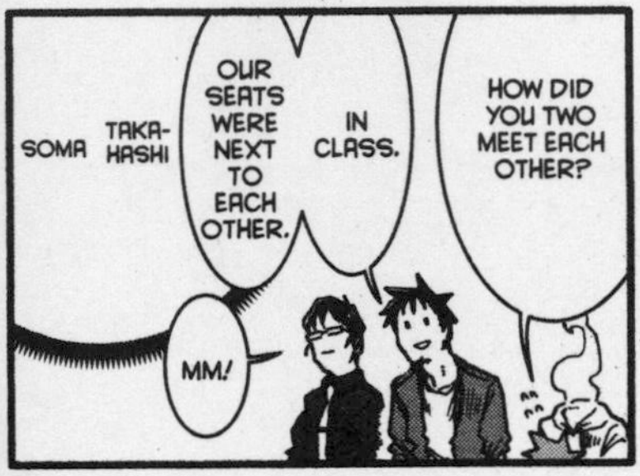
HOW DID YOU TWO MEET EACH OTHER?
IN CLASS.
OUR SEATS WERE NEXT TO EACH OTHER.
TAKA-HASHI
SOMA
MM!

Seats next to each other, page 53
In the Japanese alphabet order, the syllables "So" and "Ta" are next to each other. Thus, **So**ma and **Ta**kahashi have a good chance of being sat next to each other alphabetically, depending on who else is in the class.

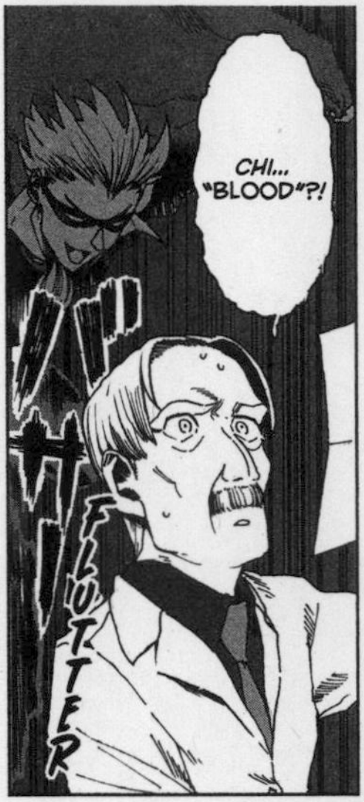
CHI... "BLOOD"?!
FLUTTER

Blood, page 60
Sakie says the answer to the riddle is *Chi ga tarinai*, or "[it] lacks *chi*." In the puzzle on this page, the syllable *chi* is missing from the names of Tochigi and Chiba (both Japanese prefectures). But *chi* can also mean "blood"—just what Van Deursen wants!

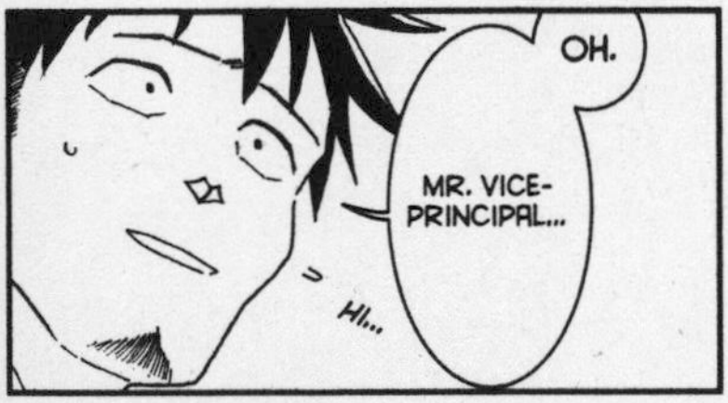
OH.
MR. VICE-PRINCIPAL...
HI...

Mr. Vice-Principal, page 87
The number-two teacher-administrator in a Japanese high school has the title *kyoto* (lit. "education chief," second only to the *kocho* or "school head"). Students as well as other teachers refer to him by this title plus the honorific "*–sensei*."

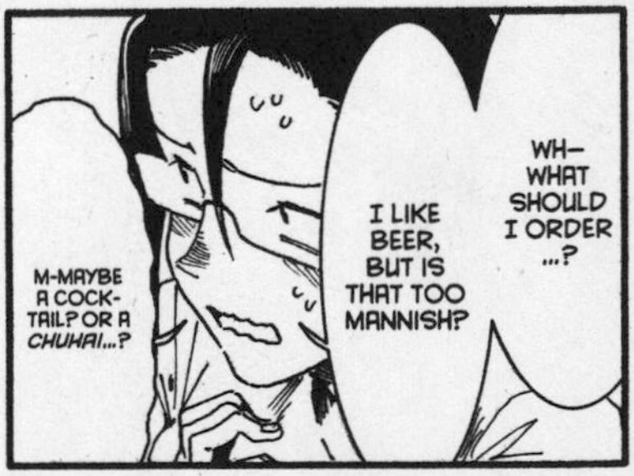
WH— WHAT SHOULD I ORDER ...?
I LIKE BEER, BUT IS THAT TOO MANNISH?
M-MAYBE A COCK-TAIL? OR A *CHUHAI*...?

***Chuhai*, page 131**
A carbonated alcoholic drink that can be purchased in can form. It's made by mixing *shochu* (a Japanese alcohol) and carbonated water, and comes in a number of fruit flavors. Definitely not for minors!

Niconico Seiga, page 133
Niconico is a Japanese video hosting and sharing service, a bit like YouTube.

Next time in *Interview with Monster Girls*...

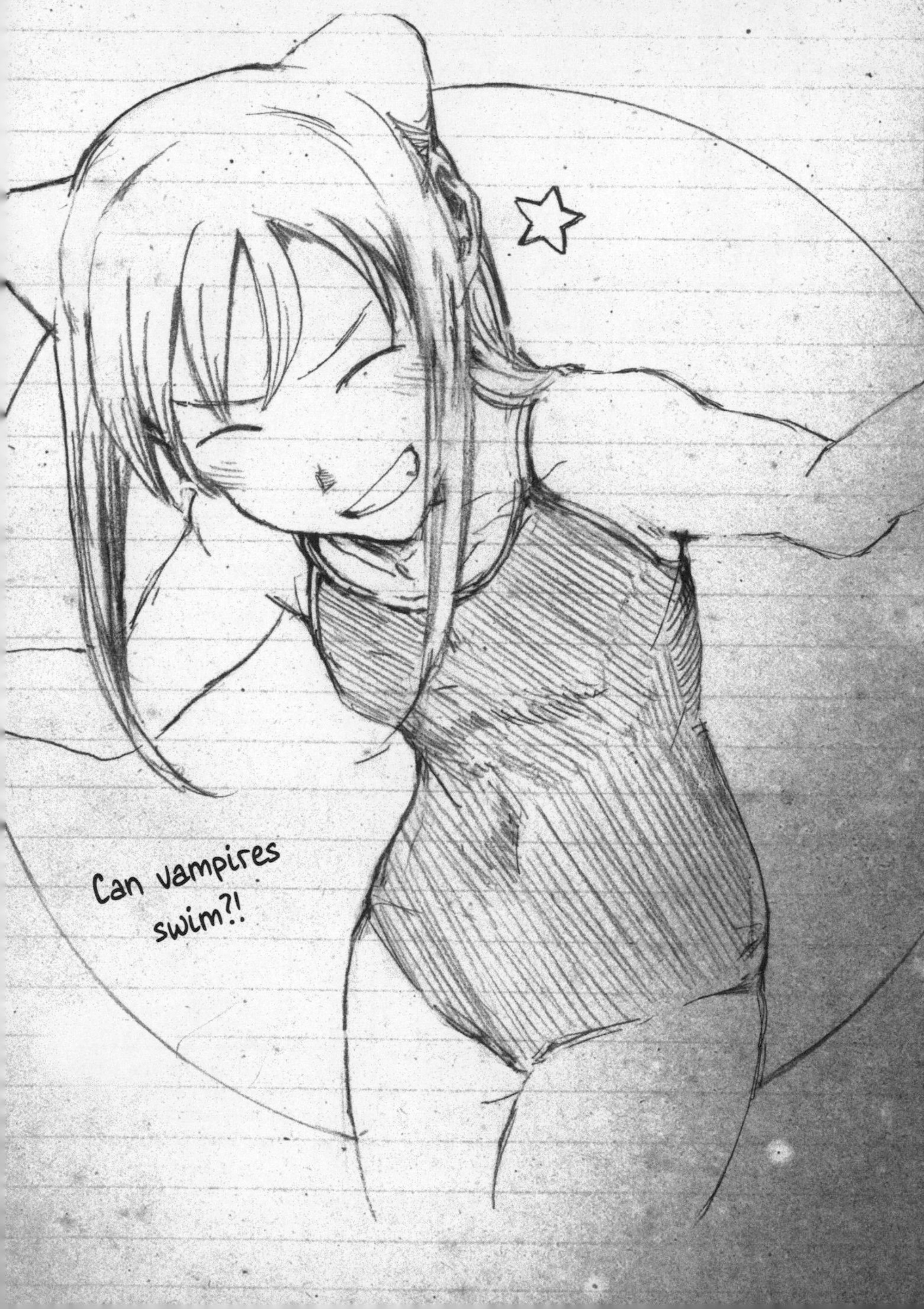
Can vampires swim?!

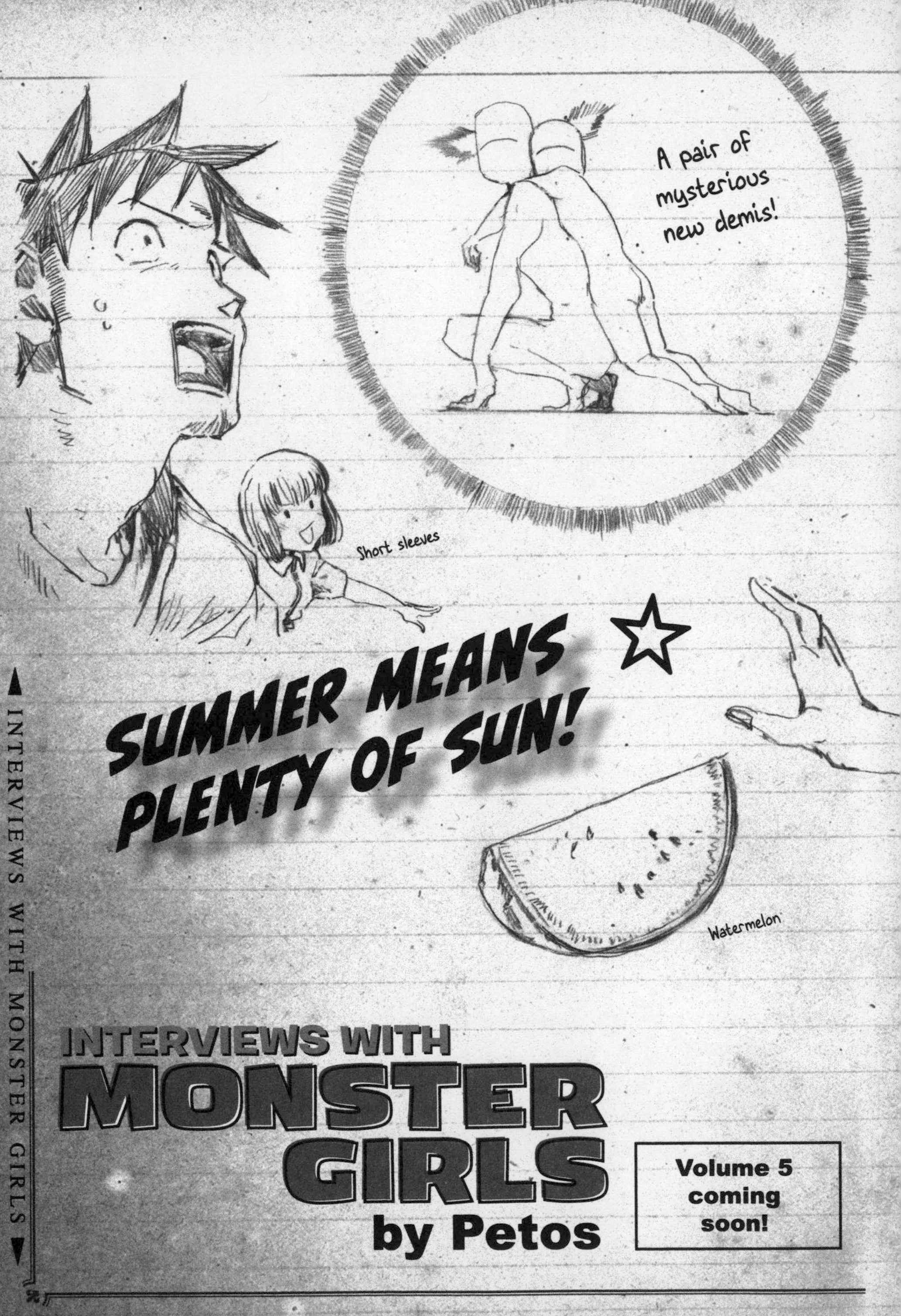

A pair of mysterious new demis!
Short sleeves
SUMMER MEANS PLENTY OF SUN!
Watermelon
INTERVIEWS WITH MONSTER GIRLS
INTERVIEWS WITH MONSTER GIRLS by Petos
Volume 5 coming soon!

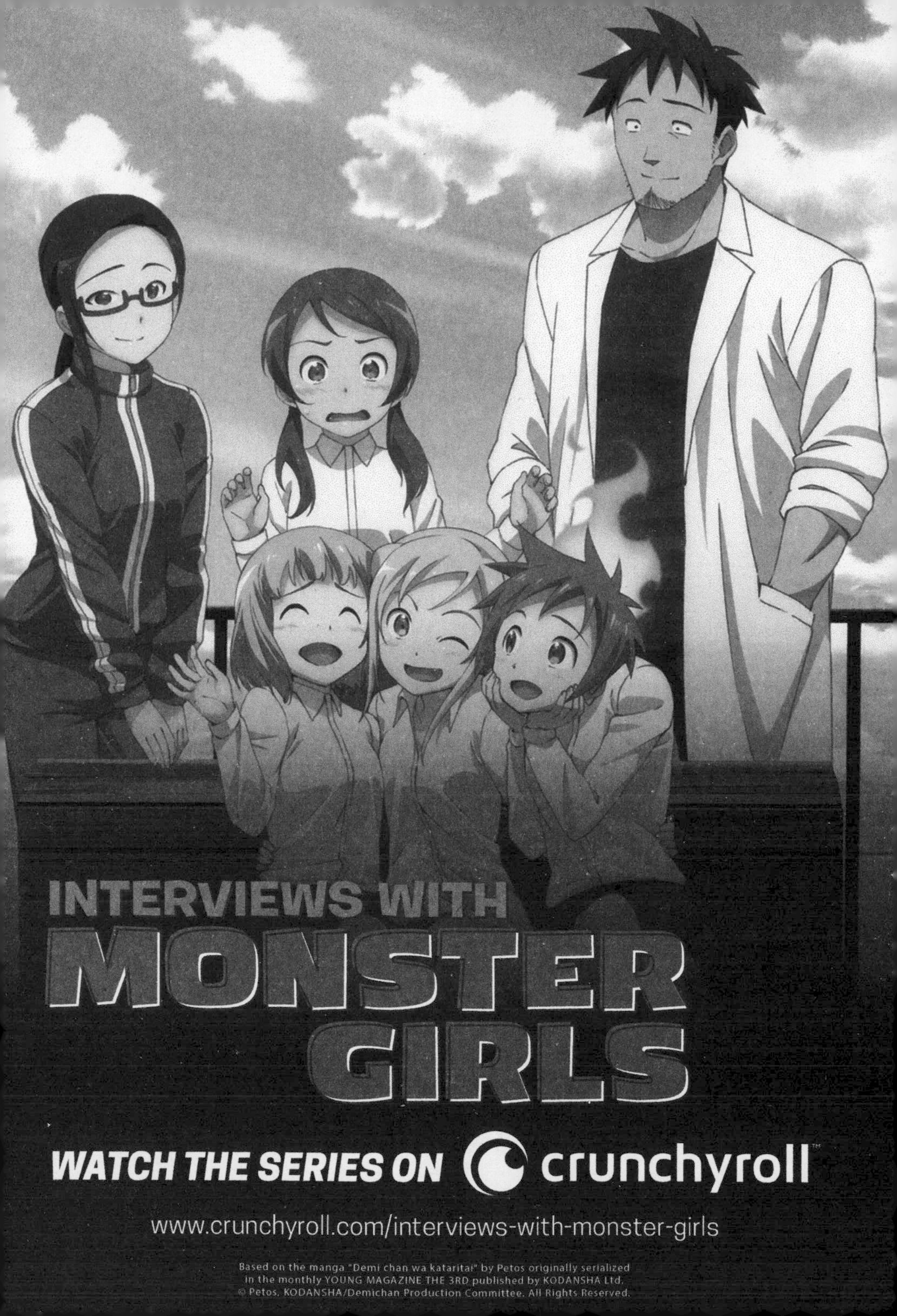
INTERVIEWS WITH
MONSTER GIRLS
WATCH THE SERIES ON crunchyroll
www.crunchyroll.com/interviews-with-monster-girls
Based on the manga "Demi chan wa kataritai" by Petos originally serialized
in the monthly YOUNG MAGAZINE THE 3RD published by KODANSHA Ltd.
© Petos, KODANSHA/Demichan Production Committee. All Rights Reserved.

Interviews with Monster Girls volume 4 is a work of fiction. Names, characters, places, and incidents are the products of the author's imagination or are used fictitiously. Any resemblance to actual events, locales, or persons, living or dead, is entirely coincidental.

A Kodansha Comics Trade Paperback Original.

Published in the United States by Kodansha Comics, an imprint of Kodansha USA Publishing, LLC, New York.

Publication rights for this English edition arranged through Kodansha Ltd., Tokyo.

First published in Japan in 2016 by Kodansha Ltd., Tokyo, as *Demi-chan wa Kataritai*, volume 4.

ISBN 978-1-63236-389-3

Printed in the United States of America.

www.kodanshacomics.com

9 8 7 6 5 4 3 2 1

Translation: Kevin Steinbach
Lettering: Paige Pumphrey
Editing: Lauren Scanlan
Kodansha Comics edition cover design: Phil Balsman

STOP!

You are going the wrong way!

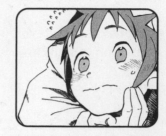

Manga is a completely different type of reading experience.

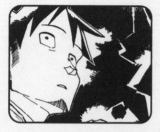

To start at the BEGINNING, go to the END!

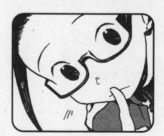

That's right! Authentic manga is read the traditional Japanese way—from right to left, exactly the opposite of how American books are read. It's easy to follow: just go to the other end of the book, and read each page—and each panel—from the right side to the left side, starting at the top right. Now you're experiencing manga as it was meant to be.